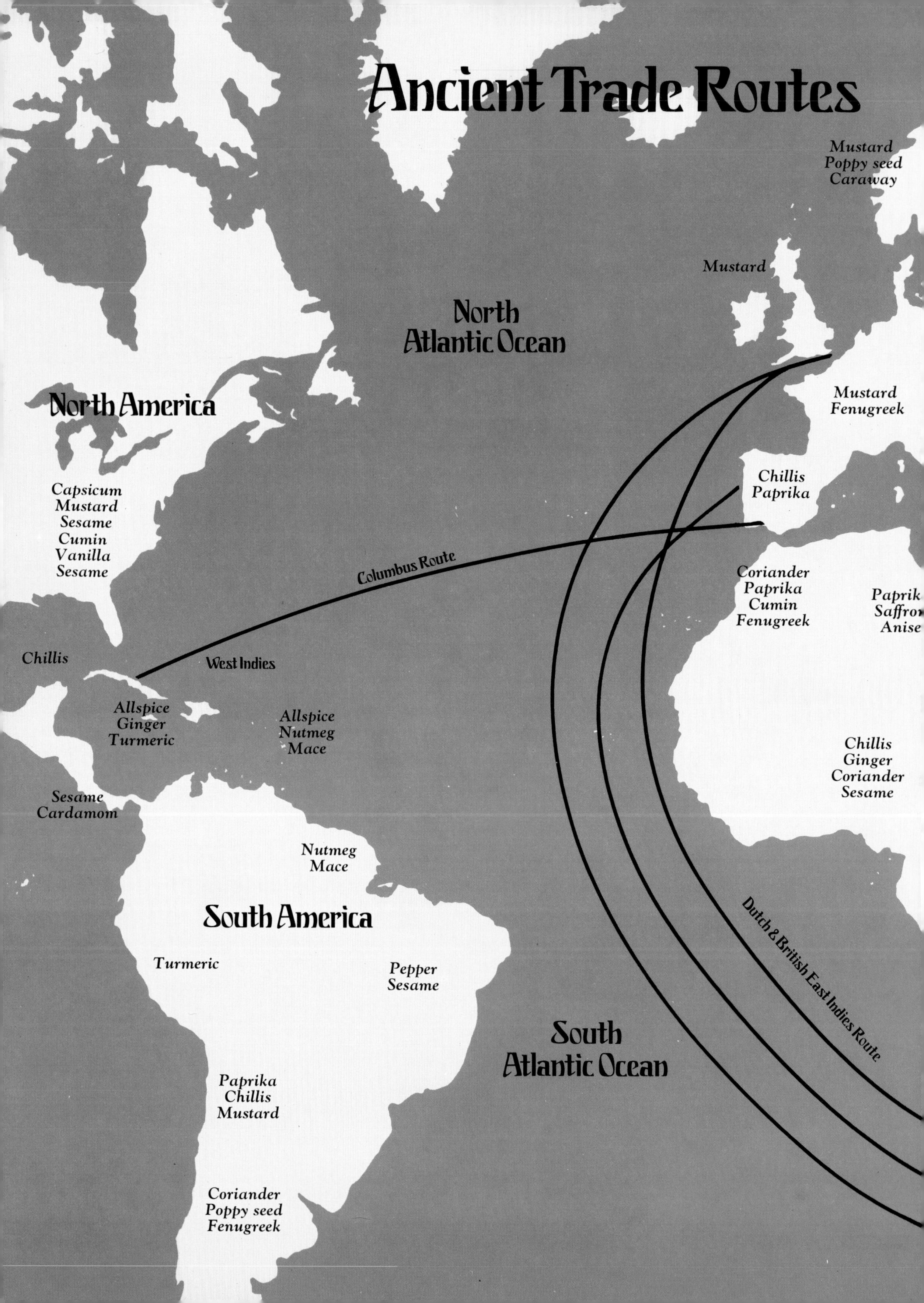

Ancient Trade Routes

Mustard
Poppy seed
Caraway

Mustard

North
Atlantic Ocean

North America

Mustard
Fenugreek

Capsicum
Mustard
Sesame
Cumin
Vanilla
Sesame

Chillis
Paprika

Columbus Route

Coriander
Paprika
Cumin
Fenugreek

Paprik
Saffro
Anise

Chillis

West Indies

Allspice
Ginger
Turmeric

Allspice
Nutmeg
Mace

Chillis
Ginger
Coriander
Sesame

Sesame
Cardamom

Nutmeg
Mace

South America

Turmeric

Pepper
Sesame

Dutch & British East Indies Route

South
Atlantic Ocean

Paprika
Chillis
Mustard

Coriander
Poppy seed
Fenugreek

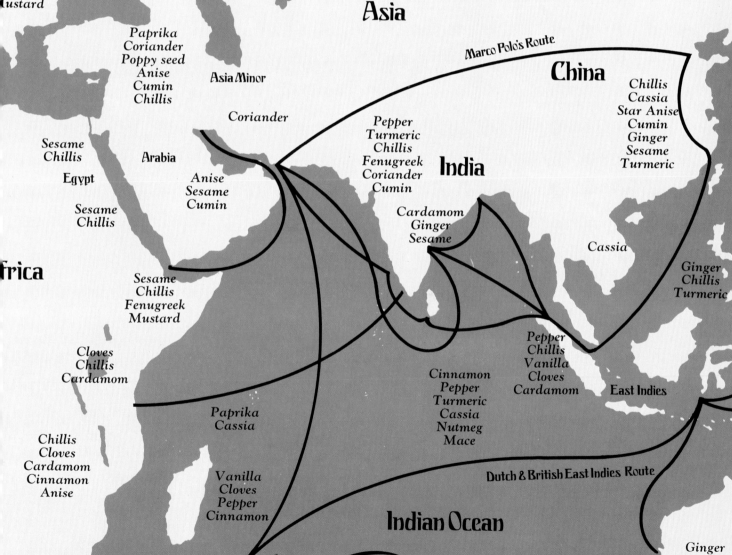

THE BOOK OF SPICES

Europe

ppy seed
araway
oriander
Paprika
Mustard

Asia

Paprika
Coriander
Poppy seed
Anise
Cumin
Chillis

Asia Minor

Coriander

Marco Polo's Route

China

Chillis
Cassia
Star Anise
Cumin
Ginger
Sesame
Turmeric

Sesame
Chillis

Arabia

Anise
Sesame
Cumin

Pepper
Turmeric
Chillis
Fenugreek
Coriander
Cumin

India

Egypt

Sesame
Chillis

Cardamom
Ginger
Sesame

Cassia

Ginger
Chillis
Turmeric

frica

Sesame
Chillis
Fenugreek
Mustard

Cloves
Chillis
Cardamom

Pepper
Chillis
Vanilla
Cloves
Cardamom

East Indies

Chillis
Cloves
Cardamom
Cinnamon
Anise

Paprika
Cassia

Cinnamon
Pepper
Turmeric
Cassia
Nutmeg
Mace

Vanilla
Cloves
Pepper
Cinnamon

Dutch & British East Indies Route

Indian Ocean

Ginger

Exeter Books

NEW YORK

Editor: Mary Bryce
Designer: Annie Tomlin
Illustrated by Caroline Austin

Published in USA 1985
by Exeter Books
Distributed by Bookthrift
Exeter is a registered trademark of
Simon & Schuster
New York, New York

© Marshall Cavendish Limited 1985

ISBN 0-671-07402-4

Printed and bound in Hong Kong by
Dai Nippon Printing Company

Some of this material has
previously appeared in the
publication *Encyclopedia of
Crafts*

INTRODUCTION

Spices have played a vital part in every civilization since the beginning of time. As our knowledge of the past increases, we realize that they were indispensable to people who lived long before history was recorded. Excavations of tombs, temples and cities that have been buried and hidden for thousands of years are constantly offering fresh evidence of the importance of spices in religious ceremonies and the embalming of the dead; in medicine and folk lore; in the preservation and cooking of food; in skin and hair care and cosmetics; and as dyes for food and fibers.

Some spices are ground to a powder at their places of origin (usually tropical); others are exported whole and milled when they reach their destination. It is convenient to have a range of ground spices to add instant flavor to any dish you are cooking, but it is well worth the extra time it takes to grind spices yourself.

We tend to put most emphasis on their use as flavorings and condiments, since spices are no longer essential for the preservation of food. We can freeze meat, fish and vegetables, or buy freeze-dried packaged foods, without having to rely on salt and other spices to keep food safe to eat. However, now that so many people are seeking to discover alternatives to the processed, prepackaged foods we have grown accustomed to, spices seem set for a welcome comeback. We can use them to make delicious preserves—chutneys, flavored oils and vinegars—and can experiment with salting and curing meat and fish.

Doubt about the advisability of relying on drugs every time we experience an ache or pain has led many people to look again at the natural medicines that were used to treat the sick for thousands of years. Health food shops usually have a section devoted to natural medicinal and beauty care products, and there are some we can make ourselves.

Looking back to nature brings us—naturally—to ancient and beautiful crafts such as making vegetable dyes to give soft and lovely colors to natural fibers. Saffron and turmeric, for example, have 'endored' (a term meaning 'to turn a golden color') not only clothes but food for hundreds of years. Experimenting with natural dyes is a fascinating hobby.

Other spices, such as frankincense, myrrh and sandalwood, have a long and important history and, burned as incense, still have religious significance today. Incense was burned as a form of fumigation and purification, and as an offering to the gods. Making incense is simple, and the ingredients are easy to obtain from church suppliers.

Although most spices thrive best in tropical climates, there are some you can grow in the garden in temperate zones, and even more if you have a heated greenhouse.

Now that so many of us want to enrich our lives with a greater knowledge of the past and of natural products, spices will once more have a wider part to play. As they are used in more subtle or adventurous cooking, in home-crafts and beauty products, maybe they will become as indispensable today as they were to our ancestors. *The Book of Spices* will encourage you to find delight in these exotic, aromatic plants.

CONTENTS

A COLOURFUL HISTORY

The colourful and romantic story of spices is woven into practically every branch of history. Reading about early religious rites and ceremonies one finds that spices, most precious of offerings, were used as an instrument in worship. The legends of the ancient world abound with stories of their magical powers. The foundation of medical knowledge is based on the healing properties of aromatic plants, which comprised the people's physic until comparatively recent times. And until modern methods of preserving and curing food were devised, spices, together with salt, played a vital part in the long-term storage of meat and fish, even before they were appreciated for their flavour.

Spices were such a highly-prized commodity, at times more precious even than gold, that their place of origin was the best-kept trade secret of all time. The search for spices not only caused a flotilla of seafaring explorations to set out on a wave of dangerous adventure, but resulted in the first drawing of the map of the globe. The first sponsored voyages were to find these Eastern riches: the first international trade agreements were to acquire them; and Britain became the first nation to draw up a minimum standard of quality for a trade that had become international.

As we use the spices we take so much for granted nowadays—a few cloves in an apple pie, perhaps, or crushed peppercorns on a steak—we might well wonder just how and why they commanded such a high price that men were prepared to pay for them with their lives. Part of the romance of their history lies in the fact that the very earliest use of spices is lost in the mists of antiquity; all we do know is that by the time the first records were kept, spices were already a treasured commodity.

Most spices are indigenous to the hot, damp tropical regions of the Orient, that is to say southern China, Indonesia, southern India, Sri Lanka and the Spice Islands of the East Indies, Java, Sumatra and the Moluccas. Some spices—notably allspice and chillis—were found when the New World was discovered in the fifteenth century and more have since been cultivated there, but very few will grow in the colder climates of Europe, especially Northern Europe. Full cultivation instructions for those spices you can grow at home are in the Dictionary of Spices later in the book.

Spices in ancient times

Not surprisingly, some of the earliest known records relating to spices come from the regions where the crops are indigenous. Among those that grow abundantly in China are ginger, cassia (a type of cinnamon), turmeric and anise, all greatly valued by the founder of Chinese medicine, Emperor Shen-Nung who lived around 2800 BC. He not only wrote a treatise on plant medicine, but held regular spice commodity markets and, practising what he preached, consumed vast quantities of ground spices every day to preserve his health and prolong his life. Legend goes further, claiming that Shen-Nung had the lining of his stomach surgically removed and replaced by a glass one, so that people could see the miracle powders at work.

Without going to quite those lengths, the Chinese have continued to put their faith in spices for medicinal purposes and for preserving and flavouring food. Confucius, about 550 BC, advised his followers not to eat any dish that lacked its proper seasoning, nor any that tasted or smelled bad. Ships plying to and from the Indian spice ports on the Malabar coast at that time carried pots planted with fresh ginger which was used to preserve the ships' stores and prevent scurvy among the mariners.

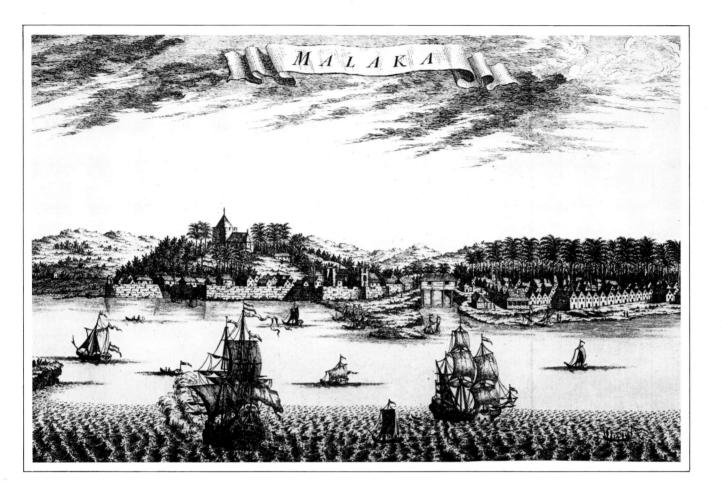

MALAKA

India was the natural home of pepper—always the world's most sought after spice—and also of chilli pepper, cardamom, ginger, turmeric, coriander, cumin and sesame, and the value of these and other aromatics, both in medicine and as food preservatives, was recognized in the earliest Sanskrit texts. Their use was 'authorized' in the *Ayurveda*, the treatise on the Hindu science of medicine, written in the fifth century BC.

One of the most primitive forms of Indian cooking, in a clay *tandoori* oven buried up to its neck in the soil, exemplifies the earliest use of spices to preserve, tenderize, flavour and colour food. The technique has been modified and is now so popular throughout the Western world that specialist restaurants enable us all to enjoy *tandoori* chicken sprinkled with salt and lime juice, marinated in yogurt and spices and coloured with hot chilli powder and paprika pepper.

Spices from China and India, with cinnamon from Sri Lanka and cloves, nutmeg and mace from the East Indies, comprised the precious cargo carried by hazardous land and sea routes to ports in the Eastern Mediterranean and Europe. The Arabs, geographically and temperamentally the natural middle men of this lucrative trade, maintained the monopoly for centuries and strengthened it by spreading fantastic tales of where and how the spices grew. For at least five thousand years caravans first of donkeys, then of camels plodded their way overland from Goa and Calicut (Calcutta), adding to their burden ivory and myrrh from East Africa and balm and frankincense from Arabia. Alternatively, the spices were carried by merchant ships through the Persian Gulf and along the Red Sea, to be taken overland from Egypt. Either way, the cargoes attracted tax, duties, tolls and colossal mark-ups at every handling point.

It was to one of these camel trains, travelling from Gilead, that Joseph, the favourite son of Rachel and Jacob, was sold by his jealous brothers for twenty pieces of silver, and resold by the merchants in Egypt.

Malacca, situated on the west coast of the Malay peninsula, controlled the European supply of spices in the later Middle Ages. At that time, it had a cosmopolitan merchant community with traders from China, South-east Asia, India, Persia and the Near East.

The routes varied over the centuries according to which nation was in ascendancy, which tracks offered the least obstruction by bandits, and other factors. Tracing any one of the complicated network of routes with a finger on a map spells adventure even today—over the Khyber Pass, through Afghanistan, Iran, south to Babylon, on to the Euphrates and west to the Mediterranean—what mystery and magic a travel brochure could evoke from the journey, even one made in modern land-roving vehicles fully equipped with tents, radio, cooking facilities, canned and packaged foods and medical supplies.

The ancient Egyptians were good customers of the Arabian traders. They burned myrrh, frankincense, bdellium and balsam to banish evil spirits and appease the gods, and the upper classes used them as disinfectant to cleanse the air they breathed. Small drops of bdellium resin, in the form of 'pearls', were carried by ladies in their bags as a type of perfume. Spices played a very important part in the embalming process and cassia and cinnamon were imported particularly for this purpose. As long ago as 2500 BC the Egyptian Pharaoh Sahure received eighty thousand measures of myrrh from 'the land of Punt', a region of East Africa at the tip of the Red Sea.

From a later document, the Ebers scroll measuring 20m (65ft), it is clear that spices such as anise, caraway, coriander, fenugreek, poppy seed and saffron (some of which grew in the Middle East) were used not just as food preservatives but as flavourings and condiments, and some as cosmetics, too.

Whenever one ruler wished to create a good impression on another, spices were sure to be among the offerings taken or sent. The Queen of Sheba, who travelled to draw on King Solomon's wisdom, flattered him with camels laden with her most priceless possessions—gold, precious stones and spices. Then Phoenician sailors of King Solomon's empire, who were renowned for their seafaring ability, set sail for India and brought back wealth to the port of Tyre.

Spices were used as the currency of homage, too, as they were when the Three Wise Men chose frankincense and myrrh, together with gold, as an offering to the Infant Jesus.

Spices in classical civilizations

The Greeks and Romans made lavish use of spices and each civilization had its written authority on the subject. About 460 BC, Hippocrates, the Greek 'Father of Medicine', wrote a treatise documenting the importance of spices in both medicine and cooking. But the Greeks had no idea where the spices came from. Herodotus, the historian, believed that cassia grew in swamps effectively protected by ferocious bat-like animals which swooped over the forests uttering strange cries, and that curls of cinnamon were used by enormous birds to build their nests on high, inaccessible slopes. The story went that the spice could only be brought down by bribing the birds with chunks of meat so large that they sent the whole nests, complete with cinnamon sticks, crashing to the feet of waiting natives.

It was the Roman writer Pliny, the author of thirty-two books on natural history, who was the first to realize that the tales of spices growing in darkest African swamps and jungles were no more than a hoax. He estimated that by the time pepper and other spices reached Rome, the price demanded was one hundred times the original cost. At last, in 40 AD, a Greek merchant discovered the secret, long known to the Arabs, that the monsoons, the seasonal winds of the Indian Ocean, blow to the east in the summer and to the west in the winter. Now spices could be brought directly to Rome in record time, cutting out some of the greedy entrepreneurs. The wealth of first-century gold and silver Roman coins excavated on the Indian coast shows what a brisk trade developed.

There followed the greatest indulgence in the use of spices the world has ever known. The Romans used them to such excess that they can literally be said to have bathed in them. Men, even the legionaries, bathed themselves in the aromatic fragrances, spice-scented ointments and creams were popular as after-bath preparations and pillows filled with pungent, yellow saffron were used to induce sleep, or at least to lessen the effects of over-indulgence in the sweet, spiced wines. And, as expense was no object, Nero was said to have burned a whole year's supply of Rome's cinnamon at the funeral of his wife.

The extravagant use of spices was not confined to the bathroom and the boudoir. A cook book written by Apicius shows that if Rome had a motto for the kitchen, it must have been 'spices with everything'. It was quite out of the question to serve meat or fish unless it was heavily disguised, not to mention overpowered, by spices and spiced vinegars. Factory flavourings were introduced, in the form of sauce *liquamen*, a

On the strength of King Solomon's reputation, the Queen of Sheba, laden with gifts including a great wealth of spices, travelled far to test his wisdom. This illustration from a fifteenth century prayer book portrays the legend that she refused to cross a stream by the bridge because she recognized its timbers as those on which Christ would later be crucified.

A sixteenth century woodcut depicts spice traders using camels to transport goods to their ships.

seasoning made from dried fish, usually anchovies, and used in place of salt, and *garum*, made from blood and the entrails of tunny fish.

Spices were so indispensable to the Romans that they carried them everywhere their conquering armies went. Their gift to Britain consisted of some four hundred aromatic plants, mustard being one of them; mustard seeds, used for preserving, were excavated at a Roman site at Silchester. Although the British came to relish a taste for spices from this time, they had known them much earlier. Coriander seeds have been found on the floor of a late Bronze Age hut, and it is known that Britain traded raw materials for spices from Asia and wine and herbs from Mediterranean countries.

Just as spices figured in the glory that was Rome, so they featured in its downfall. When Alaric the Visigoth advanced on Rome in 408 AD one of the payments he demanded to raise the blockade was three thousand pounds of pepper, then worth its weight in silver. But two years later Rome fell anyway and, with the rise of Constantinople, the trading emphasis shifted.

The most famous spice trader of all was the prophet Mohammed, who started work as a camel driver and then went into partnership in a spice shop in Mecca. When, later, he married the widow of a spice merchant he carried on a dual mission, spreading the Islamic faith and trading in the lucrative spices at the same time. The Mohammedans were largely responsible for advancing the techniques of extracting and distilling scents and oils from aromatic plants.

The Medieval use of spices

As the cloud of the Dark Ages spread over Europe, the tapestry of the spice story, woven until then in such brilliant colours, was laid aside for hundreds of years, continuing in the Moslem East but with little documented contact with the Christian West. However, with the dawn of the twelfth century, the Crusades brought thousands of pilgrims to Syria and Palestine and an enormous two-way trade developed. Ships brought food, wool, clothing and metals to the crusading soldiers and returned to Italy with spices, jewels and exotic fruit. Suddenly a way of life, which had passed into obscurity since Roman times, flourished again and the standard of living improved throughout Europe. Ports such as Venice and Genoa became rich as never before and here was the wealth on which the Italian Renaissance was founded.

Throughout the Middle Ages in Europe, one way in which wealth was demonstrated was in the vividly colourful presentation of the food. To tease noble palates dimmed by a surfeit of meat, game, fowl and fish, spices and herbs were used for their colour as well as their piquancy. Everything from roast peacock to spit-roasted minced meat balls was 'endored'— gilded with a saffron paste until it glittered like a gold crown; parsley provided a bright green colouring, sandalwood red and turnsole purple. Ginger, mustard and vinegar brought interest to meats and fish which had been dry salted or soused in brine, and ginger, cloves and other spices were infused in Hippocras, a mulled wine of the period.

English merchants travelled to the continental trade fairs to buy spices, and Venetian galleys sailed into British ports, but the British had to pay dearly for the Channel crossing. In the thirteenth century, pepper cost nearly twice as much in England as in France and peppercorns were so precious that they were counted singly and even accepted as currency in the payment of rent, taxes, tolls and dowry.

A set of household accounts for the year 1418–19 shows that Dame Alice de Bryene used five pounds of pepper, which she bought for 2s 1d per pound in London and 1s 11d at Stourbridge Fair, eighty-four pounds of mustard seed at less than a farthing a pound, three pounds of cinnamon, two-and-a-half pounds of ginger and three-quarters of a pound of saffron— used sparingly because it has always been the most costly spice of all. At this time a pound of saffron cost as much as a horse, a pound of ginger the same as a sheep, and two pounds of mace the same as a cow.

During the reign of Henry II, in 1180, a pepperer's guild of wholesale merchants was set up in London. This was later incorporated into a spicers' guild, and succeeded in 1429 by the present Grocers' Company, which was granted a Charter by Henry VI to sell goods in quantity—the term grocer deriving from the French *vendre en gros* (literally 'selling in bulk'). The Company was formed to manage the trade in spices, drugs and dyes—for many of the spices, saffron particularly, were commonly used to dye wool, linen and cloth as well as food—to select spices and medicinal products and to garble or cleanse them and ensure that they were of an acceptable standard quality.

The age of exploration
Against the background of continuing confusion and deliberate concealment about the origin of the spices, Marco Polo's journey from Venice to China was of tremendous significance. When he set out on foot at the beginning of the thirteenth century, many of the former trade links had been broken, and much of the knowledge of Roman times forgotten. And so, by the time he stood before the ruler, the Kublai Khan, he had crossed not only continents but centuries. When he returned home over twenty-five years later with tales of a market where one hundred and twenty thousand people brought their wares, of palaces, temples, silks, jewels and exotic fragrances, he was treated with scepticism. It was not until the Polo family put on a lavish feast, dressing themselves in luxurious silken robes and offering their guests a sumptuous menu spiced with Oriental delicacies that his account was accepted as fact rather than fiction. But it was not for another two centuries that the European nations finally tired of paying the exorbitant prices extracted by the middle men and decided to set out in earnest to search for the spice lands.

This determination heralded the age of exploration by sea, and throughout the fifteenth and sixteenth centuries nations entered into a race to finance voyages to discover and capture the riches. In a flurry of maritime activity, Portuguese ships discovered Madeira and the Spanish captured Mexico and Peru. Diaz, under the Portuguese flag, sailed to the Cape of Good Hope, and in 1497 Vasco da Gama rounded it, sailed on up the East Coast of Africa and, with the aid of a local marine pilot, reached the vital trading post of Calicut on the Malabar coast. The Indian ruler sent da Gama home with a message to King Manuel, 'A gentleman of your household came to my country, whereat I was much pleased. My country is rich in cinnamon, cloves, ginger, pepper and precious stones. That which I ask of you in exchange is gold, silver, corals, and scarlet cloth.' And so the Portuguese sent a merchant fleet to trade with the Zamorin—and took possession of Brazil in passing. They discovered the source of cinnamon in Sri Lanka and seized Malacca, one of the most important spice centres. By 1515, after the discovery of Madagascar, Borneo and Java, they had control of virtually the whole Far Eastern trade and brought back such quantities of bounty that Lisbon harbour had every appearance of an Eastern spice market.

The profits from this ever-increasing trade were ploughed back into exploration, enabling the king of Portugal to finance another great voyage, in which Magellan sailed almost round the world—he was actually killed by natives in the Philippines. And now the real charting of the seas could begin; the map of the world was drawn not on a flat sheet of paper, but on a globe.

Meanwhile, in 1492, Columbus persuaded the Spanish royalty to finance his voyage of discovery and with three ships he sailed West in search of India. Three months later when he stepped ashore, he found not glittering palaces but rambling, ramshackle huts and not pepper but chillis in Mexico and allspice—a berry with a flavour resembling a blend of cloves, cinnamon and nutmeg—in the West Indies. Later voyages returned with vanilla, the bean or pod of an orchid native to Central America.

The Dutch and the English began a simultaneous build-up of sea

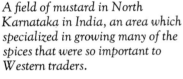

A field of mustard in North Karnataka in India, an area which specialized in growing many of the spices that were so important to Western traders.

Vanilla became an important spice after Columbus's first voyage to America. It can now be grown in Northern hemispheres in greenhouses.

power. In 1579 the Netherlands declared their independence from Spain and began to trade direct with India. The rapid influx of wealth enabled them to establish the Dutch East India Company which took control of Malacca, the Malay Peninsula and northern Sumatra. In 1577 Sir Francis Drake sailed around the world to find a North-east passage to China, and brought back a large spice cargo. The English defeated the Spanish Armada, and Queen Elizabeth granted a charter to the East India Company to handle trade with the Eastern Hemisphere.

The growth of the modern spice trade

With so much profit at stake, rivalry developed to the point of warfare between the European maritime nations. By 1658 the Dutch had wrested from the Portuguese the cinnamon trade of Ceylon, and soon after that controlled the rich pepper ports of the Malabar coast, Java and Celibes. By 1690 the Dutch had the monopoly on cloves which they grew only on the island of Aboyna and, to keep the price up, had the trees on all the other islands burned. There are even stories of mountains of cloves being burned in the streets of Amsterdam. However, in 1749 a Frenchman smuggled some 'mother cloves' (the ripe fruit) out of the country and planted them in the French colonies.

With the growth of colonization most of the spice-producing areas came under British, French or Dutch influence and the three nations enjoyed a period of great prosperity. But the wheels of fortune turned again, and by the end of the eighteenth century, the Dutch company was bankrupted and England took over the Dutch ports in India and all the Dutch East Indian islands except Java.

Britain's reputation as a leading naval power was established, and London became the centre of the spice trade, with elegant headquarters at the Commercial Sale Rooms in Mincing Lane. With so many ships sailing to India, and so many British personnel in administrative posts there, curried dishes became almost a part of the national cuisine and a great many spiced fruit sauces and chutneys were imported to accompany them.

Across the Atlantic, the end of the American War of Independence had left fast and well-equipped ships available to ply for trade and the Yankee Clippers travelled to the East Indies, trading mainly for pepper and tea. Some of the first American fortunes were founded on the spice trade at this time, one being that of Elihu Yale, who founded Yale University.

Now the growth of independence for the spice-producing countries means that the spices contribute greatly to the economies of the new states. Nutmegs and mace, for example, are practically the sole export of the West Indian island of Grenada. Great industries still flourish from small beginnings for the bulk of the world's crop of cloves comes from those original smuggled plantings in Madagascar and Zanzibar.

SPICES IN MEDICINE

It was Hippocrates who, in the fifth century BC, wrote, 'Let food be your medicine'. This is what people the world over had been doing since the earliest times. They were dependent on the plants that grew locally for their food and, when they became unwell, for their medicine, too. The use of spices in remedies must have developed through trial and error. People suffering from flatulence would have noticed that a meal including, say, anise seed or cinnamon—both now recognized as carminatives—brought relief, or that those experiencing loss of appetite were persuaded back to normal eating habits when a dish spiced with black or cayenne pepper was put before them. And so a primitive but practical understanding of medicine grew and was handed down through the generations. Present-day chemical and botanical experiments have analyzed the spices and shown why many of the medicines self-prescribed almost by instinct were effective.

Medicinal spices through history

Each of the great civilizations of the ancient world had its authority on medicine, and each seems to have come independently to similar conclusions. Chinese folk medicine dates from primordial times, probably from 20,000 years ago, and as long ago as 3000 BC had been formulated into a recognizable pattern. It is based on the philosophy that each person is an individual with a delicately balanced system composed, on the one hand, of the power of darkness, the yin, and on the other, of the power of light, the yang. Medicinal remedies must restore and keep a balance of these two opposing facets and spices are categorized accordingly.

In India the *Ayurveda*, the Hindu science of medicine, in Egypt the *Ebers Papyrus*, in Greece the works of a physician, Dioscorides, in his herbal called *De Materia Medica*, all bear witness to the importance of spices in the treatment of illness and the preservation of health.

In Roman times, Pliny wrote a number of books on the subject, and the Roman soldiers took aromatics with them wherever they went. Under Roman occupation, the monasteries in Britain and France cultivated 'physic gardens' which were the beginning of a source of medical supplies

Opium was used in China as a sedative and a relaxant, and opium dens abounded in the last century as the drug raised the poor above the miseries and exigencies of their daily lives. Morphine, codeine and thebaine are extracted from opium for use in present-day medicine.

so important in later years to the hospitals built alongside the ecclesiastical communities.

Spices have played their part in world health not only as cures, but also as indirect killers. Ironically, the Black Death, which swept across Asia and North Africa in the fourteenth century before it killed one quarter of the population of Europe, is thought to have been carried there on the ships bringing spices from the East. In a desperate attempt to protect themselves from the devastating disease, people in Britain turned to spices for help, drinking juniper wine, saffron tea, garlic soup and bathing themselves with sponges soaked in extracts of cloves and cinnamon.

Turmeric, a yellow powder, was used in Elizabethan times to treat illnesses on a 'like with like' basis.

The work of Gerard and Culpeper

A number of erudite works showing the relationship between aromatic plants and medicine were written in Britain during the late Middle Ages. One of these, by William Turner, an admirer of Dioscorides' work, deals with the subject with the strictest caution, as perhaps befits a clergyman who became a Protestant and was also a doctor of medicine, a scientist and a botanist. Turner, who lived from 1508 to 1579, left, in his *Herbal*, a standard work of immense value.

Another man whose experience embraced both the laboratory and the garden was John Gerard, who was born in Cheshire, England, in 1545, and became an apothecary to James I. As superintendent to the gardens of one of Queen Elizabeth's ministers, Gerard wrote *A General History of Plants* with a colourful appreciation of the plants as they grew and made a unique collection culled from all over Europe.

In those days only rich and well-connected people could afford professional medical advice; others had to treat themselves with plants that were readily available. And it was for these people that, in 1649, Nicholas Culpeper wrote a book describing numerous plant remedies and advocating a branch of natural medicine called 'The Doctrine of Signatures'. Following this system, people would treat themselves on a 'like with like' principle taking, for example, yellow-coloured saffron or turmeric powder to treat yellow jaundice.

Homeopathic medicine

Homeopathic medicine can be said to be in sympathy both with the Chinese folk medicine, in that patients are treated as individuals with individually-prescribed remedies, and with the philosophy of treating like with like.

The basic philosophy of homeopathic medicine is attributed to an eighteenth-century physician, Samuel Hahnemann, who lived in Saxony (part of present-day West Germany). His aim was to find ways of curing patients with kindness and natural ingredients, rather than with some of the unnecessarily brutal methods he observed among his fellow doctors at that time. His first breakthrough was the observation that a minute dose of *Cinchona* bark, the tropical plant from which quinine is made, produced in a patient symptoms very similar to malaria, for which the drug quinine was usually prescribed. It seemed that quinine could not only combat malaria, but also induce symptoms very similar to those of malaria when given to a healthy person.

Working on this observation, Hahnemann carried out experiments with other plants, metals and minerals and came to the conclusion that 'what can cause can cure'. A drug would be effective by reinforcing the life forces in their struggle against the disease.

A feature of homeopathic medicine is that doses of any prescribed drug are extremely minute. First of all, a tincture is made from the raw material, such as the root or bark of a plant, and then diluted and 'successed'—violently shaken up—several times before being made into liquids, oils or tablets.

Aniseed and Star Anise have medicinal properties recognized by both conventional and homeopathic medicine. They are especially useful in aiding digestion.

Medical scientists have been making their discoveries, too, and progress has been rapid, if not alarming, in the field of drugs. With the ready availability of literally thousands of manufactured drugs in recent years, there has been a great swing away from natural cures, and bottles and packets quickly obtainable from doctors and pharmacists were our main weapon in the fight against illness. Now, however, when many people are concerned about the likely side effects of synthetic drugs, some impossible to identify until a drug has been in use for a number of years, there is a renewed interest in natural cures.

It is not always necessary to tramp the fields and hedgerows in search of cure-all plants, since reliable herbal remedies can be bought in health-food shops, or from professional homeopaths or herbalists. However, without delving deep into the realms of true medicine, it is possible to make some harmless and pleasantly soothing teas (tisanes), infusions and decoctions from the seeds and leaves of aromatic spice plants. These are quick and easy to do, consisting mainly of lightly crushing the seeds and infusing them for a few minutes in boiling water before straining the liquid and enjoying the refreshing aroma and taste. Specific quantities, and the conditions likely to be helped by the brews, are given under the name of each spice in the list that follows.

Other old-fashioned remedies are given, too, more from general interest than from a conviction that they will truly fulfil the claims made for them. Certainly if one could believe all one read about the power of such spices as sesame, saffron, liquorice root and sunflower seeds as sure-fire aphrodisiacs, none of us would waste our money on Valentine cards any more!

The medicinal spices

Anise *Pimpinella anisum* Anise seeds have for a long time held a place in folk lore and in magic, and are now recognized to have properties useful in the preparation of conventional and homeopathic medicines. In folk medicine, crushed anise seeds were mixed with oil of cloves into a paste and applied to the back of the neck, forehead and temples to relieve nervous headaches. The very thought of it somehow makes one feel at once more relaxed! The Aztecs chewed the seeds to relieve flatulence, and success has been claimed for an infusion of the seeds for complaints ranging from infantile catarrh, stimulation of the digestion—a theory held by Italian farmers—to tension and insomnia. Certainly anise tea would be a pleasanter remedy for sleeplessness than the old Eskimo cure—swallowing powdered animal bones washed down with melted snow!

To make Anise Tea

	Metric/U.K.	U.S.
Anise seeds	1 tsp	1 tsp
Water, boiling	300ml/½ pint	1¼ cups

Lightly crush the seeds, put them in a pot and pour on the boiling water. Allow to stand for at least 5 minutes then strain the tea into a stoppered bottle and leave it to cool. Take in frequent doses of 1 or 2 teaspoons. The tea will keep in the refrigerator for two to three days.

The Romans put their faith in anise seeds to send guests away from a feast in a not-too-serious state of discomfort, serving huge and heavily-spiced anise cakes at the end of a meal.

Gerard, in his *Herbal*, strengthened some of the earlier beliefs and recommended the seeds to relieve both hiccough and epilepsy; 'Aniseed helpeth the yeoxing or hicket and should be given to young children to eat, which are like to have the falling sickness or to such as have it by patrimony or succession'.

In conventional medicine, anise is an ingredient in linctus and lozenges given for the treatment of coughs. Essence of aniseed taken in hot water can help to relieve indigestion. Oil of aniseed is used in paregoric elixir, for its antiseptic properties in liquid dentifrices and as an insect repellent.

Star anise *Illicium verum*, known as Chinese anise, is highly valued in the East. The seeds are chewed after a meal to aid digestion, and the fruit is given to relieve colic and rheumatism. In Japan, the bark is ground to a powder and burnt as incense in the temples. In homeopathic medicine, a tincture is made from the seeds.

Caraway *Carum carvi* Gypsies seem to have detected a similarity in the properties of anise and caraway—it was an old Romany custom to chew caraway seeds to aid digestion. Caraway cake, eaten now solely for its pleasantly aromatic taste, was traditionally served to farm labourers to celebrate seedtime—when the last grain had been sown. The tradition of the Shakespearean era, when a dish of caraway was served with baked apples, is still carried on at Trinity College, Cambridge, while in Scotland, 'salt water jelly', a saucer of seeds, is set at the tea table and the buttered side of bread is dipped into it and then eaten.

An old-fashioned remedy for earache was a poultice of ground caraway seeds and breadcrumbs moistened with spirit, and to relieve the pain and discolouration of bruising, the ground seeds were mixed with vinegar.

Caraway julep was taken for the relief of nervous indigestion and flatulence, and sometimes given in cases of hysteria. It makes a pleasant tonic now and almost certainly helps to settle the stomach.

Cardamom was recommended as long ago as the fifth century B.C. for the relief of urinary diseases and headaches.

To make Caraway Julep

	Metric/U.K.	U.S.
Caraway seeds	25g/1oz	1oz
Water, boiling	600ml/1 pint	2½ cups

Lightly crush the seeds and put them in a teapot. Pour on the boiling water, put on the lid and stand overnight. Strain the mixture into a bottle, discarding the seeds. Take in doses of 1 tablespoon as needed.

Caraway is rarely used in medicinal preparations now, only to correct flavours and make other substances more palatable—to sugar the pill, in other words.

There is some evidence that oil of caraway—which gives the liqueur kümmel its characteristic 'burnt' flavour—stimulates the flow of bile, which is essential to the digestion. Dioscorides, the Greek physician, mentions the use of oil of caraway as a tonic for pale girls, and in India it is used in the manufacture of soap.

Cardamom *Elettaria cardamomum Maton* The *Ayurveda*, the Hindu science of medicine written in the fifth century BC, accepts cardamom as a cure for urinary complications, as a means of removing fat from the body and a cure for piles and jaundice. Other Brahmanic texts mention it in connection with halitosis, nausea, headache and fever, and as a soothing application in cases of eye disease.

Anything that might bring relief after the excesses of the table was welcome in Roman times and Apicius, who wrote and compiled the cook books that tell us so much about the Roman diet, recommended that cardamom be taken after any gastronomic indulgences—which, in those days, presumably meant frequently and often.

The Arabs also recognized cardamom seeds as an aid to digestion and put their faith in it, too, as a means of cooling the body and as an aphrodisiac.

Cardamom coffee, called *gahwa*, is given to visitors as a symbol of Arab hospitality and as an inducement to tranquil thoughts. It is a tradition that the ritual of the coffee is not disturbed by the discussion of business terms, and so negotiations are not entered into until the coffee has been sipped and enjoyed in peace. The perfect guest may accept up to three cups of the strong, pungent brew, which is poured from small brass pots in a ceremony verging on ritual. *Gahwa* is made from roasted green coffee beans, crushed with brass pestle and mortar and put into a small brass coffee maker with hot water, broken cardamom pods, cardamom seeds, sugar and a pinch of ground cloves. The coffee is then boiled for two to three minutes, strained and served 'black' in delicate little cups, and usually accompanied by small, sweet pastries.

Chillis Chilli peppers are the fruit of *Capsicum frutescens*, a perennial plant with red, orange or yellow pods up to about 10cm (4in) long which, when ground, are known as chilli or cayenne pepper. (They are not to be confused with capsicums, the fruit of *Capsicum annuum*, which are much larger and not, in spice terms, so 'hot'.) Chillis, whether whole, crushed or ground, are eaten in the tropics for the welcome effect they have of raising the body temperature and producing perspiration; welcome because this makes the surrounding air seem less oppressive, even cool. It is chilli powder which makes a hot curry 'hot'.

The Hindu *Ayurveda* strongly recommended chilli peppers as an aid to digestion and as a cure for paralysis. Chillis are known to stimulate the flow of saliva and gastric juices and may very well, therefore, aid weak digestion and help to overcome loss of appetite. If someone is 'off their food', they might be tempted to eat a dainty meal lightly spiced with cayenne.

The way appetite is tempted in the West Indies, one of the natural homes of chilli peppers, is with *mandram*, a dish that has at once both hot and cool flavours. It consists of chilled and thinly sliced unskinned cucumber sprinkled with lime or lemon juice, Madeira and cayenne pepper and mixed with chopped shallots and chives.

Cayenne pepper is sometimes used in tonics given to prevent disease, and herbalists use it in prescribed powders and pills. An old-fashioned remedy for chilblains, is to paint them with tincture of cayenne.

Cinnamon *Cinnamomum zelyanicum*, and **Cassia,** *Cinnamomum cassia,* are two of the oldest known spices. They have similar properties, though cinnamon has always been held to be the superior. In the fifteenth-century *Boke of Nurture*, John Russell wrote of 'Synamome for lordes, canell (cassia) for commyn people'. But no such distinction was made in the Biblical reference to the two spices, when the Lord asked Moses to anoint the tabernacle of the congregation of children of Israel with cinnamon, cassia and other spices.

Medieval magicians used both spices as ingredients in their sometimes harmless and often disappointing 'love potions'.

The Chinese took cinnamon as a remedy for excessive gases in the stomach, to normalize the temperature of the liver. Dioscorides who, according to legend, was the personal physician to Antony and Cleopatra, prescribed cinnamon bark in hot rum for colds, a practice which lingers even now in country cures. Ground cinnamon is added to hot milk, sometimes strengthened with whisky or sweetened with honey, or stirred into a mixture of lemon juice, honey and hot water, and taken at bedtime to lessen the miserable effects of the common cold.

In modern medicine, cinnamon is combined with other ingredients in medicines to relieve flatulence and arrest vomiting; with chalk and astringents it is a treatment for diarrhoea and internal haemorrhage.

Cloves *Syzygium aromaticum* The people of many early cultures discovered the soothing and healing powers of cloves. Early Brahmanic texts show that in India cloves and cardamom seeds were wrapped in betel-nut leaves and chewed to increase the flow of saliva and aid digestion. The *Ayurveda* recommends taking cloves for all manner of irregularities including fevers, dyspepsia and brain ailments, for toning up the heart and to relieve kidney, stomach, spleen and intestinal disorders.

Below A detail of the bark of Cinnamomum Cassia *and* Bottom Cinnamon *sticks and powder. Both have similar properties and a mixture of cinnamon, hot milk and whisky or honey is recommended as a palliative for the common cold.*

In the third century BC courtiers seeking an audience with the Chinese emperor were required to sweeten their breath and make their presence more acceptable by chewing cloves, keeping the aromatics in their mouths for the duration of the interview. The Arabs tended to brush aside any medicinal claims made for the fruit and used them instead to offset the bitterness of mixtures prescribed in the treatment of fevers.

In the old folk medicine which verged on witchcraft, the buds, fruit and flowers of the tree, a member of the myrtle family, all had their part to play in bringing together would-be lovers, for they and the aromatic oil they produced were among the many ingredients used in 'love potions'.

For tension and headaches, country people found relief in the application of oil of cloves mixed to a paste with crushed anise seeds. Or they would inhale an infusion of cloves and hot, boiled vinegar. The same liquid was applied as a cold compress to the temples and neck. In Bolivia an infusion of a few cloves in a cup of boiling water was taken to relieve flatulence.

Cloves are now recognized to have the greatest stimulative and carminative powers of all spices and can assist the action of other medicines. Ground cloves or an infusion of cloves in water are prescribed for nausea, flatulence, weak digestion and dyspepsia. The volatile oil is a powerful antiseptic, and can be applied as a local anaesthetic in the manufacture of toothpaste and mouthwashes, as well as in the preparation of antiseptics and soap. It is often used in its concentrated state as a very effective relief for toothache.

Coriander *Coriandrum sativum* In early Hindu medicine coriander was mentioned as a treatment for constipation and insomnia, and an aid to child bearing. In medicine now, it is frequently used to mask the taste of other laxatives and to lessen the griping tendencies. Liberal use of the seeds is not recommended, because they can have a narcotic effect. In small quantities, both the seeds and leaves—highly pungent and much used in Indian cooking—can assist in the relief of flatulence. A few of the seeds mixed with a spoonful of honey and taken before meals, or infused in lemon juice and hot water, will be found helpful.

Cumin *Cuminum cyminum* The seeds, which are an essential ingredient in *garam masala* spice blends and curry powder, have long been appreciated by the Indians for their stimulative effects. Early Hindu medicine prescribed them for jaundice, piles and practically every organic complaint.

Herbalists in the Middle Ages wrote of the comforting, carminative properties of the seeds, and they were used to treat flatulence, weak digestion, colic and dyspeptic headaches. However, cumin seeds fell out of favour for individual use, because they were found less palatable than other spices with similar claims. For external application, where taste is of no account, they still have their uses. The bruised seeds are mixed to a paste and applied to relieve the pains in the side known as 'stitches' and, together with other drugs, form a stimulating linament. Apart from that, their medicinal use is now confined almost solely to veterinary practice. For example, an application of cumin seeds, bay salt and common salt is used to treat a condition known as scabby back and breast in pigeons.

Fenugreek *Trigonella foenum-graecum* The Latin name of this plant (also reflected in its common name), a native of western Asia, means Greek hay. It is sometimes mixed with hay to sweeten the fodder given to cattle and is prepared as a conditioning powder to make horses' coats shine.

However, it is as a treatment for almost countless human conditions that fenugreek merits attention here. In ancient times, in Asia and the Mediterranean countries to which the spice was indigenous, it was used to reduce fevers and soothe intestinal inflammation. Tribesmen mixed the crushed seeds to a paste and applied the poultice to battle wounds, boils and other 'open' disorders of the skin. Oriental physicians prescribed fenugreek for pregnant women in cases of difficult labour, and in Egypt it

Top Coriander seeds have a sweet flavour and are sometimes used in medicine to mask the bitter taste of other laxatives.

Above Cloves have powerful curative properties and the oil is sometimes used in the manufacture of toothpaste and mouthwashes.

Top *Fenugreek was taken by Turkish women to guarantee a rounded plumpness and was also sometimes mixed with hay for fodder for cattle. It can be used as a conditioning powder to make horses' coats shine.*

Above *Juniper berries were used to stimulate the appetite and to cleanse the blood.*

was given to improve lactation. Ground fenugreek mixed with cotton seed was also given to increase lactation in cows.

Fenugreek had a heavy responsibility in Turkish family life, where it was used by the women to sweeten their breath and banish body odours. They took a mixture of the seeds and honey to improve their allure.

In the Middle Ages, a fenugreek preparation was recommended as a cure for baldness, and it is still used in Java as a hair tonic.

Culpeper was the first European herbalist to note its many medicinal properties and listed its efficacy as a diuretic, carminative and aphrodisiac.

One of the most important uses for fenugreek is in the breaking up of mucus in the body. In Albania, an infusion of the seeds is mixed with onion juice and lemon juice and taken to relieve inflammation of the mucous membranes, for head colds and sinusitis. A Bavarian medical practitioner described fenugreek as 'a liquid mucus solvent' and showed that it could remove collected mucus from the intestinal passages, organs and bloodstream, and help to dissolve fat in the kidneys. Any way of taking the seeds is said to be helpful in this connection—chewing them, particularly after a heavy meal, and drinking as a light infusion, or tisane.

To make Fenugreek Tea

	Metric/U.K.	U.S.
Fenugreek seeds	2 tsp	2 tsp
Water, boiling	200ml/⅓ pint	¾ cup
Honey (optional)	1 tsp	1 tsp
Lemon juice (optional)	½ tsp	½ tsp

Put the seeds in a cup, pour on the boiling water and allow to stand for 5 minutes, stirring occasionally. Strain the infusion, stir in the honey or lemon juice if used and drink while still hot.

This spice, which has figured in the self-help cures of so many cultures, and is still used by herbalists, is keeping pace with medical progress, for it is being used in experiments in the compilation of oral contraceptives, possessing as it does a steroidal substance, diosgenin.

Ginger *Zingiber officinale* Ginger has its roots in medical annals throughout the ages. In early Chinese medicine, it was recommended as a heart strengthener, and Dioscorides referred to its warming effect on the stomach and its properties as an aid to digestion and an antidote to poison. In early Hindu medicine, it was recommended for liver complaints, flatulence, anaemia, rheumatism, piles and jaundice. And, given the seal of Islamic approval, ginger was mentioned as a medicine in the Koran.

A pleasant way to enjoy the soothing powers of ginger is to make tea.

To make Ginger Tea

	Metric/U.K.	U.S.
Bruised root ginger, or powdered ginger	15g/½oz	½ oz
Water, boiling	600ml/1 pint	2½ cups

Put the bruised root or powdered ginger in a pot and pour on the boiling water. Leave for half an hour, then strain the liquid and leave it to cool. Take in doses of 1 fluid ounce (2 tablespoons) at a time.

American Indians drank a similar decoction of root ginger to relieve stomach upsets. Gypsies, whose culture has always been rich in remedies from the soil, have a cold 'cure' which is a blend of ginger, white horehound, hyssop and coltsfoot, and in Asia Minor for the same ailment, ginger, cinnamon, mustard seed and cayenne pepper are mixed to a paste with honey and spread on a piece of flannel to cover the chest.

Horseradish *Armoracia rusticana* Not strictly a spice, but a highly aromatic root, horseradish has been recommended as a stimulant since the Middle Ages. Because of its high Vitamin C content, it was effective in the prevention of scurvy. Horseradish syrup was taken as an expectorant medicine for coughs following bouts of influenza and an infusion, together with mustard seed, recommended for dropsy.

According to gypsy medical lore, horseradish leaves combat food poisoning and the ground root is effective against coughs, colds and bronchitis. To relieve neuralgic pain, a bag of scraped horseradish root was held against the source, and a compress of grated root with a little water used to alleviate tension pain in the back of the neck.

Juniper *Juniperus communis* Legends abound about the magical and holy powers of the juniper tree. A strong infusion of the berries in water was used as an antidote to poisonous bites, bee stings and insect bites—and if it worked, one can see how one of the tales of magic originated.

In Mongolia, strong belief is put in the power of juniper as a relaxant, and a decoction of juniper leaves and ground root is given to pregnant women at the onset of labour.

The berries are said to stimulate appetite and aid digestion, and thought to be cleansing for the blood. A strong decoction made from the stems of the plants was given as a remedy for piles and bleeding gums, and colicky babies were treated with a mild juniper berry tea, also found to be effective against cramp.

With their fragrantly sweet smell, juniper berries can be used as a disinfectant. In the nineteenth century they were burned and used to freshen the air in Swiss schools in the winter, when it was too cold to open the windows and allow air to circulate in the classrooms. The berries are still used sometimes for this purpose in invalids' rooms.

Folk lore has passed on belief in the efficacy of juniper berries in the treatment of dropsy; sometimes the berries were infused with either bruised ginger root or grated dandelion root.

Mustard There are three main types of mustard, Black mustard, *Brassica nigra*, Brown mustard, *Brassica juncea*, and White mustard, *Brassica alba* or *Brassica hirta*. All three are members of the cabbage family. Mustard seed is well documented as a virtual cure-all by the early Greeks, Romans and Egyptians. In 530 BC Pythagoras recommended it as an antidote to snake bites and scorpion stings, one of the most deadly killers, and over a century later Hippocrates documented the internal and external medicinal uses of the seeds. Roman soldiers had mustard as part of their diet, and it was used, in plaster form, to relieve rheumatism and arthritis.

Culpeper, in his *Herbal*, affirmed Pythagoras's theory about snake bites, and further recommended a paste of crushed mustard seed and honey to apply to bruises or pains in the neck.

Many a Victorian household was run on the assumption that a mustard bath or foot bath would keep colds at bay and relieve any symptoms already present. The theory was that the heat of the mustard drew the blood away from the congested area—the head or chest. Mustard bath powder is still sold commercially, the packet stating that the bath 'will be found pleasant, soothing and refreshing, especially after outdoor exercise and when feeling cold, tired or stiff'. The preparation is sprinkled on hot or cold water in the proportion of one half to one ounce per gallon of water. It is said to be relaxing and to tone up the skin. People take mustard baths, too, to relieve the pain of severe bruising and to draw out the bruise. Country people, especially farm workers and gardeners, put mustard leaves inside socks to promote circulation of the blood and thus keep the extremities warm in harsh wintry weather.

According to folk medicine, white mustard seeds were used as a laxative, and a strong infusion of the seeds in water was given in cases of chronic bronchitis. Mustard seed tea, a weaker infusion, was a refreshing gargle for a sore throat and a remedy for intestinal and digestive disorders.

Below *A traditional gypsy remedy advocated a concoction of mustard seeds, wholewheat flour and warm water for colds, congestion and kidney ailments.*

Top *and* Above *One of India's most important spices, pepper has diverse properties and over the centuries has been used to treat a wide range of disorders from jaundice to arthritis.*

Gypsies use chopped mustard leaves and the seeds to preserve and flavour food and, as a side effect, to aid digestion. An old gypsy remedy for constipation consists of chewing mustard leaves and sipping cold water at the same time—not an easy thing to do. For colds, congestion, bladder and kidney complaints, gypsy lore favours a plaster of one part of mustard seed mixed with four parts of wholewheat flour and warm water.

Nutmeg and **Mace** The large evergreen tree with the botanical name *Myristica fragrans* produces both nutmeg and mace—the mace grows around the thin shell surrounding the nut. Nutmeg has been prescribed in India for thousands of years as a cure for headaches, intestinal disorders, fevers and bad breath. Since the ninth century, Arab medical sources have claimed nutmeg to be a remedy for kidney ailments and stomach complaints, and acknowledged it as an aphrodisiac.

In the twelfth century the streets of Rome were fumigated with nutmeg before the coronation procession of Emperor Henry VI passed by. And sixteenth and seventeenth-century herbalists used nutmeg in many of their therapeutic cures. Grated nutmeg was mixed with lard and used as an ointment applied in the treatment of piles. Now, a relic of country lore, it is sometimes grated on top of malted or hot milk drinks to soothe head and chest colds.

Pepper *Piper nigrum*, the black pepper indigenous to India features in early Brahmanic texts where it is mentioned in the treatment of urinary complaints, disorders of the liver, piles, jaundice and as a means of removing fat. It has been used for centuries as a stimulant, carminative, to treat constipation, diarrhoea, cholera and arthritis, and as a digestive aid. It is hard to believe that a single spice could have such diverse properties.

Gerard, in his *Herbal*, showed that he was a follower of the Greek physician when he wrote that, 'All pepper heateth, provoketh, digesteth, draweth, disperseth and cleanseth the dimness of the sight, as Dioscorides noteth.' One can hardly have a better testimony than that!

Pepper is not greatly used in modern medicine, but is sometimes added to quinine.

Poppy seed *Papaver somniferum* Since ancient times, the red poppy has been the symbol of fallen warriors and now after two world wars, the Flanders poppy (*Papaver dubium*) has been adopted as the symbol of peace on Armistice Day, November 11th.

Since the Stone Age, poppy seed has been used to stimulate the appetite and at the time of the Olympic Games in Greece the competitors were given the tiny blue-black seeds mixed with wine and honey as part of their training diet, to encourage them to eat and grow strong! The drug opium, which can be obtained from the dried milky-white juice in nearly-ripe capsules, was known for its medicinal and narcotic properties to the Egyptians, Greeks and Romans. However, as the seed is not formed until after the capsule has lost this opium-forming matter, it has no narcotic effects.

Saffron *Crocus sativus* Because it has always been by far the most expensive of spices, the use of saffron has rarely been lavish, though in Greco-Roman times it was scattered on the floors to perfume theatres and public halls before a performance. According to Hetodt, a German medical practitioner in the seventeenth century, there was no sickness, from toothache to the plague, that saffron was not capable of eradicating. And at that time it was considered in other European countries to be an effective stimulant and antispasmodic and a remedy for measles, dysentery and jaundice—the latter an example of the 'like with like' cure, treating jaundice with a yellow-coloured spice.

In Ireland, country women dyed their sheets with saffron—even a very little produced a strong colour—believing that it strengthened the limbs of their children.

Saffron has also been used as a colourant in medicines. And in Arab countries, the combination of saffron, asparagus, egg yolks, milk and honey produced a delicious yellow-coloured concoction with allegedly irresistible results!

Salt The mineral sodium chloride, essential to human and animal life, makes salt one of the few raw materials of our diet which is basic to our needs. It has been used for centuries as a vital preservative for foods of all kinds and, effective in this important way, has contributed greatly to overall good health, especially in hot climates where food would normally deteriorate quickly.

In Roman times, a mixture of salt and spices was taken to settle the stomach. Old remedies involving salt include drinking heavily salted water to induce sickness in cases, for example, where something harmful has been eaten. And there is an old Cornish recipe for an eyebath to soothe eyes irritated by grit or smoke in the atmosphere. To make this, measure 600ml/1 pint (2½ cups) of water from the tap and leave it to stand uncovered overnight. This will draw off the chlorine in the water. Bring the water to the boil, add 1 tablespoon of sea salt and stir it until it has dissolved. Allow the salt water to cool a little, then pour it into a sterilized bottle or jar. Cover and use it in an eyebath or soaked on a pad of cotton wool (sterile cotton).

Sesame *Sesamum indicum* Probably the oldest crop grown for edible oil, sesame was mentioned as long ago as 1550 BC in the *Ebers Papyrus* and there are earlier records of its production in the Tigris and Euphrates Valleys.

The use of sesame goes back into the realms of mythology, when, according to Assyrian beliefs, the ancient gods drank sesame wine before they created the earth—presumably to give them the strength to undertake the mammoth task before them. The God of Death, Yama, pronounced sesame a purifier and symbol of immortality, to be used at funerals and ceremonies of expiation.

Sasruta the Elder, who is believed to have practised as a surgeon in India in about the fourth century BC, applied sesame poultices to wounds after an operation, and had the floors of his operating rooms and clinic strewn with the aromatic plants as fumigation.

Folk lore recommends sesame leaves steeped in boiling water to make an eyebath or compress for sore and tired eyes.

Throughout ancient times sesame was thought to have desirable properties as a sexual invigorator and aphrodisiac. In Arabia a mixture of sesame seed, liquorice root and stoned and chopped dates was simmered in water, sweetened with honey and taken three to four times a day—or as needed! And the women of ancient Babylon relied on a mixture of sesame seeds and honey, a delicious sweetmeat, to increase their sexual desire and fertility. Without making too many claims in the field of romance, sesame seeds may well help in improving lowered vitality—and their nutty flavour makes them pleasant to eat in any case.

Turmeric *Curcuma longa* This bright yellow spice is known in Europe as Indian saffron, because it has the same colouring qualities as real saffron.

In Malaysia, ground turmeric was mixed to a paste with water and smeared on the abdomen after childbirth, both for its believed healing properties and to ward off any lurking evil spirits.

In Asia, the spice is still used as a remedy for liver troubles and a tonic for ulcers, as well as externally for the treatment of skin disorders and as a depilatory. Country folk medicine recommends a recipe for turmeric boiled with sugar and milk as a remedy for the common cold.

Vanilla *Vanilla planifolia* In the sixteenth and seventeenth centuries, when it was first introduced into Europe, vanilla was considered to be a stimulant, stomachic and an antidote to poison. And, because of its pleasantly mild flavour, no doubt, was popular in sweet mixtures believed to be aphrodisiacs.

Below The poppy plant and Bottom the poppy seeds. Opium is derived from the dried milky-white juice in nearly ripe capsules and has been in use for centuries. Poppy seeds were used to stimulate the appetite.

SPICED DRINKS

Hot, fragrant, spicy wines—what a lovely, reassuring picture they conjure up! Carol singers stamping their way through the driven snow, and being rewarded with a steaming glass of mulled wine; a late-night drink around the log fire on Christmas Eve, with a glass of hot punch discreetly left near the glowing embers for Father Christmas, or a party to give friends the warmest welcome of all.

Few drinks—with the exception, perhaps, of champagne—allow guests to slip more readily into the party mood, or make them feel more instantly at home. Yet mulled wines need not be particularly alcoholic. Many of the recipes actually call for the wine to be diluted with fruit juice or even water. And they certainly need not be expensive, for no one on earth would recommend adding cloves, nutmeg, orange juice, lemon peel and honey to a fine vintage wine. If you want to give the drink a little more 'kick' you can mull a fortified wine such as sherry or port—many of the traditional recipes use these wines—or add a little brandy or liqueur to the punch. This depends entirely on your taste, your purse—and whether your guests have to drive home afterwards.

Spiced drinks of the past
Spiced wines were very popular in Roman times; so popular, it seems, that a whole range of other spices was called upon to restore calm to troubled heads and stomachs.

Throughout the Middle Ages, wines were commonly flavoured with sugar and spice, but this was simply to make them palatable. At that time, the art of winemaking and viticulture left a great deal to be desired. What was misleadingly termed 'wine of vintage' was simply the unfermented grape juice, the must, corked into the barrel the moment fermentation had started. Other casks, left to their own devices for a few months before being corked into the barrels, were sold at a considerably higher price as 'wine of rec'. But without a proper understanding of the treatment of casks, with no glass bottles, and scant regard for sterilization of equipment, the wine was harsh and bitter. If it was not drunk within a year of the grape harvest it turned to vinegar.

No wonder the favourite drink of the day was Hippocras, a spiced mull based on red or white wine, which was served at the table of the English King Richard II. A contemporary recipe gives instructions for infusing the wine with cinnamon sticks, powdered ginger, cardamom pods and cloves, each tied in a separate cheesecloth bag and suspended in the sweet wine as it heated over the fire. Such blends were called piments, and recommended —in moderate quantities—by apothecaries, as medicinal cures and aids to digestion—a case of a little of what you fancy doing you good!

Wine was even taken at breakfast in those days. A favourite morning tipple was 'soppes of wine', a bowl of spiced wine with chunks of bread crumbled into it. In poorer homes, this was substituted by 'milk mess', with the bread broken into a bowl of hot and sometimes spiced milk.

By the summer, when even the addition of sugar and spices left the wine pretty well undrinkable, ale came into its own. Brewed from corn, oats or barley, either individually or blended, it was probably not a bad drink in its own right, but mulled ale had an enthusiastic following. Tankards of the brew were heated by a hot iron from the fire plunged into the foaming liquid, and the spices were added to the quaffer's taste.

The adequate spicing of drinks took on such importance in Britain that a whole range of products was crafted to cater for the fashion. People who travelled about the country dared not trust the generosity of penny-pinching hotel- and inn-keepers, so they took their spices with them. Miniature nutmeg graters in the shape of acorns, barrels and mace (a play

Hot Toddy is a warming and welcoming drink to offer guests on cold, wintry evenings. The heavy, silver tureen and cups are eminently suitable for mulled wines.

25

A traditional Scandinavian punch, Glögg combines wine, spirit and fruit with ginger, cardamom, cinnamon and cloves to make a deceptively strong but delicious drink.

on words) and exquisitely fashioned from expensive hardwoods, silver, enamel and tortoiseshell are collectors' items today. Pocket-sized fruitwood boxes swivelled to reveal precious hoards of individual spices, and at home cinnamon casters and beautiful spice boxes and cabinets were standard equipment.

Where spiced drinks were concerned, quantity as well as quality must have been the order of the day, judging by an eighteenth-century description attributed to an innkeeper in *The Beaux Stratagem*. He spoke of a gigantic silver tankard, 'near upon as big as me; . . . and smells of nutmeg and toast like an East Indian ship'.

How to make mulled wines
You don't need any special equipment at all to serve mulled wines, or hot punches; you are not actually making the wines, only flavouring them. The choice of wine is important, of course; the wine you mull must not be so good that it will be offended by what you are going to do to it! Look in the wine shop or licensed retail store for inexpensive wines from California, Portugal, Spain, Italy or South America. If they are described on the label as fruity, full-bodied, 'stout' or 'round', so much the better. Mulled wines should taste (though need not actually be) strong. These days it is customary to make hot punches from red wine, and those long, cool summer fruit cups from white wine, but you can, if you wish, mull both white wine and cider.

You will probably already have all the spices you need in the kitchen. As you come to know the blends you enjoy and the degree of spiciness you like best, you can vary the recipes at will (you will find a selection of detailed recipes later in the book). Most recipes use two or three spices, usually ginger, cinnamon, cloves, mace, nutmeg and mixed spice, and you could experiment with cardamom, coriander, allspice and juniper berries. Unless you have a palate for the really unusual, avoid hot spices such as peppercorns and chillis. They not so much spice as fire the wine!

You can use spices whole or ground. Either way, you can tie them in
cheesecloth or muslin and hang them in the wine—as you do with a
bouquet garni of herbs in a casserole—then remove them when the wine
has absorbed the aroma and is ready to serve. Or you can stir the whole or
powdered spices into the wine with the honey or sugar. Although whole
spices floating on top of the wine, mingling with thin slices of orange,
lemon or apple, look decorative, a mouthful of cinnamon stick or root
ginger is not always a pleasing experience, so it is best to strain them off
before serving. Powdered spices, of course, form part of the brew, and
are *there* when the wine is drunk. The flavour of the wine is stronger and
slightly mustier, and the mull is more cloudy—it's a matter of preference.

The flavour of both oranges and lemons is a perfect complement to the
sweet spiciness of punches—orange is a little more traditional. How you
impart the orange flavour is a matter of choice, too, and always has been.
One famous hot punch, called The Bishop, is based on non-vintage port

Nutmeg can be bought whole or ground but if bought whole, grind it using the small holes on a cheese grater or a special nutmeg grater.

flavoured with orange. Dean Swift favoured using roasted oranges:

'. . . fine oranges
Well roasted with sugar and wine in a cup
They'll make a sweet Bishop when gentlefolks sup.'

Dr Johnson described the concoction as mulled port with Seville oranges, sugar and spices. Other authorities like to serve the mull with an orange pricked with cloves, like the prickles on a hedgehog's back—a very good way to tame the whole cloves when serving the wine—and others, perhaps with a little more patience at the preparation stage, prefer to rub the zest of the orange with lumps of sugar to sweeten the mull.

To add a sense of drama to an occasion, people sometimes add a little brandy to a bowl of steaming punch and set it alight, to be carried in triumphantly, blue flames leaping, like the Christmas pudding.

The Bishop, Sir Roger de Coverley and Negus, all evoking caricatures of portly gentlemen, are among the stronger mulls, based on port. The last one is said to have been invented in the eighteenth century by an East Anglian Member of Parliament, Colonel Francis Negus, who hit on the idea of diluting the port, and hopefully the tempers of his political contemporaries, at his dinner table. Sweet sherry and Madeira make heart-warming mulls, too, but most people settle for *vin ordinaire*, red wine of unremarkable quality, which can be strengthened with a small proportion of one of the fortified wines or with brandy, to give a feeling of largesse to the occasion. But there are many recipes which much more economically suggest diluting the wine with orange, grapefruit or pineapple juice, or with water—and these are probably the blends to go for when a party is to include a large number of young people. Even the most sophisticated drinkers have difficulty in detecting the strength of a drink when it is both spiced and sweetened—until, perhaps, it is too late.

Mulled wine must be heated gently, and never allowed to reach boiling point; this destroys both the flavour and the alcohol. Choose a large saucepan—enamel is ideal—but do not use aluminium. Pour in the wine, fruit juice, water or other liquor and stir in the sugar, honey and spices, or tie them into bags to dangle in the brew. Allow the wine to heat very slowly until it is just below simmering point. By this time it will have absorbed the sweet, pungent flavours. Taste it to be sure that it is neither too sweet nor too bitter. If it is, correct the balance by adding more fruit juice (lemon or lime juice is ideal if it is really over-sweet) or honey or sugar, stir and gently reheat. If you have used loose whole spices, strain the wine through fine muslin or cheesecloth.

The traditional way to serve the wine is in a large punch bowl, but not many of us have them. A large soup tureen or casserole dish does the job equally well, and you can use a ladle or small china or pottery jug for pouring. Or you can funnel the heated wine back into the bottles (heat them first) and stand them in a large pan of simmering water to keep a ready supply. Wrap a tea cloth round the bottles of heated wine and pour it with all the panache of a top wine waiter serving a vintage claret.

Do not be tempted to use your best glasses. The wine must be served

piping hot, and high temperatures and fine crystal do not really go to-gether. Pottery goblets are ideal, or beer glasses which have handles. Warm the glasses first and move a silver spoon from one to the other as you pour in the wine.

Hot, fragrant, spicy wines—with these simple instructions you have all the makings of a friendly gathering. Make your hospitality generous, but not so generous that your guests go away with the telltale signs referred to in *The Knight of the Burning Pestle*,

'Nose, nose, jolly red nose,
And who gave thee this jolly red nose?'
'Nutmegs and ginger, cinnamon and cloves,
And they gave me this jolly red nose.'

For a hot drink with a difference, try Wassail Bowl which is made with beer, sherry, spices and apples.

PRESERVING FOOD

As we take a selection of out-of-season fruit and vegetables from the freezer, open a can of meat or fish, or choose a complete freeze-dried meal from the supermarket shelves, it is difficult to imagine what it was like to plan meals before these methods of food preservation were known.

Basic methods of preserving meat and fish, by drying in the wind, smoking, dry salting or pickling in brine (salted water) were known to most primitive peoples, and by the time the Romans invaded Britain much more sophisticated methods of preserving were commonplace. In the Roman cook book of Apicius there are recipes for pungent vinegars made aromatic by the lavish use of spices, and for pickling such humble vegetables as turnips.

Commercial refrigeration and food canning were unknown until about a century ago, and even then were not available to people in rural communities cut off from the march of progress by poor access roads, lack of communication or simply lack of money. There are still plenty of people who can remember and reminisce with pride about the days of frantic and anxious activity as each home-grown crop was harvested, or an animal was slaughtered in the autumn (fall). For where money was short, the barren winter months could prove too costly to keep a backyard animal. And so until very recently methods of food preservation had changed little. Salt was the staple preservative, spices were used in many of the pickling solutions and preserved food which had lost much of its original flavour in the processing was cooked in spiced broth to make it palatable again.

Another very recent innovation is the production of seeds which give a succession of vegetable crops which can be harvested over a period of several weeks or months. Before that, it was a short harvest and a frantic one while people worked long hours in the kitchen to cope with the glut.

The pantry shelves would fill up with dry salted beans, pickled red and white cabbage, sometimes spiced with cloves, chillis and peppercorns, picked cauliflower, marrow and ginger, mixed pickles and chutneys of every kind. For whereas the prime vegetables were needed for pickling in the various spiced vinegars, any slightly damaged 'windfall' vegetables could be used to make the glowing rich red, brown and amber chutneys which would give flavour to the cold meats.

Some fruits could be kept in storage throughout the winter. Apples and pears could be dried and hung like paper chains in a cool, airy place. Other fruits—plums, greengages, peaches and damsons, for example—would be bottled in spiced vinegar or syrup to emerge as tempting as the day they were harvested. We sometimes forget, too, that jams, jellies, fruit butter and cheeses and fruit and vegetable curd were not only ways of providing delicious tea-time confections, but also of preserving the crops.

Those were the days when the term self-sufficiency had real meaning, and could represent the difference between survival and, if not starvation, at least uncomfortable months of hunger and monotonous diet.

The most valuable food of all was the backyard animal, and cottagers, however small their plot, tried to keep at least one pig, top favourite for the kitchen because of the range of products that could be made from the meat. Sometimes within a community householders would agree to stagger the pig slaughtering so that each family could offer the others a piece of fresh meat; in that way they all saved some of the chore of processing the meat for storage. The remainder would be salted, pickled, cured—often by a recipe which was kept a closely-guarded secret within a family—gelatine would be made from the trotters or feet, brawn from the

This attractive array of preserves reflects how fulfilling preserving home-grown produce can be and is also a practical way of dealing with a glut of vegetables and fruit from the garden.

head, and sausages packed tightly into skins and smoked over the kitchen fire.

Fewer people had the opportunity to keep cattle, but when a bullock was killed the meat had to be preserved to last for many months. Joints for short-term keeping would be lightly salted, then steeped in a brine and vinegar pickle flavoured with mixed spices. In this way, the meat would keep for a few days in hot weather or a week or two in the winter. For longer-term preservation, the joints were dry salted, then steeped in brine or a 'sousing drink' for several days, then finally hung in a cloth to smoke over the kitchen or living-room fire. Many old farmhouses still have large S-shaped hooks hanging in the inglenooks to bear witness to this type of husbandry.

Fish has always been one of the most difficult foods to handle because it remains in peak condition for such a limited period. In the Middle Ages herrings already preserved by salting were imported from the Baltic and North Sea regions and the British were reported to be 'wonderfully fond' of them. The monasteries, castles and larger households had ponds and pools where pike and carp were cultivated—an early example of fish farming—and eels were bred in the ditches, so fresh fish was constantly available. Coastal communites preserved the catch by salting so that the fish could safely make the long, slow and tedious journeys to the urban areas. Fish was in great demand because in Medieval times all Fridays, some Wednesdays and Saturdays and the whole of Lent were proclaimed meatless days by the church.

Spices were in great demand, too, to flavour all the meat and fish that had lost so much of its original taste in the processing. In Roman Britain and, after the Dark Ages, again throughout the Middle Ages, food was considered barely fit for consumption unless it was completely masked by

Preserving fish is a most difficult process since fish does not keep in peak condition for very long. This photograph, taken in 1910, illustrates the popular 'Scotch cure' which consisted of brining the fish for a period of eight days. When the barrels were full of herrings, they were sealed with tight-fitting lids.

cooking in heavily spiced broths and served with overpoweringly pungent sauces.

The first European settlers in America took with them their knowledge of preserving food, and the spices they had become accustomed to using in the process. In the Pennsylvania Dutch community where even today the people, largely of German origin, farm the land without the aid of any form of mechanization, the preserved mixed pickles, known as chow chow, have endured as a regional speciality borne of necessity. Throughout America, salted meat and fish were sweetened with molasses, the locally grown sweetener, and this gave rise to the many regional recipes for curing ham with the characteristic blend of sweet spiciness.

The developments which have given us the convenience of modern ways of preserving food do not mean that earlier methods are entirely superceded and unnecessary. Just because we have electricity in our homes, it does not mean that we do not sometimes prefer the romance of candle-light or the gentle flicker of an oil lamp! And so as we harvest an abundant crop from our gardens, buy fresh food cheaply in bulk, or buy a whole animal from the butcher, it is useful to know the many tasty ways the food can be preserved with salt and spices.

Salting beans

If you have a good crop of beans and no freezer, there is no need to resort to distressing waste. You can salt the beans and store them for up to six months. Choose young, fresh runner (snap) or green beans, wash them under the cold tap and dry them on kitchen paper towels. Green beans can be preserved whole; all but the smallest runner (snap) beans should be sliced. Rinse and dry the beans thoroughly before salting. Use kitchen salt in the proportion of 450g (1lb) to every 1.50kg (3lb) of beans. Wash, rinse and dry the beans, and choose any non-metal container, such as the large glass jars that used to line confectionery shop shelves, or the kind of earthenware crocks you can buy cheaply in second-hand shops. Place a layer of salt in the bottom, then a layer of beans and fill the jar with alternate layers, pressing the beans down well as you go. Finish with a layer of salt and cover the vessel with heavy plastic tied with string or secured with a rubber band. You can also cover the crock with a lid if it has one. After two or three days when the beans have settled, top up the jar with more layers of salt and beans, then cover again.

To cook the beans, rinse them well under the cold tap, then soak them in warm water for 2 hours. Drain and cook them in boiling water for 20–30 minutes, until they are tender. Drain the beans and serve as usual.

Spiced sauerkraut

The German way of preserving finely-shredded cabbage spiced with caraway seeds or juniper berries is a very simple process and the sauerkraut, cooked with sausages, is a delightfully different way of serving the vegetable. Trim the stalk and tough outer leaves from a white càbbage and shred it finely. Allow 15g/½oz (2 Tbs) of salt to each 450g (1lb) of cabbage. Sprinkle a layer of the salt in a wooden tub or an earthenware crock, add a layer of cabbage and a few caraway seeds or juniper berries, and continue to the top, finishing with a layer of salt. Cover the container with a clean cloth then with a heavy weight and leave it to mature for three weeks in a warm temperature, such as in an airing cupboard, linen closet or kitchen with an all-night burning oven. For the necessary fermentation to take place, the temperature should be 20–25°C (70–80°F). As fermentation proceeds, a scum will rise to the top and this should be removed every few days. If the level of the brine falls, top it up to the original level with a solution of 50g/2oz (½ cup) of salt to 1 litre/2 pints (5 cups) of water.

Fresh sauerkraut should be cooked within 3 to 4 days—try it boiled with your favourite frankfurters or spiced sausages. To preserve the vegetable,

Pickling spice is a mixture of whole spices – mustard seeds, coriander seeds, allspice, dried chillis, mace, peppercorns and ginger root – and is used to spice the vinegar for chutneys and pickles. It can be bought ready-made but it is more fun to make your own with the spices mentioned above.

follow the normal bottling (canning) procedure. To do this, drain the liquor from the container, bring it to the boil in a pan, add the processed cabbage and simmer it. Pack the cabbage into warm, sterilized jars, top them up with some of the liquor and cover them with the caps. Process the jars in boiling water for 25 minutes, test the caps for a proper seal, then tighten the rings or fix the clips and store.

Pickling vegetables with spices

The time-honoured way of pickling vegetables in spiced vinegar has in no way been superceded by other methods of preserving. Nothing quite compares with a selection of crisp, colourful and lightly spiced vegetables to serve with cold meat, and particularly with the Christmas or Thanksgiving Day turkey.

All types of vegetables are suitable for preserving in this way. Large ones, such as cauliflower, cabbage and marrow (squash) are divided into florets, shredded or diced, according to type. Small ones such as pickling onions, mushrooms and baby carrots may be left whole. It is a matter of preference whether vegetables are pickled individually or combined. Usually the highly coloured ones, red cabbage and beetroot, are served alone, but most others are blended with at least one different vegetable to give variety of texture, shape and flavour.

Vegetables must be salted before pickling, to remove excess moisture—this helps to retain crispness—and prevent the formation of bacteria. Those with a high moisture content, such as courgettes (zucchini), marrows (squash) and cucumbers, should be put into a bowl with layers of block or sea salt in the proportion of about 1 tablespoon to each 450g (1lb) of vegetables. Others must be completely covered in brine solution made from 450g (1lb) of salt to each 5 litres/1 gallon (5 quarts) of water. This should be boiled to dissolve the salt, cooled and then strained. The vegetables are left to salt for up to two days, then thoroughly rinsed in cold water before being packed into clean jars. Jars must be of the type used for fruit preserving, or have screw-on lids and be lined with special vinegar-proof paper. The type of seal used for jams and marmalades is not suitable for this type of preserve.

Apples and pears, and stone fruits such as cherries, peaches, greengages, plums and damsons can be pickled, too, and are delicious accompaniments to meat dishes. To retain the plumpness and firmness of stone fruits, they should first be pricked all over with a needle. All fruits should be lightly cooked before being packed into jars.

You can use malt or cider vinegar or, for a lighter colour and more delicate flavour, particularly attractive with fruit pickles, wine vinegar. The spices you use will not only help in the preserving process but contribute significantly to the flavour of the individual pickles, so it is fun to experiment with different combinations. You can buy a mixture known as pickling spice, but this gives a uniformity to your preserves. Always use whole spices—ground ones would give cloudy results with less flavour. The basic recipe for spiced vinegar is 50mm (2in) cinnamon stick, 1 teaspoon whole cloves, 2 teaspoons allspice berries, 1 teaspoon whole black peppercorns, 1 teaspoon mustard seed and 2 to 3 bay leaves to each 1 litre/2 pints (5 cups) of vinegar. For a 'hotter' pickle, you can add dried whole chillis and for variety try cardamom, coriander or cumin seeds, and pieces of fresh root ginger.

To prepare the spiced vinegar, put the spices and vinegar into a pan, cover it and bring the vinegar just to the boil. Remove the pan from the heat and allow the spices to infuse for $2\frac{1}{2}$ to 3 hours. The vinegar is poured cold on to vegetables which are to retain their crispness, but can be reheated and poured hot over fruit. In all cases make sure the vegetables or fruit are completely immersed in the spiced vinegar. Cover the jars with vinegar-proof paper, then with well-fitting metal lids.

Some of the spices that can be used for preserving: ginger, chillis and mustard seeds.

Shelled, hard-boiled (hard-cooked) eggs can be preserved in spiced vinegar, too, and make a popular accompaniment to cold dishes. The spiced vinegar is poured cold over the eggs which should be stored for at least a month before serving.

Salting pork

If you buy pork in quantity for freezing, it is a good idea to pickle some joints and make what is called unsmoked or 'green' bacon to add variety to your bulk purchase. This is a very easy and quick process. Directions are also given to cure ham.

The best joints to choose for pickling are flank or belly (bacon). The meat must be of the best quality and fresh. Choose glass or stoneware crocks for the processing, and sterilize them before you begin. Make a brine from 2kg (4lb) of coarse salt, 60g/2½oz (½ cup) of saltpetre and 6.5 litres/1¼ gallons (7½ quarts) of water. Bring to the boil, simmer until the salt has dissolved and the liquid become clear, then skim. Cool the liquor. Place the pork in the sterilized vessel, cover it completely with the cooled brine and cover the crock. Leave it to steep at a temperature of 3–4°C (35–38°F)—in the refrigerator or a very cold larder or cellar—for 24 hours. Remove the pork, squeeze the excess moisture from it and dry it on kitchen paper towels. Store it in the refrigerator and use it within 1 week. It is good boiled in stock with vegetables, whole spices and herbs.

Curing ham

There are almost as many recipes for curing ham as there are regions where this means of preserving pork was carried out, the ingredients varying according to the products that were locally available. The principle is that the meat is first steeped for a short time in brine, then for several days in a spiced and sweetened liquor and finally hung in a cloth over a smoking fire or in a special smoke box.

One of the most popular 'cures' is the Wiltshire ham, which is given its characteristic flavour by the use of beer and black treacle or molasses. For a 4–5kg (8–10lb) boned ham, you will need a solution of 650g (1½lb) coarse salt, 20g/¾oz (¼ cup) saltpetre, 1 litre/2 pints (5 cups) beer, 450g (1lb) treacle or molasses, 10 to 12 juniper berries and 15g (½oz) crushed black peppercorns. Boil these ingredients together, and leave them to cool. Meanwhile, soak the ham for 1 hour in the brine solution described for pickled pork. Remove the ham from the brine, rinse it well and place it in a sterilized glass or earthenware crock. Cover it with the cooled beer solution, cover the vessel and leave it at a temperature of 3°C (35°F) for two days for every 450g (1lb) weight of ham. Turn the ham in the vessel every other day and when the time is up, remove it from the solution, dry it with clean muslin or cheesecloth and place it in a strong cotton bag. Leave the ham in a cool place to dry for 24 hours, then hang it near a fire made of hardwood, or in a special smoke box and 'cool smoke' it at 25–30°C (75–85°F). If the smoking is continuous, 24 hours will be long enough, but intermittent smoking could mean leaving the ham to process for as much as a week. Store the smoked ham in a cool, dry larder with a free circulation of air. To serve the ham, remove the skin carefully, score the fat with a diamond pattern and stud each angle with a whole clove, then either roast or boil according to preference.

Salting beef
When buying beef in bulk for the freezer, you can add extra variety by salting some of the smaller joints. This is what the early American settlers did when they killed a beast—but they called it corned beef. To salt a joint weighing about 2.25kg (5lb), make a solution of 900g (2lb) salt, 1 table-spoon of saltpetre, 125g/4oz (½ cup) sugar and 3 litres/6 pints (5¾ quarts) of water. Bring the solution to the boil and pour it into a container. You can salt any joint of beef, but silverside, topside or brisket are traditional. Put the beef in the crock and make sure it is completely covered with the solution. Cover the container and leave it in the refrigerator or a cold place to steep for 4 to 5 days. Rinse the beef under cold, running water to remove the salt.

Spiced beef
This is a marvellous way to prepare beef to cook and serve cold for a buffet, or it can be pot-roasted with mixed root vegetables. Soak the beef in brine, as above, for 24 hours, remove it and pat the meat dry. Mix together 2 tablespoons each of sea salt, black pepper, crushed bay leaves, ground cloves and ground coriander. Rub this mixture thoroughly into the surface of the meat. Return the meat to the brine and soak for a further 4 to 5 days. Remove the beef from the liquid, pat it dry and rub 2 tablespoons of ground mixed spice well into the surface, before cooking.

Salting fish
Keen fishermen who want to preserve their catch to enjoy on later oc-casions, or people who can buy fish fresh and cheaply at the quayside might find it interesting to try this old method of salting. The prime requirement is that the fish should be perfectly fresh. Herrings are ideal for the process. Measure 3½ litres/6 pints (7½ pints) of hot water, 550g (1¼lb) salt and 125g/4oz (½ cup) of sugar. Put the salt and sugar into glass or earthenware bowls, pour on the hot water and stir until the salt and sugar have dissolved. Allow the mixture to cool before adding the fish. Each 800ml/1½ pints (3¾ cups) of the solution will be enough to preserve 6 to 8 herrings, depending on size, so you can process a large 'catch' in several crocks at the same time. Gut, bone and clean the fish, hold them under cold, running water, then put them into the cooled brine. Cover the vessels and put them in the refrigerator or a cold pantry. Leave them in the solution for 7 to 10 days, again depending on size. Eat the fish within two weeks at the most. To vary the flavour, you can add a few lightly crushed peppercorns, fennel seeds or bay leaves to the brine.

An attractive display of cured and smoked hams: (1) Bradenham hams (2 and 6) York ham, one of Britain's best known cooked hams (3) Suffolk ham (4) Parma ham, Italy's most famous raw ham (5) Boneless ham (6) See (2) (7) Westphalian ham, a German smoked ham served raw (8) Canned ham, pressed in jelly.

CASTING A BEAUTIFUL SPELL

For thousands of years, spices have been associated with beauty, purity, cleanliness and colour. Aromatic plants of various kinds have been entrusted with the beauty care of queens—kings, too. Their fragrances have been relied on to sweeten the body, mask unwelcome odours in the home and, in the form of incense, purify religious temples. The sometimes vibrant and often subtle colours have been extracted to dye wool, cotton and silks which were woven by traditional craftsmen into clothes, rugs and other furnishings of immense charm.

Of course, the earliest uses of spices in these many ways were a question of making a virtue out of necessity, when people were entirely dependent on the natural products that grew locally or could be imported through the old-established trading routes. Nowadays, when every aroma and colour can be reproduced with synthetic substances, we can preserve our complexions, waft about surrounded by sweet-smelling fragrances and drape ourselves and our homes in magnificently-coloured materials without the help of a single natural product—if we want to. But unless one is a scientist or a chemist at heart, beauty from a bottle does little to compare with the satisfaction of capturing an aroma or a colour from the natural products around us. If you have a love of nature, and a little more than average patience, a few simple experiments into making your own soap, incense and dyes can lead to lasting and rewarding hobbies.

As befits a lady's beauty secrets, the exact formulae of the first cosmetics and beauty products are veiled by the passage of time. But as more towns and cities of the ancient world are excavated and our knowledge of the past unfolds, so some of these secrets are at last being told. It is clear that cosmetic preparations in one form or another were known to all the ancient peoples. Sometimes the use of ointments and oils was largely to protect the skin and hair against the ravages of hot, dry climates; sometimes they had a religious significance—in ancient Egypt certain unguents could be made and distributed only by priests—and some had magical associations, as in the case of warriors who smeared their bodies with pungent oils before going into battle, relying on the mystical powers to ensure victory.

Fashion played its part, too, and in every society there was a pacesetter. Cleopatra fortified herself—and presumably weakened the political resolve of others—by appearing awe-inspiringly decorative at all times. She used face masks to soften and clarify her skin, rubbed fragrant oils on her body, painted her lips and cheeks with red ochre and accentuated her eyes with generous applications of kohl on the lids and lashes. Other tricks of the trade at the time were the use of butter and barley flour paste to eradicate skin blemishes (the Romans used white lead and chalk for the same purpose), ground pumice stone to polish the teeth, and henna, a safe, deep, reddish-brown vegetable dye, to colour the hair, nails, palms of the hands and soles of the feet.

Bathing for beauty

The Egyptians considered frequent baths essential to good health and purity, and always washed before and after meals. In Syria it was the custom for the king to join his subjects in mass bathing pools. Legend has it that on one occasion, in a fit of largesse, Antiochus poured his expensive bath oil over the heads of his admiring subjects—who presumably were loathe to wash it off for months afterwards. The Romans, too, liked to be seen to be clean, and in the public baths vied with each other to have the most fragrant of oils. The emperor Heliogabalus, renowned for his personal extravagance, took to bathing in saffron-scented water and emerging with a gentle golden, though impermanent, tan.

Perfumed baths became popular in England in the seventeenth century, when women gathered bath posies to scent the water, then rubbed themselves down with spiced vinegar. Recipes for these bath posies were as individual as the gardens where they grew. They would include some fragrant petals such as rose, thyme and lavender, possibly bay and mint leaves and dried lemon peel, sprinkled with a few drops of oil of spikenard and 'fixed' with musk or ambergris. These delightfully fragrant mixtures, similar to pot pourri blends which were placed in open bowls to scent the rooms, were tied into cheesecloth bags and trailed in the tepid bath water. This is a charming idea to copy, tying the mixture into disposable cheesecloth bags to hang under the tap. Lovely spicy mixtures to try include rose petals scattered with a few cloves, lightly crushed juniper berries stirred into young marigold leaves and fenugreek seeds blended with lemon balm leaves. Middle Eastern harem women preferred to eat their fenugreek seeds, though—they were thought to be the secret to rounded plumpness.

People who find that frequent baths have a drying effect on the skin—destroying the acid mantle which gives some protection from disease—can benefit from an ancient remedy, the addition of a little sesame oil to the water. Fragrant bath oils are very easy to make, and will last indefinitely in tightly-stopped bottles. You can make them with either a dispersing oil, which dissolves in water, or a floating one, which clings to your body when you get out—and makes your skin gleam. Dispersing oils have the advantage of not leaving a ring around the bath. Castor oil is an example of this type, but only in its treated form, known as Turkey Red oil. Mix together three parts of Turkey Red oil to one part of your favourite aromatic oil, bottle it and use 1 teaspoonful at a time in the bath water. For a floating oil, one that is lighter than water, you can use almond or avocado oil—full of Vitamin E which nourishes the skin—with aromatic oil in the same proportion. These bath oils, stored in pretty bottles with carefully hand-written labels, make delightful and highly personal gifts. You can surprise your friends with the elusive fragrance of oil of nutmeg or oil of cumin.

Mary Queen of Scots bathed in wine, but most of us would be content with cider vinegar which has the same effect and restores the acid mantle to the skin. Add two to three tablespoons to the water, or rub the cider vinegar diluted with six parts of water all over the skin before taking a bath. This treatment is especially good for dry skin. Salt added to the bath can remove dead cells and generally tone up the skin; for a real 'spa' treatment, mix together 225g/8oz (1 cup) of Epsom salts (Magnesium sulphate) and 450g (1lb) of Magnesium chloride with a few drops of oil of patchouli and dissolve in warm bath water.

Natural spice cosmetics
The first cosmetics must have been made from the natural vegetable oils and animal fats available. The first cleansing cream—a mixture of olive oil, wax and rose water—was blended by a Greek physician, Galen. Ladies all along the Mediterranean came to know the value of sesame oil as a dry skin food which penetrates and softens the skin. This polyunsaturated nut oil is a highly beneficial aid to sun-tanning because it absorbs most of the ultra-violet rays of the sun. Resistant to water, it is also ideal to use when swimming.

If you are buying myrrh to experiment with making incense—discussed later in this chapter—you might like to try the wrinkle preventative favoured by Athenian ladies. They burned a little myrrh powder on a stone and allowed the astringent resin fumes to penetrate and nourish the

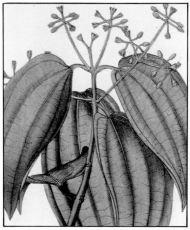

Top *Sesame produces a nourishing oil which when added to a bath keeps one's skin supple.*
A detail of the leaves and flowers of the cinnamon tree. Cinnamon was one of the ingredients used to make up the chrism – a holy oil used to anoint the Tabernacle and its priests.

Making your own soap is a simple process and you can scent them according to taste as many essential spice oils produce a delightful fragrance.

skin in the form of a fragrant, cleansing steam facial.

Spicy soapmaking

It is thought that soap was first discovered by accident in Rome about 1000 BC when the fat from sacrificial animals was mixed with the ashes from the fire. Gradually spices were added to colour and perfume the soap and examples have been found in a soapmaker's shop in Pompeii.

The craft of soapmaking is one which we can easily practise in our kitchens and enjoy every day. Think how satisfying it is to lie in a bath wallowing in a natural fragrance you have blended yourself. The permutations of colour and scent are endless, you can use all kinds of disposable moulds to make the soap into attractive shapes, and even carve initials or little drawings as decorations.

At its simplest, soap is a combination of a fatty acid, normally tallow, and alkali, caustic soda (lye). The necessary chemical reaction takes place when the melted tallow and the caustic soda and water solution are mixed together at the same lukewarm temperature, so it is important to follow the instructions carefully.

Melt the tallow the day before you intend to make the soap—or earlier if it is more convenient. It will keep for several weeks in the refrigerator. Put the pieces of fat in a heavy pan, discarding any discoloured parts. Set it over a low heat until most of it has rendered, then strain it through two layers of cheesecloth or muslin lining a strainer. Leave it in a bowl to set. Each 250ml/8fl oz (1 cup) of melted tallow will be enough to make one large tablet of soap.

Before starting to make the soap, gather together all the kitchen utensils you will need, a wooden spoon, a hand whisk or electric mixer, a heavy saucepan and 2 mixing bowls. You will also need a standard measuring cup and a tablespoon. Protect all the surrounding kitchen surfaces with several layers of newspaper, and yourself with a large apron and a pair of rubber gloves.

To make one large tablet of soap

	Metric/U.K.	U.S.
Cold soft water (rain water, or tap water softened)	125ml/4fl oz	$\frac{1}{2}$ cup
Caustic soda (lye)	2 Tbs	2 Tbs
Tallow	250g/8oz	1 cup

Melt the tallow in the saucepan. Before measuring out the caustic soda (lye), read the manufacturers' instructions carefully. Caustic soda (lye), particularly in its dry form, can burn the skin. If you spill a speck on your hand, wash it off immediately under the cold tap and rub the skin with lemon juice or vinegar. *Never* leave the packet within reach of children.

Pour the water into a mixing bowl and add the caustic soda (lye). Stir the mixture with a wooden spoon until the soda dissolves as the mixture becomes hot. Allow both the matted tallow and the caustic soda (lye) solution to cool to lukewarm—test by putting your hand underneath the containers. Then pour the fat in a steady stream into the caustic soda (lye) solution, stirring slowly. Beat it with a whisk, watching carefully for the sudden transition from a shiny liquid to a thick, opaque mixture—soap. Pour it quickly into the mould and allow it to set overnight. Release the soap from the mould and place it in a warm, draught-free area such as an airing cupboard or linen cupboard to mature for at least two weeks.

If you like, you can carve the mature soap with the sharp point of a craft knife. Initialled soap tablets make a highly personal gift for friends. Collect the soap scrapings and use them in a metal soap saver.

To scent your soap

You can add essential spice oils to this basic recipe, making lovely fragrances of your own, and colour the soap with powdered spices or bottled food colouring. As soon as you have poured the melted tallow onto the caustic soda (lye) solution, add a few drops of oil of cloves, patchouli, nutmeg, caraway, or a few pinches of sandalwood powder. To colour the soap, add a pinch of turmeric or saffron powder for yellow or bottled food colouring. Stir the oils or colourants in thoroughly, otherwise they will form lumps or beads on the surface of the soap. To make honey spice soap which has a soft creamy colour, measure 1 tablespoon of olive oil, 1 tablespoon of sesame oil and 1 tablespoon of honey. Top up to the 250ml/8fl oz (1 cup) with melted tallow and, when the mixture is lukewarm, pour it on to the caustic soda (lye) solution.

Bottom left Food colouring can be added to soap to make it visually appealing.
Bottom right A mixture of tallow and caustic soda (lye) combine to make a thick, opaque mixture which, when set, makes a tablet of white soap.

The mystery of incense

Another way to scent your home with the sweet smell of spices is to make incense, which creates a lingering atmosphere evocative of the mystic East. It was, in fact, burned in Egypt, Babylon and China in magical and religious rites and introduced into the Christian church in the sixth century, where it was held to be a symbol of purity, virtue, and the ascent of prayer to God. Frankincense, the basis of church incense, produces phenol carbolic acid when it burns, so it was valued for its practical qualities as an antiseptic, too, and it was said that churches where incense was burned were never attacked by woodworm.

There are two basic types of incense; one is a simple blend of ground spices and fixatives which can be sprinkled on to charcoal glowing in a fire or a thurible, those beautifully decorative brass church ornaments. Or you can blend the spices with charcoal and gum and form them into cones or sticks to burn indoors.

You can buy the ingredients of traditional church incense, frankincense and myrrh, from church suppliers and sandalwood, the one so reminiscent of the East, from Indian stores. Much more cheaply, you can blend your own mixtures from your kitchen or garden spices. Although you can use ordinary charcoal for the shaped incense, there is a quick-lighting type which is chemically treated and ideal for the purpose. If it is to be burned indoors, charcoal should have a good draught—which is why church thuribles are swung backwards and forwards—and only be used in a well-ventilated room as the fumes can be harmful.

To make incense without charcoal

	Metric/U.K.	U.S.
Sandalwood powder	25g/1oz	1oz
Gum benzoin	25g/1oz	1oz
Cardamom seeds, ground	15g/½oz	½oz
Cloves, ground	15g/½oz	½oz
Cassia bark, ground	15g/½oz	½oz

For a basic incense mixture, blend these ingredients well together. Gum benzoin, which acts as a fixative, has an aura of well-cared-for antique furniture and you will find that the cassia chips are very reminiscent of cinnamon sticks.

For variety, you can add experimental ingredients of your own choice, such as grated dried orange or lemon peel, bay leaves, eucalyptus leaves and resin, dried lavender, crushed scented barks or one or two drops of cedarwood or nutmeg oil. For a more authentic church-like aroma, you can use a two-to-one mixture of frankincense and myrrh as the basis, adding sandalwood or the suggested barks or oils as variations.

To make incense shapes

	Metric/U.K.	U.S.
Charcoal, quick-lighting	175g/6oz	6oz
Gum benzoin, powdered	25g/1oz	1oz
Sandalwood, powdered	6g/¼oz	¼oz
Cassia, ground	6g/¼oz	¼oz
Mucilage of gum tragacanth, compound tragacanth powder or gum arabic		

Crush the first four ingredients together and mix them well. To bind the mixture into a pliable 'dough', use mucilage of gum tragacanth (which, because it has chloroform and alcohol in it, has to be made up by a pharmacist), compound tragacanth powder (a sucrose, starch and tragacanth mixture, also from pharmacists), or gum arabic. Your choice might very well be decided by local availability. The last two preparations have to

be mixed first with water, then stirred in to form a stiff paste.

To this basic mixture, you can add other aromatic ingredients of your choice (see the suggestions for making incense without charcoal) until you have a 50/50 mixture of charcoal and other ingredients. Once the mixture forms a stiff paste, mould it into cones or other shapes and leave them on a warm shelf for two or three days to dry. Wrap the shapes in plastic or aluminium foil so that they retain their scent in storage. To use the incense, stand the shapes on a non-inflammable base such as a tin plate or a brass bowl or dish.

The sweet smell of incense wafting through your house will evoke all the mysteries of the East, but always burn charcoal-based incense in a well-ventilated room as the fumes can be toxic.

Natural dyes extracted from plant material give clothes lovely hues.

Creating spicy colours

Before manufactured colourants were available, people used natural plant material to dye yarn and cloth. Saffron was used to dye the soft, flowing robes of the Buddhist monks—turmeric gives a similar effect—and powdered fenugreek seeds to give a paler shade. As a symbol of Chinese hospitality and welcome, saffron powder was sprinkled on the clothes of visitors; not always a welcome gesture, presumably.

The principle of plant dyeing is to make an extraction of the colour by simmering the plant material—flowers, leaves, berries, bark or powder—

in water. It is not an exact science and it takes a trained eye to see just when the infusion is strong enough and when the yarn has been simmered for long enough. The moisture content of the plant, the soil in which it was grown, the weather and the softness of the water are other factors which affect the final colour—and give the home craftsman some delightful surprises.

All natural fibres 'take' well, but wool is the most successful. White woollen garments can be given a new and brighter lease of life or the wool unpicked and rewound into skeins. Balls of wool need to be rewound into skeins, too, and lightly tied into a bundle. You can sometimes buy un-bleached wool and, by dyeing it in batches with different plants, create your own fashion range of subtle and blending colours.

Apart from the plant material, you will usually need what is known as a mordant, a substance which enhances or deepens the colour and sets it fast. These are discussed later. As long as you are not using poisonous plants, you can use your kitchen utensils—pans and a strainer. You will also need rubber gloves, a stick for stirring each colour and rain water or softened tap water.

The amount of plant material you will need varies with each plant, but as a general guide, allow 125g (4oz) to each 25g (1oz) of wool. Powdered spices, flowers, petals and leaves might need as little as 20 minutes' sim-mering, but the tougher parts of the plant, such as bark and hard berries, can take up to 3 hours. Crushing tough plant material first helps to draw out the colour.

First of all you must weigh the wool to be dyed, then weigh the appro-priate amount of plant material. Put it in a large pan, cover it with soft water and bring it slowly to simmering point. Top the pan up to the original level with more hot water as it evaporates. When the colour is the strength you want, strain the liquor through a strainer and discard the plant material. Allow the dye to cool to hand-heat to use it straight away. To store it for later use, let it cool completely before putting it in covered jars in the refrigerator.

Top *Wool is the easiest of natural fibres to dye and skeins of wool can be dipped into a pot of dye, but make sure the yarn is loosely tied. It can then be knitted or crocheted into a garment of your choice.*

Dyeing without a mordant

Some plants will give a lasting and satisfactory result by what is called the 'direct' dyeing method, that is to say without the addition of a mordant. These include ground turmeric (saffron is too expensive), the outside skins of onions, the tops and flowers of golden rod and of ragwort and the berries of white snowberries, which all give a yellow extract. Bilberries, blueberries and sloes give rose, pink and purple, depending on the length of time the plant material is simmered, and the whole plant of common grey wall lichen gives brown.

First, thoroughly soak the woollen garment or the yarn. Put the wet wool into the dyebath—a large saucepan or preserving pan—cover it with the dye and raise the temperature of the liquid very gradually to sim-mering point. Keep it simmering, stirring from time to time, until the wool is the colour you want. Lift it out on the end of a stick to gauge the colour, and remember that it will dry several shades lighter. Gently squeeze the wool to remove most of the excess liquid, then plunge it into warm, soft water and rinse it thoroughly.

Dyeing with a mordant

Plant materials other than those mentioned above need 'fixing' with a chemical that has an affinity with both the fibre and the dyestuff. It takes experience to know in just what way a mordant will change a dye colour. Two of the best mordants to use are alum and iron, both obtainable from pharmacies. Alum generally speaking brightens natural dye colours; iron tends to darken most colours and can turn yellow dyes to green.

To mordant with alum (Potassium aluminium sulphate) use 25g (1oz) or

Below *A crocheted skirt of beautiful, vivid colours, all of which have come from natural dyes.*

Top *The leaves of lily of the valley produce a lovely shade of green, besides being an attractive plant to have in your garden.*

Above *Blackcurrant fruit used with a mordant produces varying shades of rose, pink and purple.*

1¾ teaspoons of alum for each 125g (4oz) of wool. The mordant is normally used before dyeing. Pour enough soft water to cover the wool into a pan, measure out the alum and stir it in thoroughly. Add the wet wool and heat the dye bath so slowly that it takes about an hour to reach simmering point. Keep it at this temperature—no more—for a further hour, gently stirring the wool occasionally. Remove the pan from the heat and allow the liquid to cool to hand-hot. Without wringing the wool, gently squeeze out the excess moisture. To dye the wool straight away, treat this as the 'wet wool' stage and proceed as described. Or dry the wool in a towel and store it in plastic bags containing moth repellent for dyeing later. Remember to wet the wool thoroughly again before dyeing.

To mordant with iron (ferrous sulphate, also known as copperas and green vitriol) measure the mordant in the proportion of 4g (⅛oz), just under 1 teaspoon, to each 125g (4oz) of wool. The iron is added to the dye for the last 15 to 30 minutes of the dyeing time. Lift out the wool on the stick, add the iron and stir it well before replacing the wool. Bring it back to simmering point slowly and then proceed as described above in the instructions for dyeing with a mordant.

The natural colours you can achieve

Yellow Turmeric powder and the outer skins of onion 'take' very quickly, yielding a pale yellow after a few minutes and a rich shade in 20 to 40 minutes. Other plant materials to dye direct are the tops and flowers of golden rod and of ragwort and the berries of white snowberries. Those which need a mordant are barberry twigs, the bark of black oak, the tips and flowers of yellow broom, the tops of queen of the meadow, the tops and flowers of St John's wort, the tops and flowers of tansy and the leaves and the tops of weld before they seed.

Blue The most popular and beautiful plant dye for blue is indigo. You can extract colour from most parts of the tree, or buy the plant extract. You can also use the leaves of woad, as ancient Britons did, and the berries of mahonia. They all need a mordant.

Brown Without a mordant, you can use the whole plant of grey wall lichen. With a mordant, you can use the bark and big bud of hickory, the hulls of black walnut (be prepared for them to take up to 3 hours to release the colour), larch needles, mahogany sawdust or wood chips, the leaves of mountain laurel, oak bark and pyracantha twigs.

Orange If simmered for longer, and mordanted, the outer skins of onion will give an orange extract. You can also use coreopsis flowers, orange dahlia flowers, the roots of lady's bedstraw and of madder.

Rose, pink and purple You can dye direct with the fruits of bilberry and sloe. With a mordant, try the fruits of blackcurrant, black huckleberry, blackberry, elder and wild grape vine.

Red For a successful red, one of the most luxurious-looking of natural colours, all the plant materials need a mordant. Try the roots of bloodroot, so aptly named, flowers of red dahlia and of geranium, the bark of hemlock, the roots of lady's bedstraw, madder roots, pokeweed berries and the fruity protruberances of prickly-pear cactus.

Green Use the young tops of bracken, the chip-wood of fustic, the tops and flowers of golden rod (mordanted with iron), the green part above the ground of horsetail, the black berries of ivy, lily of the valley leaves, nettle leaves and tops, privet leaves and the leaves and tops of weld.

Black or grey With suitable mordants, alder bark, buckthorn berries, butternut nuts, logwood bark and yellow flag iris roots will give shades varying from pale grey to almost black.

To test whether a plant material will give you a successful dye, simmer a little wool with the plant and watch as it turns colour. You will often find that you can achieve some pleasant surprises, and shades that even now cannot be prepared commercially.

SPICES IN
YOUR KITCHEN

With a good selection of spices in your kitchen, the whole world of cooking is at your fingertips. You can bring constant interest and variety to your dishes, turn the cheaper types of meat and fish into delicacies, and give your family and friends all the culinary excitement of foreign travel. You can experience the splendour of a Medieval banquet with saffron-coloured fish dishes and hot, spiced wines, evoke all the gaiety and colour of South America with fiery, palate-tingling dishes and red-hot sauces, or present a perfectly balanced vegetarian meal in the Oriental manner, where the spices play an important but not dominating role.

So that you are always sure to extract the maximum possible flavour from your spices, it is important to follow a few simple rules about storing and using them. Most of the seeds, bark and roots we use as spices are dried. This means that they will have a fairly long shelf life and will actually keep almost indefinitely. But they gradually lose their aroma and in most cases are past their best after about three months. For this reason it is best to buy or grow your spices in small quantities, so that you are constantly replenishing your supply.

Whole spices retain their flavour much better than ground ones so the ideal is to buy whole spices little and often—never be afraid to ask for 15g or 25g ($\frac{1}{2}$oz or 1oz) of the ones you use least. Both light and heat affect the flavour, and so the least efficient means of storage is the decorative rows of glass jars that look so attractive on kitchen shelves. Since glass jars are so obviously practical and can be washed between each new supply, look for dark-coloured ones like old apothecary jars—if you want to keep them on show. Otherwise, put colourless glass containers away in a cupboard out of the light. If your kitchen is hot and steamy—and particularly if you have an all-night-burning oven—then it is in any case not the best place for your spices. Find a suitable place where the spices will be kept at a lower temperature. The effort of having to take extra paces to reach your spices will be more than rewarded in terms of flavour when you use them.

Buying ground spices

If, for quickness and convenience, you do choose to buy ground spices, it pays to buy a reputable branded make. Usually the higher price will be an

An assortment of ground and whole spices which are so necessary to everyone's kitchen. A mortar and pestle is especially useful in grinding spices.

indication that the product has been carefully graded and will be purer and more pungent. When you buy ground spices as fragrant, colourful powders, it is virtually impossible to be able to assess the quality when they are sealed into plastic bags, cardboard drums or glass containers. But because of the relatively high value of spices, the practice of dilution—or adulteration—with cheaper ingredients has been rife for centuries, and even now has not been stamped out entirely. However, the major spice importers who sell their products under brand names implement the strictest quality control. Not only do they, in a large number of cases, visit the spice plantations and buy the crop 'on the bush', but they also carry out tests at every stage thereafter. Delivery trucks are inspected, looking for any traces of impurities on the floor of the vehicle; then the spices are tested under laboratory conditions for impurities, moisture and acid content, colour and flavour. Only after a spice has passed with flying colours will such a firm accept the consignment.

Spices ground in the factories of these firms are subjected to analytical tests both during and after the process, too, and spice blends are constantly analyzed to check the balance of ingredients. And so, in terms of care, satisfaction and value for money, you generally get what you pay for.

Grinding your spices

Most spices are very easy to grind at home. An ordinary pepper mill will cope with most of the seeds (although the minute black poppy seeds slip through the teeth without a blemish!). A hand-operated rotary grinder, the type with a little drawer at the bottom to collect the powder, is also efficient, and gives the authentic aura of an Eastern spice market. These will cope with all your spices except poppy seeds, cinnamon and mace. For poppy seeds you need a special grinder, which you can buy in some countries abroad. Cinnamon and mace, along with all the other seeds, can be ground quite satisfactorily in a manual or electric coffee grinder.

If you find that your ground spices are not quite as finely powdered as you would wish, sift them before use, either through a metal or nylon strainer or through a piece of coarse cheesecloth or muslin.

Freshly-grated nutmeg, infinitely more aromatic than the ready-ground spice, is invaluable in many rich fruit cakes, baked puddings or as a last-minute garnish to soups and sweets. You can buy special little graters just for the purpose—or you might like to invest in an antique one if one of your hobbies is collecting old kitchen utensils and tableware. Otherwise, just use the smallest mesh of an ordinary kitchen grater, grating only the amount you need for the moment and storing the nutmeg away again in a lidded container.

When you want to crush the seeds without actually grinding them to a powder, a pestle and mortar are the traditional tools to use. Specialist kitchen shops usually sell the old-fashioned heavy stone ones, or you can buy them in decorative olive wood or even brass. These are particularly useful when you want to make a paste of pounded spices with a liquid such as lemon or lime juice, the 'wet masala' featured in many of the Southern Indian dishes. Another way to crush spices is by putting them in a heavy quality plastic bag, double sealing the ends, and giving them a good hard roll with a rolling pin.

A very good way to keep alive the flavour of your spices is to infuse vinegar and cooking oil with the flavours and to keep them, tightly corked, ready to use in salad dressings, marinades and to brush meat and fish before grilling (broiling).

To make flavoured vinegar

Use whole spice seeds such as coriander, fennel or fenugreek—one type of seed for each bottle of vinegar. Lightly bruise the seeds in a pestle and mortar or with a rolling pin. Use about 2 tablespoons of seed to 1.5 litres/

Below Dried ginger root is either crushed with a mortar and pestle or finely grated before use.
Bottom Fresh ginger is peeled and sliced or diced before use. It can occasionally be pounded.

2 pints (5 cups) of vinegar. White distilled vinegar will give you a purer impression of the spice flavour, while malt or cider is a much stronger brew. Put the crushed seeds into a jar, shake it well and put it in a warm, dark place such as an airing cupboard or linen closet for two weeks, shaking it occasionally. Taste the flavour at the end of this time—it should be fine. If you want a stronger spice, strain off and discard the seeds and start again, pouring the warmed vinegar onto a fresh batch. Finally, strain off the seeds and store the spiced vinegar in a tightly-corked bottle.

To make flavoured oil

You can flavour cooking oil in a similar way, keeping it on hand to give an unusual lift to marinades and salad dressings and to brush grilled (broiled) foods. Crush 2 tablespoons of spice seeds and put them in a jar. Pour on 250ml/½ pint (1¼ cups) of sunflower, corn or olive oil and 1 tablespoon of wine vinegar. Seal the bottle with a cork or screw cap and shake it well. Leave it in the sunlight to infuse for two or three weeks, shaking it

Where possible, spices should be bought loose and stored in airtight containers out of the light. If you have to buy them in ground form, buy in small quantities so as to avoid loss of freshness.

well twice each day. Strain off the seeds and pour the oil into a clean bottle. Cover it with the lid or a cork.

Heating spices for full flavour

Some spice seeds, such as fenugreek, coriander, cumin and poppy, improve in flavour if they are gently heated before being pounded, ground or used whole in cooking. To heat spice seeds, use a small non-stick pan over a low heat. Put in the seeds and shake the pan from time to time until the seeds are heated through and pop slightly. Then use them as directed in the recipes.

Some seeds—sesame is a good example—change their personality considerably if they are toasted over a higher heat or put into a medium oven. Seeds scattered on bread or cakes to be baked will, of course, toast as they are cooked; for seeds to garnish soups, mashed vegetables or mousses, toasting adds a nutty flavour and a contrastingly crunchy texture.

Spices in Indian cooking

The very smell of toasting spice seeds wafting through the kitchen brings to mind the great variety of regional Indian dishes, so much more subtle and delicious than our generic term 'curry' can ever imply. Curry powder is never used in authentic Indian cooking, though various blends of the sweeter spices, known as *garam masala*, are included, usually added to a dish towards the end of the cooking time. When the hotter spices— peppers and chillis—are included, they are added first, so that the heat is drawn off, as it were, into the main ingredients. An Indian cook would consider it an unpardonable sin to offer a dish in which any spice tasted raw.

Cloves, cardamom, cinnamon, fennel, cumin, nutmeg, mace and turmeric in any combination and varying proportions are usually used to make *garam masala* blends. You can mix together your own spices and grind them freshly, just before you use them, or a little in advance to save time at the last moment.

In Southern India where many people still follow a vegetarian diet, more fresh spices—coriander leaves, for example—are used, and the protein is largely made up of lentil dishes—*dhal*. Blends of spices are mixed to 'wet masalas' with lemon or lime juice or coconut oil, and plenty of rice is provided to soak up the sauce.

Tandoori chicken, now such a popular dish in restaurants in the Western world, emanated from the north of India, where many meat dishes absorb the flavour of the spices in marinades before being crisply cooked over glowing charcoal.

Chutneys and pickles are an important part of Indian cuisine, not only because they can provide perfect complements to the main dishes, but because they are a practical way of preserving fruit and vegetables that, in a tropical climate, have such a short season.

Spices for Chinese cuisine

There is a tendency to regard Chinese cooking as bland by comparison with Indian; or perhaps it would be more accurate to say there *was* such a tendency, before Szechuan dishes were introduced to restaurants in Europe and America. In this northern region of China, red-cooked dishes pulsating with Szechuan pepper are in complete contrast to the gentle dishes which rely for effect on an harmonious blend of soft and crisp textures, bright and pale colours, large and small ingredients. The equivalent of the Indian *garam masala* in China is called 'five-spice powder', a blend of finely ground anise, Szechuan pepper, fennel, cloves and cinnamon. The proportion of the hot pepper in the blend, of course, determines the 'heat' of a dish. Nothing about Chinese cooking is ever a hit and

miss affair, and the use of spices is no exception. The ancient cult of Taoism, the Way of Nature, determines the compatibility of foods with each other and in relation to spices. Followers of the cult would never, for example, serve lamb's liver spiced with pepper, nor flavour a dish containing rabbit with ginger in any form.

Latin American hot spices

If the word compatibility were to be applied to Latin American cooking, on the other hand, it might well be said that every ingredient—meat, fish, fruit, or tortillas, the daily bread of the Central American countries—is compatible with chilli peppers. When Columbus went in search of black pepper and other Oriental spices, and found America instead, he found a civilization already used to eating fire, with palate-stinging sauces sold by Indian peddlers in the markets, truly a downright lethal trap for the unwary traveller.

Experimenting with recipes from the countries where the spices originated, and from other parts of the world where they were traded over land and sea, it is fascinating to see how these aromatic plants have fitted in so many different ways into the various culinary cultures. With a selection of spices in the kitchen, you can capture in your own home the flavour of the Caribbean with lamb curry laced with mango, pumpkin and rum; of Spain with a paella succulent with shrimps, chicken, peas, beans and saffron; of the Middle East with honey cake enriched with cinnamon, allspice, cloves and candied peel, and of the Viennese Empire with traditional *sachertorte*, chocolate cake essentially flavoured with vanilla. Your cook's tour can take you to Russia with lamb and prunes gently simmered with cinnamon, nutmeg, coriander and lemon juice, or perhaps with bread dipped in allspice butter, or spread with quince and clove preserve. And for a taste of Scandinavia, you could try cardamom-flavoured waffles made with sour cream or, in a more lavish mood, *Gravlax*, pressed cured salmon with a sweet and sour mustard and dill sauce.

So many dishes in so many moods—and they can all be created from your store of spices.

SPICES YOU CAN GROW

Most spices grow in the hot, moist, tropical climates of the Eastern and Western Hemispheres, so in Northern gardens it is not possible to recreate all the exotic, pungent aroma of a plantation of cloves in the Moluccas or pepper vines rambling as far as the eye can see. However, on good, well-drained soil in a sunny position, you can grow several spices that favour a mild climate and, given a long, hot summer, can count on more successes; anise and sesame seeds, for example, will only ripen to their full pungency in a good long spell of hot sun.

With a greenhouse or cold frame you can widen the scope still further. In an unheated greenhouse you can sow and bring on seeds to plant out in the garden or greenhouse border later, and in a heated greenhouse, where conditions can be brought closer to the heat and humidity of the tropics, experiment with some of the real 'exotics'.

Obviously, the closer conditions are to their natural habitat, the more plants will flourish. Full details of the soil and cultivation requirements are given under the name of each individual spice in The Dictionary of Spices. When you read that a spice is indigenous to the Middle Eastern or Mediterranean countries, you will get an idea of the conditions it enjoys: generally speaking, a light, well-drained soil and a sunny position. Unfortunately, stodgy, heavy clay is no more a favourite with spice plants than it is with those of us who have to work on it. If that is your problem, it is best to plant your spices in troughs or large pots filled with light, specially prepared soil. Stand the troughs or pots against a south wall, or on a balcony rather than on a windowsill. Because of their largely straggling habits spice plants are not the neat little kitchen window decoration that some herbs can be.

Most of the spices we can grow produce generous quantities of seeds,

Coriander is very easy to grow and is a resilient annual plant.

on full, umbrella-shaped clusters or in tightly-packed pods, so two or three of each type of plant will usually produce enough seed to dry and use in one year. If, of course, you have space and want to turn your spice-growing hobby into a way of giving your friends an entirely personal, home-grown present, then go ahead and grow rows and rows. Don't be tempted, though, to grow a crop for about five years' use in your own kitchen. The dried seeds gradually lose their aroma completely, and there are few sadder sights in a kitchen than a spice rack without a single spicy smell.

Flowering spice plants

Many spice plants have such pretty flowers that it is a pity to consign them to the vegetable patch, along with the runner (snap) beans. The annuals give very good value in the flower garden before the seeds develop. Sesame has white flowers splashed with red or yellow, anise and fenugreek have creamy-white flowers, and the poppy grown for culinary seed, *Papaver somniferum*, rewards you with short-lived white, lilac or purple blooms. Coriander, a hardy annual which can be grown on slightly heavier soil than the others, has pale mauve flowers, and caraway, a biennial, great clusters of minute white flowers, rather like sheep's parsley. All these plants are of medium height, growing 60–90cm (2–3ft) high, and so should be planted towards the centre or back of a flower bed, depending on the other flowers you grow. If you have very tall flowers, such as hollyhock, foxglove and delphinium, of course, they will tower over your spices. Cumin, described as a low-growing annual, reaches about 30–60cm (1–2ft), and so could be in front of the others. With its white or rose-coloured flowers, it makes a pretty plant just behind, say, an edging of lavender or sweet-smelling pinks.

Another low-growing plant is the saffron crocus, which once established can be reproduced quite rapidly from the tiny cormlets which form at the base of the bulb. Plant the cormlets in rich, sandy, well-drained soil, 15cm (6in) apart, and be on the look-out, in the autumn (fall) for the splash of bluey-purple flowers that will suddenly burst out between the shiny green leaves. The golden stigmas are your treasure trove, and should be picked as soon as the flowers open.

Top Saffron is best bought whole in little threads which are the dried stamens of the saffron crocus. Above The saffron crocus yields blue-purple flowers in the autumn (fall).

Harvesting spice seeds

Harvesting spice seeds requires a certain amount of judgement. Clearly, you want to leave the seeds on the plant as long as possible to develop and ripen. But leave them too long and the plant will do the job that Nature intended for it, scattering the seed far and wide. Fine for next year's crop, but not so good for this year's spice jars! Cut all the umbrella-shaped clusters, such as anise and caraway, poppy, too, close to the ground. Tie the stems in bunches and hang them upside-down for the seeds to complete their ripening process. Avoid losing any falling seed by tying muslin or cheesecloth loosely round the seedheads, by hanging the bunches over a tray, or by standing them, head down, in a large crock or clean, dry bucket. Where necessary, shake out the remaining seed by hand or, in the case of cardamom, pick off the dried seed pods. They are best stored complete with the seeds inside, otherwise they quickly lose their aroma.

Other seeds need further drying before storing. The natural way to do this is to spread them on trays to dry in the sunshine, but the danger with this is that the wind might blow them away. A tray on a south-facing windowsill or in the airing cupboard or linen closet is usually the answer.

When the seeds are dry, store them in airtight jars or bottles, preferably away from the light and in a reasonably cool, dry room.

Sowing the seeds

You can plant some spice seeds straight into the ground where they are to grow.

Coriander likes soil well manured the previous year. Sow the seeds in spring, 6mm (¼in) deep; rows should be 30cm (1ft) apart. You can pick some of the fresh, pungent leaves to use in curries and chopped in salads. The seeds should ripen by late summer. Choose a damp day, when there is dew on the ground, to cut off the stems.

Anise seed, also sown in spring, likes light soil with plenty of lime and a sheltered, south-facing position. This is one of the spice seeds which will ripen only in a good summer; without a crystal ball, you can't actually know this when you plant them.

Fenugreek is one of the richest of spice aromas, indispensible in curry powder. The seed should be planted in spring in well-drained soil. The cream flowers bloom during early and late summer and are followed by long, flat pods, eaach one containing about sixteen seeds. Uproot the plants and hang them to dry before threshing the pods and drying out the seeds ready for storage.

Caraway seeds should be sown *in situ* and can take a light clay soil. Since the plants are biennial, and will not flower until the following year, be sure to mark the position where they are lying dormant, or you might accidentally dig them up. Plant the seed either in the late spring or the autumn (fall), and thin the seedlings to 15cm (6in) apart. Keep the patch well weeded and give the plants a light dressing of fertilizer the following spring. This will encourage them to produce flowers in late spring and ripe seeds in summer. Harvest the stems on a dull day, either by uprooting the whole plants or cutting the stems at ground level.

Mustard Although a field of mustard is one of the most marvellous sights of the countryside, the individual plants are rather disappointing, a bit like tall, scraggy cabbage plants. These really could be candidates for the vegetable patch. Both black and white mustard seed need a sunny position. Black mustard prefers light soil with plenty of moisture, and white mustard fares better in a heavy, sandy soil with less watering. Plant the seeds in the spring, thinning them to about 45cm (18in) apart, and take care to harvest them before the pods burst.

With a cold frame or greenhouse
If you have a cold frame or greenhouse, you can sow other spice seeds and bring them on for later repotting or transplanting into the open.

Cumin seed should be planted in pots or trays under glass in the spring, and transferred to a bed of warm, dry, rich soil in a sunny position. The plants develop in 3 to 4 months, producing slender, branching stems and

Bottom left *Caraway seeds should be sown in late spring or autumn (fall) and result in great clusters of tiny white flowers as illustrated by the photograph* Bottom Right.

Capsicum annuum, *the Christmas pepper, is one of the many varieties of sweet pepper which is delicious in salads.*

long, narrow, deep green leaves. The small umbels of white or rose-coloured flowers are followed by the fruits, usually referred to as seeds, which develop to a yellowy-green colour and are covered with tiny hairs.

Sesame seeds should be sown in the greenhouse in spring. Prick out the seedlings as soon as they are large enough to handle. Pot them on into small pots, one per seedling, and then into 12–15cm (5–6in) pots in a temperate greenhouse. Alternatively, you can transplant them into rich soil in the warmest spot in the garden—ideally beneath a south-facing wall. You need luck with the weather for the seeds to ripen; without it, be grateful for the lovely flowers.

Capsicum is a favourite crop for greenhouse owners. Any one of the varieties of sweet peppers makes a delightful salad or vegetable. Though they are perennials, in temperate zones they are treated as half-hardy annuals. Sow the seed in the greenhouse in spring in potting soil, and keep the trays at a temperature of 16°C (60°F). Pot the seedlings singly into 7.5cm (3in) pots, then on again into 17.5cm (7in) pots or into well-fertilized soil in the greenhouse border—the growing bags you can buy in garden centres are ideal. Give the plants frequent dressings of nitrogenous fertilizer, and support the plants with canes as they grow. In a good summer, capsicum plants will thrive in a sunny border out of doors, but do not transplant them until early summer and keep them well watered. Cut the fruits when they are firm and a good size. It is usual to discard the seeds when preparing sweet peppers for salads or cooking, but you can enjoy them, fresh or dried, as an extra spicy seed.

Cardamom plants will flourish in a greenhouse where you can provide high humidity during the spring to autumn (fall) seasons and dryish conditions in the winter. The plants are grown from divided pieces of rhizomes planted in early spring in a soil made up of four parts turfy loam, one part sharp sand and one part leaf mould—any good gardening shop will advise you on this. The plants, perennial shrubs, will rarely reach more than 30cm (1ft) in height, but will reward you with beautiful spikes of flowers, white with a blue and yellow lip, and highly-scented pointed leaves. You can grow cardamom indoors as a house plant, away from direct sunlight in a warm room—the shuttered elegance of old country houses seems to be the right milieu!

Cinnamon It is interesting to try growing miniature cinnamon trees in a greenhouse. The temperature should be 21–27°C (70–80°F) from the spring right through until the autumn (fall) and then, when the growing season is over, down to about 16–21°C (60–70°F). Plant cuttings should be taken from young shoots in April and rooted in a closed propagating frame at a temperature of 27°C (80°F). They must have this initial heat if they are to flourish. Later on pot the young plants in a half-and-half mixture of turfy loam and peat to which a little sand has been added. The trees can be grown either in large pots or in the greenhouse border, and should be given plenty of water during the growing season. They will develop dark green, glossy leaves which are delightfully fragrant, and small yellow flowers before the dark purple berries.

Nutmeg If you are in an experimental mood you could try growing nutmeg trees in a warm greenhouse. The tree bears the male and female flowers on separate plants. As you need one of each for fruit to develop, plant several cuttings to be sure. Plant cuttings of ripened shoots in sand in a propagating frame with gentle heat underneath, then transplant the young plants into a mixture of sandy loam and fibrous peat. The greenhouse temperature must not drop below 13°C (55°F). Even if your trees do not bear the nutmeg and mace you would like to grate into your puddings or flavour your pickles, your efforts will be rewarded with the lovely scented evergreen leaves and pale yellow flowers in early summer.

Indoor spice seed crops
Some spice seeds are fun to grow indoors as quick salad crops.

Mustard As a slight graduation from growing white mustard seed on damp blotting paper or a piece of flannel, as everyone must have done at some time, you can grow the crop in bowls or seed trays filled with fine, sandy soil or bulb fibre. Weekly sowings between autumn (fall) and spring will give you an economical round-the-winter crop. Sprinkle the seed thinly on top of moist, well-firmed-down soil; do not cover with more soil. Either place the container in a drawer or closet or cover it with a piece of wood to exclude the light. Keep the seeds moist with a light sprinkling of water and bring them into the light once germination has started. Cut the crop when the sprouts are from about 7.5cm (3in) high.

Fenugreek is another indoor crop that gives marvellous value. The seeds take about 4 to 6 days to sprout and give a yield 6 to 8 times their original weight—a very good return on capital. Try growing the seed in jars; it works like a dream. Put 3 tablespoons of the seed in a large glass jar and cover it with a piece of clean old nylon or cheesecloth secured with an elastic band. Fill the jar with tepid water, drain it off through the covering and keep the jar on its side. Repeat the watering and draining treatment night and morning. When the sprouts are from about 5cm (2in) long, tip them into a colander and wash them well. They are an unusually spicy ingredient for salad, or can be served as a crisp vegetable. Plunge them into boiling salted water, bring it quickly to the boil again, and drain off the sprouts straight away. Serve them dotted with butter and sprinkled with ground black pepper.

A DICTIONARY OF SPICES

Most spices grow and reach their full, pungent maturity in the hot, sunny, moist climates of the tropical countries where they are harvested by hand, threshed and winnowed in ways that have not changed for centuries, and dried in the baking sun. More modern methods and machinery are gradually being introduced, but on the whole the spice harvest is still faithful to local tradition.

Some of the spices described on the following pages can be grown in our colder climates, and some can be successfully raised if a heated greenhouse is available to provide nearly-natural growing conditions. Those spices that can be grown in garden or greenhouse are marked with an asterisk. Some, such as caraway and sweet peppers, will produce a very satisfactory crop. Others, such as anise and sesame, will be rewarding only in a good summer. And still others—cinnamon is one—will produce a miniature tree and never reach full maturity.

But if you have space to spare, green fingers and a love of cooking, experiment by growing a few of your own spices. Even if they do not attain the full aroma of those grown in the tropics, you will have the satisfaction of achievement that will more than compensate.

Brassica hirta (or alba)

MUSTARD WHITE

Brassica nigra

MUSTARD BLACK

Both members of the cress family, and both having yellow flowers, black and white mustard are distinguished by the colour of the seed. Black mustard has reddish-black seed; white mustard seed is yellowish-orange. There is another type, known as brown, or wild mustard. These rather oily seeds are sometimes mixed with the cultivated ones in commercially prepared 'made' mustard or powders. The spice is one of the earliest known food preservatives and medicines.

Habitat A native plant of Southern European and Mediterranean countries, mustard is now extensively cultivated as a field crop in the United States and all over Europe. Black mustard is grown on light, sandy loam and white mustard on heavier sandy loam. Both plants need good sunshine. The plants are rather tall and straggly, and are not considered attractive garden crops.

White mustard seedlings are the ones grown with cress, a popular crop for children to cultivate on damp cotton. They can be grown out of doors, too, as a crop to be harvested a few days after germination.

Cultivation To grow the crop for seed, plant the seeds in spring and water well; white mustard needs more moisture than black. Both types of mustard will bear yellow flowers on straggly plants, then black mustard will develop smooth, narrow pods containing a row of small seeds and white mustard hairy pods with larger seeds.

To sow the seed for the salad crop, sprinkle it onto finely raked soil firmed down and lightly watered, but do not cover the seed with soil. In bad weather, protect both seed and seedlings under glass.

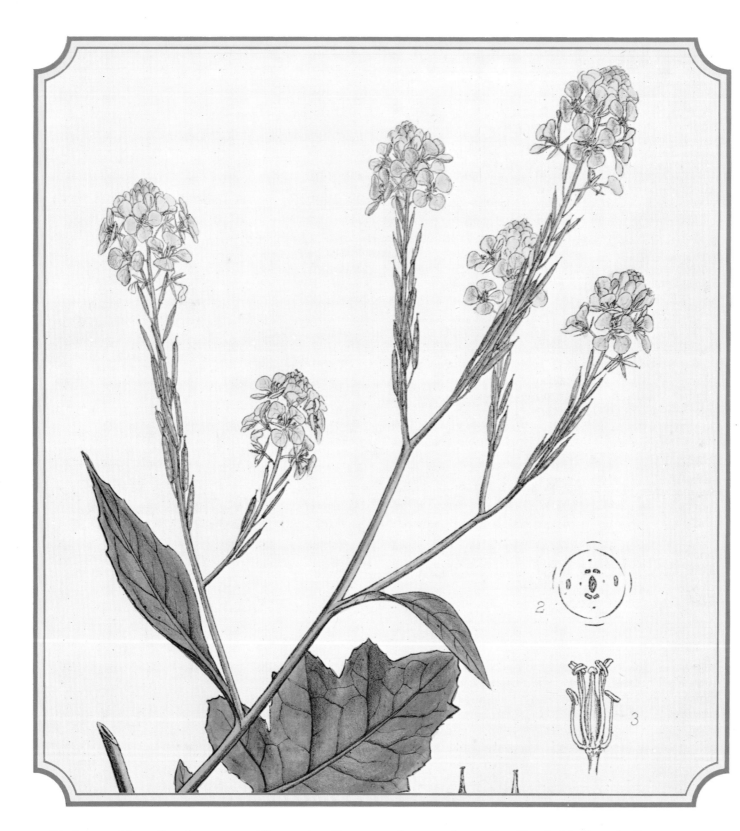

Black mustard has yellow flowers and its seeds are reddish-black. Only when liquid is added to dry mustard powder or the seeds does the characteristic 'hot' flavour evolve. White mustard seeds are added to the black and ground to provide commercial mustard powder.

Harvesting You must harvest the pods of both black and white mustard before they burst or they will scatter their contents everywhere. Wait until they are fully developed, but not quite ripe. Hang the plants to dry, then thresh out the seeds and dry them in the sun or a warm place.

To harvest the salad crop, cut the seedlings when they are about 7.5cm (3in) high.

Uses Black mustard seeds are used whole in pickling spice mixtures. White mustard seeds, much less aromatic, are mixed with the black and ground to provide the commercial mustard powder. A ground cereal such as wheat flour is added to act as a preservative and absorb the natural oils. Prepared or 'made' mustard, the ready-made condiment, is the dried powder mixed with salt, other spices and wine or vinegar. Dry mustard powder or seeds have no 'hot' flavour. It is not until liquid is added and enzyme activity takes place that the characteristic pungency is evident. Different countries and regions have their own traditional mustard recipes; for example, French mustard is made from the black seeds alone.

Made mustard can be spread on fish, poultry or meat before roasting or barbecuing for a 'devilled' finish, and a pinch of mustard powder added to salad dressings. It is used as a preservative in commerical salad creams and mayonnaise.

The leaves of field mustards can be cooked and served as a vegetable.

Salad mustard, often grown at home with cress, is used as a delicate garnish for savoury dishes, in mixed salads, or in sandwiches combined with egg, cheese or fish paste.

Capsicum annuum
CAPSICUM

Widely cultivated throughout the world, this half-hardy annual herbaceous plant grows from 30–90cm (1–3ft) high and bears fruit ranging from 1–24cm ($\frac{1}{2}$–11in) long. It includes all the red, yellow and green peppers, some long and thin and some small and round, which are eaten in salads and as a vegetable, and the red peppers which are ground and sold as paprika.

Habitat The plants require warm, moist conditions.

Cultivation Sow the seed under glass in potting soil in early spring, in a temperature of 16°C (60°F). Pot the seedlings singly first into 7.5cm (3in) pots and then into 17.5cm (7in) pots, or into a greenhouse border. Support the plants with sticks and feed them with nitrogenous fertilizer. The plants may be grown out of doors in sunny weather. Plant them out in summer and keep them well watered. In dry weather, spray them from above, too.

Harvesting Cut the fruits when they are firm and of a good size. This will depend on the variety.

Uses Remove the strips of white 'pith' and the small white seeds inside. Cut up the fruits to use in salad or in casserole dishes. Whole peppers can be stuffed with a rice and meat mixture and baked.

Dried, ground sweet pepper, paprika, is a feature of Hungarian cooking, especially goulash. It is not 'hot' in the way that chilli pepper is, and combines well with egg, fish and meat dishes, particularly pork, veal and chicken. A little paprika pepper is an attractive garnish on light-coloured cream soups such as potato or Jerusalem artichoke.

Capsicum frutescens
CHILLI PEPPER

The same family as the sweet peppers, chilli peppers are indigenous to Central and South America, Mexico, the West Indies, India and China. They have small red, orange or yellow pods which vary enormously in intensity of flavour; they are all more highly spiced than sweet pepper, and some are so hot that they can burn the skin—or the tongue.

Habitat Tropical and temperate climates.

Cultivation The perennial plants, wlth thick, woody stems, grow to a height of up to 2m (6ft). They are usually grown in dense rows.

Harvesting The mature fruits are harvested over a period of several months. They are dried in the sun, either on concrete areas or hanging on

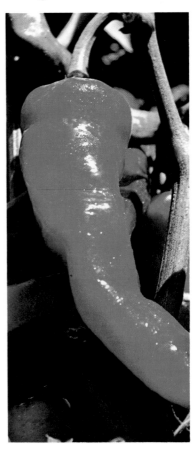

Chilli plants, besides producing a useful crop for the kitchen, are very decorative with their gaudy red hanging fruits. Care should be taken in handling certain varieties as they can leave an unpleasant burning sensation on the skin.

long strings, like colourful garlands.

Uses The various types of chillis cover a wide range of pungency. They are used both fresh and dried as a condiment in India, South-East Asia, Mexico and South America, even eaten raw. Ground chilli powder, or cayenne pepper, varies in strength, too, and should be used in such dishes as curries and chilli con carne with the utmost caution. A whole dish can be rendered quite unpalatable by the addition of too much of the spice. A very small pinch of the ground pepper is used to garnish egg dishes, cream soups, fish mousse and some shellfish dishes.

Carum carvi
CARAWAY

This biennial plant grows to about 60cm (2ft) high and has soft, fern-like leaves and white umbels of flowers. The fruits split into two seeds, which are considered as a spice. Caraway grows in Europe, North America, Russia and India.

Habitat A sunny position in any dry, well-drained light soil.

Cultivation Sow the seeds in a permanent position in the autumn (fall) and thin them to 23cm (9in) apart. Weed around the rows carefully and keep the plants watered in dry weather. They will flower and produce seed the following year. Caraway will re-establish itself with self-sown seed.

Harvesting Allow the seeds to ripen on the plant—usually in summer— then cut the plants off at ground level and hang them in a dry, airy place. When the seeds have dried, shake them on to a sheet of paper and store them in airtight jars away from heat and strong light.

Uses Caraway cakes, bread, biscuits or cookies, now enjoyed for their delicious, characteristic flavour, were served in Roman times to aid digestion. Caraway tea is said to have the same benefit. The seeds are used to flavour cheese, cabbage (particularly sauerkraut), dumplings and Hungarian goulash, and are added to rich game and meat dishes.

The young leaves can be chopped into green salad, and the roots boiled and served as a vegetable. Caraway seed oil is an important ingredient in the German liqueur, kümmel.

Cinnamomum zeylanicum　　　　　　　*Cinnamomum cassia*
CINNAMON　　CASSIA

The two spices have similar properties, but cinnamon, always thought to be superior, has now almost replaced cassia. Cinnamon originated in Sri Lanka (Ceylon) and is now also cultivated in South India, the Malagasy Republic (Madagascar) and the Seychelles. The tree, a member of the laurel family, can grow to a height of 10–12m (30–40ft). It has long, aromatic leaves but is cultivated for the spice, the dried inner bark.

Habitat Wet forest areas.

Cultivation In the tropics, the seeds are planted in round clusters of four or five, with gaps of about 3.5m (10ft) between groups. The seeds germinate after about 3 weeks, but the first harvest does not take place until the fourth or fifth year. The trees are usually cut back to a height of 2–2.5m (6–8ft).

The trees can be raised in northern climates in a greenhouse, but will never reach full maturity. Put the plants in a 50/50 compost of peat and turfy loam with a little sand added, in large pots or a greenhouse border. Keep them warm and moist—21–27°C (70–80°F) during the spring and summer, and 16–21°C (60–70°F) for the rest of the year is ideal. Propaga-

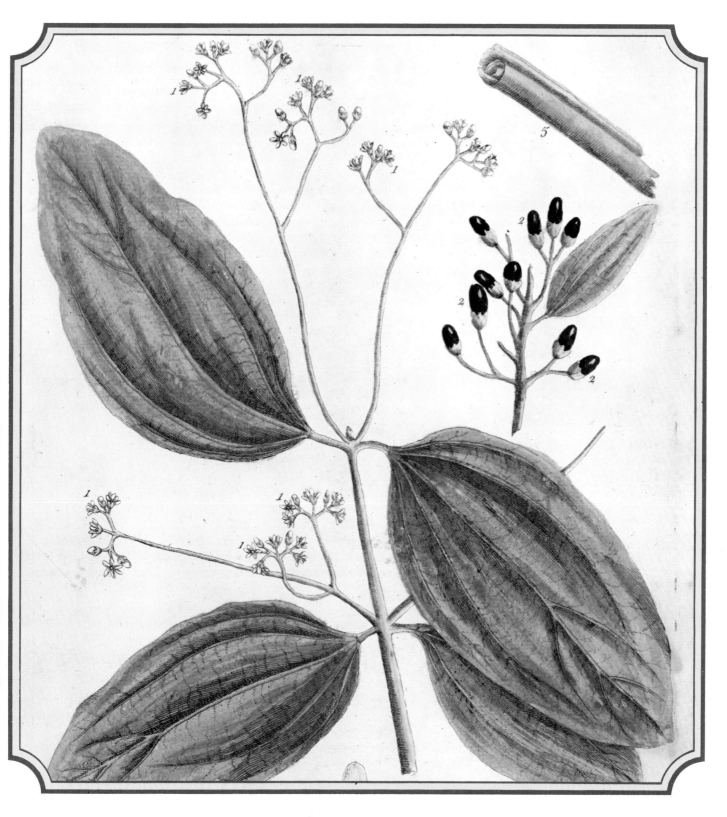

tion is by cuttings, carefully taken from the young shoots of the plant, in mid-spring.

Harvesting The bark is peeled off in long strips with special curved knives. Bundles of bark are left for 24 hours to ferment, then the crumbly outer layer scraped off. As the inner bark dries, it curls like a quill.

Uses Pieces of stick cinnamon are used to spice pickling vinegar and in mulled wine drinks. Ground cinnamon is used in cakes, especially rich fruit cakes, biscuits (cookies), steamed puddings such as Christmas puddings, and in milk puddings.

Cinnamon trees can be grown in Northern climates in a greenhouse and although they will never fully mature, they will still produce an abundant supply of cinnamon. Stick cinnamon is used in pickling vinegar and mulled wines, while the ground variety is best in desserts.

61

Coriandrum sativum

CORIANDER

The plant is an umbelliferous hardy annual plant with fan-shaped feathery leaves and clusters of pale mauve flowers. The pungent leaves are used in Indian dishes, soups and stews, but the plant is mainly grown for the round, aromatic seeds, which are used as a spice. Coriander is a native of the Middle East and was grown in the Hanging Gardens of Babylon. It used to be cultivated on a large scale in the Eastern counties of England.

Habitat A sunny location with a medium or heavy soil, well manured from a previous year. Freshly-manured soil is not suitable.

Cultivation Sow seeds in spring or autumn (fall), 6mm (¼in) deep in rows 30cm (1ft) apart. The plants will grow about 30–90cm (1–3ft) high—autumn (fall) sowing produces stronger, healthier plants.

Harvesting Cut the clusters as soon as the seeds start to ripen, usually in summer or early autumn (fall). Hang them upside-down in a warm, airy place to dry, then shake them on to a sheet of paper. Store the seeds in airtight jars away from strong light and heat.

Uses The seeds, which are said to be an aid to digestion, are used in dishes as varied as sauces, pickles, chutneys, cakes and some confectionery and candy, and are the pungent ingredient in some spiced sausages and other meat products.

Crocus sativus

SAFFRON

The world's most expensive spice, costly because it takes about 250,000 stigmas from about 76,000 of the blue-violet autumn crocus flowers to yield 450g (1lb) of saffron. A native of Southern Europe and the Middle East, saffron was cultivated in Britain in the Middle Ages and a large industry grew up in East Anglia, where the growers were called 'crokers'. At the price it is, it is well worth trying to grow the crop and harvesting your own little gold mine!

Habitat The world's production now comes largely from Spain and Portugal. The saffron crocus favours a light, rich sandy or loamy soil with good drainage. It needs a sunny position and, since it does not flower until the autumn, might need protecting by cloches or Hotkaps from heavy rains or early frost, which would completely damage the crop.

Cultivation Carefully separate the young cormlets which form at the base of the bulb-like corms and plant them 15cm (6in) apart, in well-cultivated soil, in late summer or early autumn (fall).

Harvesting The crop should be harvested as soon as the flowers open. Each one has three bright orangey-red, funnel-like stigmas. Pick them carefully by hand and separate them from the flowers. Spread the stigmas on a tray and dry them in an airing cupboard or warm linen closet, away from draughts. Store them in airtight jars as soon as they are dry and thread-like.

Uses Saffron was one of the earliest known colourants, producing a beautiful range of yellow and orange shades for food, cotton, silk and wool, and was used as a cosmetic, notably by Cleopatra.

The spice is sold whole, the thin, thread-like strands packed in tiny sachets, or in ground form. But, because of the high cost of the spice, ground saffron is liable to be adulterated with additives. (In Germany in the fifteenth century people convicted of adulterating the spice were burned at the stake.)

Coriander is a hardy annual; it is mainly grown for its seeds which are used in a wide variety of culinary dishes. The leaves, to a lesser extent, can be used in Indian dishes, soups and stews.

The dried threads should be crushed with a pestle and mortar, then soaked in hot liquid—the stock or sauce that is to form part of the dish. Saffron is an essential colouring and flavouring ingredient in dishes such as Spanish paella, French bouillabaisse and traditional English saffron cakes and buns. A thread or a pinch of ground saffron added to the stock or water gives a beautiful golden colour to rice and is usually used in Indian biryanis.

Saffron is one of the world's most expensive spices as thousands of flowers are required to produce one pound of saffron. It has been in use for centuries in food, medicine and dyes, but nowadays its main function is in cooking.

Cuminum cyminum

CUMIN

A native of the Middle East, this delicate annual plant is mainly grown for the seed-like fruits, which are a pungent and highly aromatic spice, slightly reminiscent of caraway. Pliny, unwilling to make such a comparison, considered cumin the king among condiments.

Habitat Warm, sunny position in rich, well-drained sandy loam.

Cultivation Sow the seed in pots, then harden them off in a cold frame before transplanting to a warm, sunny bed. The plants grow 30–60cm (1—2ft) high on very slender stems and are delicate, so they should not be crowded by more vigorous ones.

Harvesting When the plants begin to wither, cut the stems just below the clusters of fruit, and hang them in a warm, airy place to dry. Store the seeds in airtight jars away from heat and strong light.

Uses The seed should be slightly warmed before use, to increase the aroma. Either whole or ground, it is an essential ingredient in curries; in the East it is known as 'jeera'. It is also used to flavour rye bread, pickles, chutneys, sausages and other meat products, and Dutch and Swiss cheeses. It is mixed with ground chilli powder in American spice blends called 'chilli seasoning'.

In the past, cumin seed was a symbol of fidelity, believed to keep lovers faithful and poultry from straying beyond the farmyard bounds!

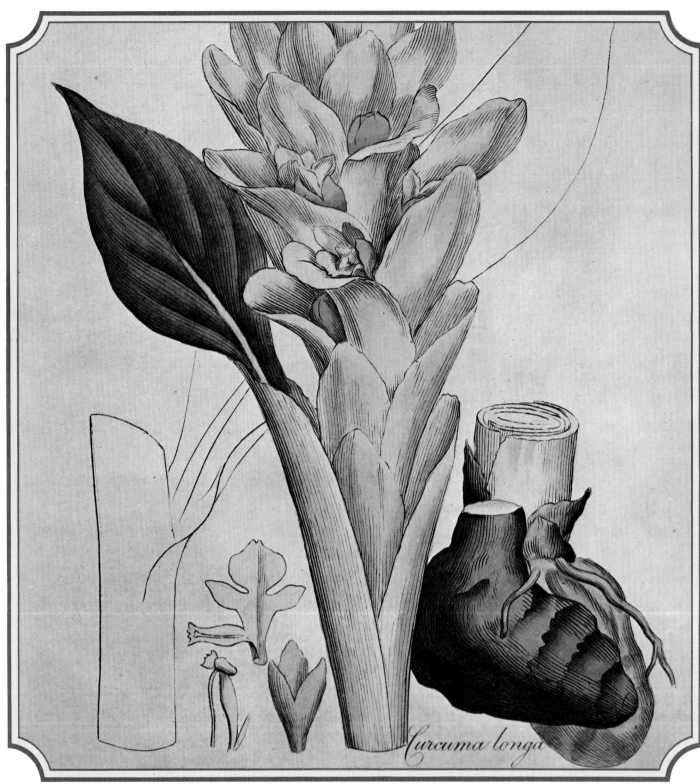

Curcuma longa

Derived from the dried root of a plant native to India, turmeric is ground to produce a vivid yellow powder. In certain dishes, it can be used as a substitute for saffron as it is so much cheaper. It also has successful dyeing propensities.

Curcuma longa
TURMERIC

A native of South Asia, turmeric is a perennial tropical plant of the ginger family. For many centuries it has been used not only as a spice but as a colourant, the bright yellow powder of the ground rhizomes being one of the earliest known vegetable dyes.

Habitat Humid, tropical hilly areas.

Cultivation The plant is propagated by dividing and planting small pieces of the round, orange rhizomes.

Harvesting Turmeric has large lily-type leaves and pale yellow flowers. It is harvested about 10 months after planting, when the stems begin to fade. During processing, in which the rhizomes are cured, boiled, cleaned and dried in the sun, they lose three-quarters of their original weight.

Uses Turmeric is sold already ground to a fine powder. Since it is so much cheaper than saffron, it is most unlikely to be adulterated. It is an essential spice in curry powder and is also used in Indian sweet dishes for both its colour and flavour. It is used in mixed pickles, particularly the mustard pickle known as 'piccalilli', chutneys and rice dishes such as pilaffs. Turmeric is said to have certain medical properties and is used to treat ulcers and liver disorders. Externally, it is used as a cosmetic by Eastern women, who prefer to give their cheeks a golden rather than a rosy glow.

Ellettaria cardamomum

CARDAMOM

A native of South India and Sri Lanka (Ceylon), the plant can grow 2–6m (6–18ft) tall. Cultivated in the colder climates of northern countries, how-ever, it would rarely reach a height of more than 30cm (1ft). The flowers, in loose spikes, are white, edged with yellow and blue. The small, ovoid green fruit capsules contain 15 to 20 hard, almost black seeds which quickly lose their aroma when released from the capsule. This is why cardamom seeds are marketed inside the capsule.

Habitat The plants can be cultivated in a very warm, shaded greenhouse. The humidity must be high during the spring and summer, but the plants need to be dry during winter.

Cultivation Propagation is by division of the creeping rhizomes. Plant them in pots in early spring in a mixture of one part of sharp sand, one part of leaf mould and four parts of turfy loam. If no greenhouse is available, the plants may be grown as houseplants in a warm, shady room free from draughts.

Harvesting In plantations, the three-sided, beige-coloured capsules are harvested by hand, five or six times a year, when they are three-quarters ripe. They are washed, then dried in the sun or in artificially-heated rooms.

Uses The small black cardamom seeds are the essential flavouring ingredi-ent in Danish pastries and are used in a wide range of cakes. In Arab countries they are infused in strong black coffee to offset the bitterness and sometimes chewed as a confection, and to aid digestion. They are also used in some Indian spice blends and to flavour pulaos and biryanis. The seeds are very hard and should be pounded before use in cooking.

Juniperus communis

JUNIPER

A hardy, perennial shrub which can grow to the size of a small tree, juniper grows wild in North America, Europe and Asia. The whole plant —reddish-brown stems, needle-like leaves and pungent berries—is aromatic.

Habitat A sloping situation on well-drained, chalky or lime soil is ideal. The plant does not do well in intense shade, but will tolerate barren conditions.

Cultivation Each berry contains three seeds. Sow the seed, or set out small plants 1.2m (4ft) apart in the spring. As male and female flowers rarely grow on the same shrub, you need at least two trees for fertilization. The male flowers are like green catkins and the female ones like cones. Occasional dressings of organic fertilizer will help to promote growth. You can propagate the plants by cuttings. The plants can also be grown in tubs or large pots.

Harvesting The berries are green at first and may not mature for two or three years. Pick them when they are black.

Uses Juniper berries are used to flavour gin and to make beer. They can be used fresh or dried and should be lightly crushed to extract the flavour. They are used in marinades for pork, veal, beef, venison and other game and poultry. They are also an essential ingredient in the Alsatian dish Choucroûte Garni which is a dish composed of sauerkraut, pork and various vegetables.

A tisane of the berries infused in hot water is said to be helpful in promoting activity of the kidneys. Juniper berries were burned as a form of disinfectant.

Myristica fragrans

NUTMEG MACE

This evergreen tree, a native of the Moluccas and other East Indian islands, and for the past 150 years extensively cultivated in the West Indies, produces two spices. It has a yellow fleshy fruit, rather like an apricot. Inside the ripe fruit, the nutshell is covered by an interlaced membrane, the mace, and inside the shell, the 'kerneal' of the fruit is the nutmeg. When it is harvested, the mace is bright red, but it mellows to golden yellow when dried. Nutmegs, thimble-sized and almost egg-shaped, have been the subject of flagrant imitation, wooden shapes having been passed off for them by unscrupulous pedlars in America. Mace and nutmeg are the only two spices found growing on the same plant.

Habitat The trees are said to thrive best where they are within sight of the sea. In the tropics, they grow in sheltered valleys up to 300m (1500ft) above sea level, in rich, sandy, well-drained soil.

The trees can be cultivated in a heated greenhouse with a minimum winter temperature of 13°C (55°F). They will bear pale yellow flowers in early summer.

Cultivation The trees are propagated by seed, and in the tropics the seedlings are transplanted to the fields, where they can bear fruit for as long as 90 years.

Plant seed in a 50/50 mixture of sandy loam and fibrous peat. The male and female flowers are borne on separate plants so, to achieve fruit, you will need at least one of each. You can graft shoots from the trees of one sex to trees of the other, and can propagate by taking cuttings of ripened shoots. Insert these in sand in a propagating frame.

Harvesting In the tropics, gathering the spice crop takes place over many months, sometimes by collecting the fallen ripened fruits. Traditionally, the fruits are shaken into baskets attached to long poles. The nuts are spread out to dry in the sun, then the mace is removed by hand, flattened and dried separately. When the nuts are dry enough for the kernel to rattle in the shells, they are cracked open and the pungent nutmeg removed. They are then carefully graded according to quality.

Uses Nutmegs are sold whole and the most aromatic way to use the spice is by grating it freshly as it is needed, using either a nutmeg grater or the small, fine holes on a cheese grater. The spice is added to mulled wine drinks, eggnog, egg and fish dishes, hot and cold milk drinks, milk puddings, cakes and biscuits (cookies), boiled green vegetables, soups, sauces, Christmas puddings, spiced breads, pies, pastries and doughnuts. Ground nutmeg is also available but is never as aromatic, so for the best

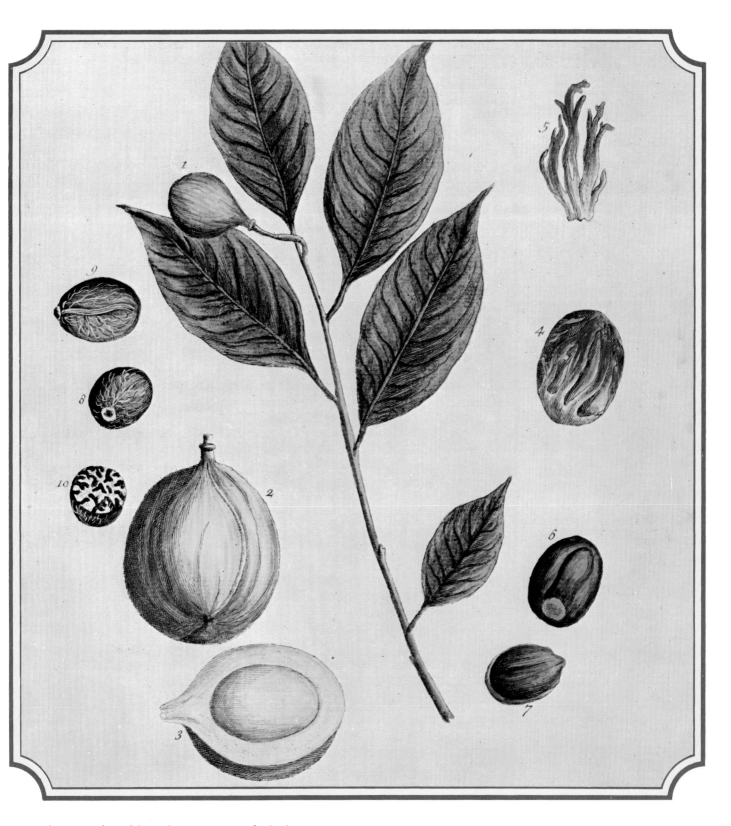

results it is advisable to have a store of whole nutmegs.

Mace is sold whole, when it is called blade mace, or ground. It is particularly suitable in savoury egg, cheese and vegetable dishes, and gives the characteristic spiciness to Bechamel sauce. Blade mace is often included in pickling spice blends. Ground mace sparingly added to the cocoa or chocolate ingredient of chocolate cakes or desserts can deliciously enhance the flavour. It is also an essential ingredient of potted shrimps and many other potted meat and fish dishes. It is useful to remember that Mace can be subsituted for Nutmeg in most sweet recipes.

The same tropical tree produces both nutmeg and mace, the former being a hard, dry seed which is light brown. It is better to buy nutmeg whole as it keeps for a long time and ground nutmeg is never as aromatic. Mace can be bought whole (blade mace) or ground.

Papaver somniferum

POPPY SEED

The poppy from which the tiny blue-black culinary seeds are taken is the opium poppy, an annual which is native to Asia. The drug was—and still is—taken from the milky juice in the unripe heads of plants grown in sunny climates. It is no longer present when the seeds are ready to harvest, so these are in no way narcotic. And it does not develop in plants grown in colder regions.

Habitat Poppies grow well in herbaceous borders where not only the short-lived purple, pale lilac or white flowers but also the greyish-green leaves are attractive. Soil should be moist, rich and well cultivated. Poppies like a position in full sun.

Cultivation Sow the seeds in spring in clumps or rows towards the back of the herb garden or border, because they grow to a height of 60–90cm (2–3ft). Cut off the urn-shaped seedheads before the seeds ripen, or they will scatter and take over the entire patch the following year.

Harvesting The seeds will be ready to harvest in late summer. Cut off the stalks below the seedheads and hang them in bundles to dry, with a tray beneath to catch any seeds as they fall. Shake the remaining seeds out and store them in airtight jars away from strong light and heat. There will be about 900,000 seeds to 450g (1lb).

Uses Poppy seeds are scattered on some breads, buns, cakes and biscuits (cookies) as both decoration and flavouring, and used extensively in Jewish and Central European cooking in dishes such as noodles and desserts. They are generally used whole but can be ground—in some countries you can buy a special grinder for the exceptionally fine, hard seeds. Without one, soak the seeds in water overnight, then put them in a plastic bag and roll them heavily with a rolling pin. To bring out the full flavour, toast the seeds lightly in the oven or in a frying pan over a low heat for a few minutes.

Pimenta dioica

ALLSPICE

Exclusively grown in the Western hemisphere, the spice is a native of Latin America and the West Indies, where it was discovered by Spanish explorers in the sixteenth century. Although the tree will grow in other parts of the world, it will not bear fruit. The name allspice recognizes the fact that the berries smell like a blend of cinnamon, cloves and nutmeg.

Habitat Limestone hills.

Cultivation In Jamaica, the trees are planted 6.5m (20ft) apart. They reach full maturity after 15 years and may bear fruit for over 100 years. In Mexico and Central America the trees are almost all wild.

Harvesting The unripe but fully-grown fruits are harvested 3 to 4 months after flowering, when they are reddish-brown. They are dried in the sun for 7 to 10 days before being cleaned and packed for export.

Uses Allspice berries have a long history as a food preservative, especially of meat. They are one of the ingredients in mixed pickling spice and are packed with barrels of fish shipped from Scandinavia. They are used to flavour cakes, soups, meat, vegetables, especially sauerkraut, and in the manufacture of Benedictine and Chartreuse liqueurs.

Pimpinella anisum

ANISE

The plant is a medium-tall annual herb of the parsley family, but is usually grown for the minute oil-bearing seeds, called aniseed, which are classed as a spice. There are about 100,000 seeds to every 450g (1lb) weight. Anise is a native of the Middle East and grows wild in Greece and Egypt.

Habitat Anise will grow well in a good summer in light, dry, loamy soil, in a sunny position.

Cultivation Sow the seeds in mid-spring. The plants will produce small white flowers and delicate, fern-like leaves.

Harvesting The seeds will ripen only in a hot summer, when they will turn greyish-green. Carefully cut the whole flower stems and hang them upside down in an airy place to dry. Shake the seeds over a sheet of paper and store them in airtight jars away from heat or strong light, which would affect the flavour.

Uses The seeds give the liquorice-like flavour to the liqueur anisette, as well as to Pernod and the Greek aperitif, ouzo. They are used in salads, to garnish root vegetables, and in cakes, biscuits (cookies) and bread. Anise tea is reputed to soothe indigestion.

Piper nigrum

PEPPER

The world's most important spice, both black and white pepper are produced from a climbing vine which is a native of India and the East Indies. The spice was one of the earliest trading commodities between the Orient and European countries and many seafaring expeditions were launched in search of it.

Habitat The pepper vine, a perennial evergreen climber, grows in damp jungle and is now extensively cultivated in the tropics of both hemispheres.

Cultivation The vine is propagated by cuttings grown in nurseries, then planted 2.75m (8ft) apart with posts or small trees to support the 10m (30ft) long climbing shoots.

Harvesting The first small spice crop may be gathered in the third year. The black pepper is the entire peppercorn, or berry, which includes the

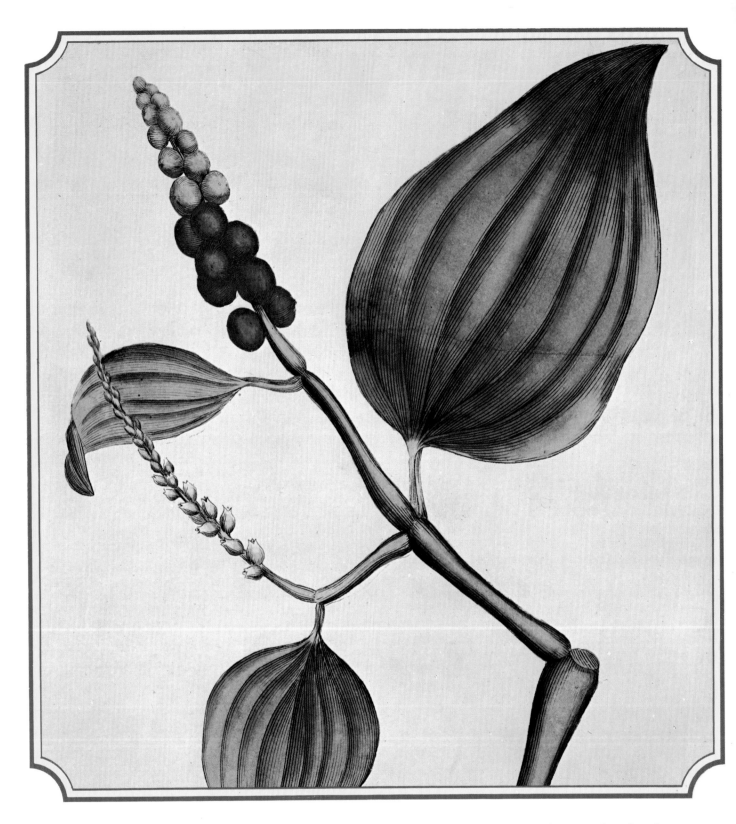

Pepper, a native of India and the East Indies, comes from a climbing vine. Black peppercorns are picked while unripe and left to dry and darken. White peppercorns are left on the vine to mature and the husk is then removed, revealing a smooth core.

dark outer hull. The berry clusters are harvested 9 months after flowering and, for black pepper, picked in their unripe, green state. It is only in the natural drying process that they darken. For white pepper, the berries are left to mature on the vine, then soaked to soften the outer hull. This is then rubbed off to reveal the greyish-white inner peppercorn, which lightens in colour as it is dried.

Uses One of the best-known of all spices and condiments, both black and white peppercorns are used in mixtures of pickling spice, added to the stock in which meat or fish is cooked, and freshly ground to flavour all kinds of savoury dishes. Both black and white pepper are available ready ground, but the flavour is less pungent. Whole green peppercorns, which have not been dried, can be bought in jars, preserved in brine.

Sesamum indicum
SESAME

The annual plant, native to Africa and Indonesia, was immortalized by Ali Baba in his famous command, 'Open, Sesame', which revealed a cave of priceless jewels. The value of the plant is in the versatile seeds it produces, which vary in colour from almost white, through golden-brown and pale orange to greyish-black. The seeds are sold whole, either raw or toasted, as a ground meal, and as a paste, *tahina*, whigh features in many Middle Eastern dishes. Sesame oil is a high-protein vegetable oil.

Habitat Light, friable soil, preferably a sandy loam, with a warm climate and moderate rainfall. In a good summer, the plant should grow more than 60cm (2ft) high and produce white, mauve or pink flowers.

Cultivation Sow the seeds in a greenhouse in spring and prick them out singly into pots when they are big enough to handle. To continue growing in a greenhouse, pot on into 12–15cm (5–6in) pots containing a well-drained potting mixture. To grow outside, plant the hardened seedlings in rich soil, ideally near a south wall.

Harvesting The plants will flower in the late summer. Harvest the seeds when the upper pods are fully developed but still green and spread them on a tray in a warm, dry place to dry. Shake the seeds out and store them in airtight jars away from heat and strong light.

Uses The seeds are sprinkled on breads, cakes, biscuits and cookies where they give a pleasant nutty texture. *Tahina* is used extensively in Middle Eastern cooking and as a spread instead of butter—it tastes a little like peanut butter. Sesame oil can be used as a salad or cooking oil, and is a good skin moisturizer; Cleopatra is said to have found it so.

Syzygium aromaticum or *Eugenia aromatica*
CLOVES

A native of the Moluccas, or Spice Islands, and now cultivated in the Malagasy Republic (Madagascar), Tanzania and the West Indies, this large, evergreen tree—or at least its highly-prized flower buds—caused many voyages, adventures and battles.

Habitat The trees grow best in volcanic, loamy soil in areas with an average rainfall of 250cm (100in) a year.

Cultivation The seeds germinate within 4 to 6 weeks, and the trees are planted 6.5m (20ft) apart.

Harvesting The spice crop is the unopened flower bud, which must be picked before the pinky-green blossom opens. The buds are literally harvested by hand—by brushing clusters against the palm. When dried, the buds turn dark brown and retain only one-third of their original weight—it takes 5,000 to 7,000 dried cloves to 450g (1lb) weight. The best grade have round, capped domes.

Uses Whole cloves are natural partners to apple dishes of all kinds; they are used to decorate and flavour whole baked ham, and mixed with other spices for pickling and mulled wine drinks. Ground cloves are used with dried fruit in cakes, steamed puddings and mincemeat, and in milk puddings and sauces. In Indonesia, cloves are mixed with tobacco in a thriving cigarette industry.

Sesame has been immortalized for ever in the legend of Ali Baba and his famous command. For centuries, it has been valued as a spice and also for the oil it produces. It is high in protein and also makes an effective skin moisturizer.

A leguminous tree native to Africa, tamarind is valued for its leaves which produce a yellow or red dye, its timber, and the seeds and pulp from the brown pod which are used in cooking.

Tamarindus indica

TAMARIND

Known as the Indian date, tamarind is a leguminous tree which grows freely in India, tropical East Africa and the West Indies.
Habitat Damp, humid tropical regions.
Cultivation The tree can grow to a height of about 2.75m (8ft), bearing seed pods 15–20cm (6–8in) long which ripen to dark brown.
Harvesting The leaves, flowers and pods are all harvested for their separate uses.
Uses Tamarind leaves are used to make a red or yellow dye, and both the leaves and flowers are eaten in salads. The main culinary use, however, is of the pods once the seeds have been removed. This pulp, which forms a black sticky mass, is sold in Indian food shops and is invaluable in the preparation of some curries and chutneys. The pulp contains about 10 to 12 per cent of tartaric acid, and it is this that gives tamarind the sourness for which it is valued. To obtain the souring agent without the tough fibres of the broken pods, infuse the pulp in a little hot water, then press it through a strainer to squeeze out the juice. The pulp is said to have mildly laxative properties.

Trigonella foenum-graecum

FENUGREEK

This annual leguminous plant of the pea family, a native of South-Eastern Europe and Western Asia, has also been cultivated in India, Mediterranean countries and North Africa, both for the seed, a spice, and as a forage for cattle.

It can be grown in other mild climates, and indoors as a sprouting salad crop.
Habitat A mild climate, well-drained loamy soil and a sunny position.
Cultivation Sow the seed in spring, either in seed boxes or under glass. Transplant the seedlings in light soil in a sunny spot. The plants should bear cream-coloured flowers, beautifully scented, in mid-summer and then develop long, flat pods, each one containing about 15 seeds. To grow the spicy seeds as a salad crop, sprinkle the seed in light potting soil in seed boxes or on damp flannel or cotton.
Harvesting When the seed pods are fully developed, pull up the plants and hang them upside-down to dry—as one does with dwarf bean plants. Break open the pods and dry the seeds in the sun if there is no wind, on a tray in the airing cupboard, linen closet or a warm, south-facing windowsill. To use the seedlings as a salad crop, cut them after a few days' growth, at the two-leaf (cotyledon) stage, using sharp scissors and cutting just above the seeds.
Uses Rich in vitamins and protein, the reddish-yellow seeds are an important part of Oriental vegetarian diets. Ground fenugreek seed—methi—is an ingredient in curry spice blends, and in America is used to flavour imitation maple syrup. Middle Eastern women eat the roasted seed to make them plump, and it flavours the calorie-packed sweetmeat, *halva*. Fenugreek tea is said to aid digestion.

The salad crop, cut after a few days' growth, has a slightly pungent and light taste and can be eaten raw or quickly blanched in boiling, salted water. The leaves of the fully-grown plant are too bitter to eat as a vegetable, but are sometimes served with a curry sauce.

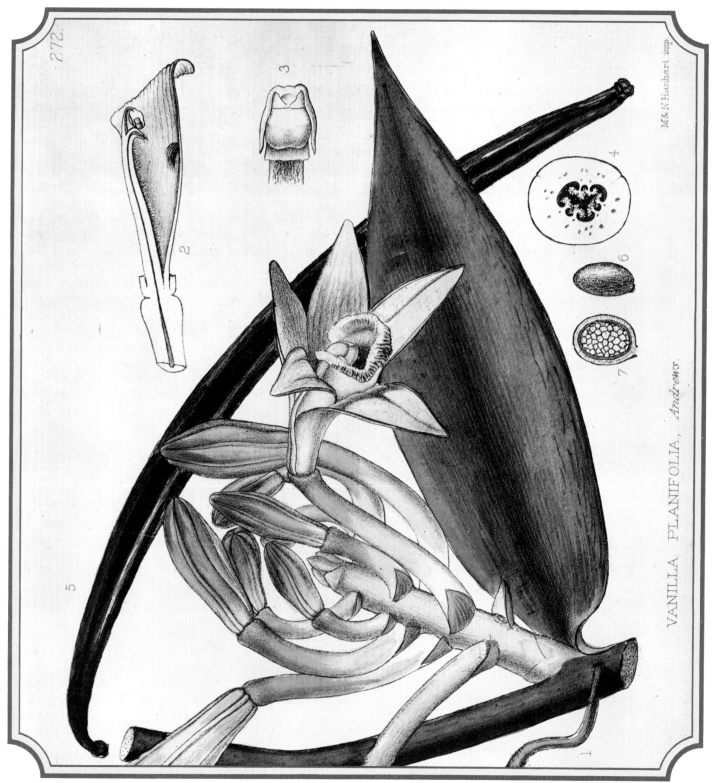

VANILLA PLANIFOLIA., *Andrews.*

M&N.Hanhart imp.

Vanilla planifolia
VANILLA

A native of the humid forests of tropical America, vanilla is one of the flavourings discovered by early explorers of the New World. It was brought to Europe by the Spaniards, who had found the Aztecs using it as a flavouring for chocolate. Now 80 per cent of the world's crop is grown in the Malagasy Republic (Madagascar).

Habitat Hot, humid, tropical regions with good drainage. The plants

Vanilla, a perennial climbing vine, produces pods which are either dried or made into a liquid extract. Vanilla pods can be used several times and pieces of the pod may be infused in milk in the making of cakes and custards.

73

must be protected from the wind.

Cultivation The vine is grown on supports of posts or trellis, and propagated by cuttings 30–120cm (1–4ft) long. The crop will not bear fruit unless pollinating insects are present, as in Mexico and Central America. In other regions, pollination must be done by hand. In these plantations, therefore, the vines are pruned and trained to a convenient height. The first crop is harvested after 3 years and the vines replaced after ten years.

Harvesting Each vine may bear up to 1,000 pale yellow flowers. These are nipped out to leave clusters of about seven flowers, and no more than fifty on each vine. The pods are picked when they are 15–25cm (6–10in) long, before they are ripe, when they are beginning to turn from green to yellow. They are matured by being alternately sweated and dried. The curing process takes about six months.

Uses One of the most versatile of flavourings, vanilla is used commercially in the manufacture of chocolate, ice cream, puddings and tobacco.

A pod of vanilla stored in an airtight jar of sugar subtly flavours it. To flavour sweet sauces, boil a pod with the milk, remove it, wash and dry and store to use again.

True vanilla extract is made from the cured pods chopped and percolated with alcohol and water, and is very expensive. Cheap synthetic substitutes sold as vanilla flavouring can be made from wood pulp, waste paper pulp, coal tar, oil of sassafras and chemicals.

Zingiber officinale
GINGER

Originating in South Asia and cultivated in ancient China and India, ginger now grows in most tropical countries. It is an erect, perennial plant growing to a height of 60–120cm (2–4ft) from thick, knobbly rhizomes, and was the first spice imported into Europe.

Habitat Ginger plants need heavy rain and plenty of sun—a warm, moist tropical climate and a situation up to 850m (2500ft) above sea level.

Cultivation Propagation is by dividing the rhizome into pieces 2.5–5cm (1–2in) long. The shoots grow up to about 1m (3ft) high and bear highly-scented flowers.

Harvesting The ginger is ready to harvest 9 months to 1 year after planting, when the plant begins to wither. The rhizomes are dug up with a hoe. The spice is obtained from the rhizomes, which are marketed fresh, dried, ground or preserved. You can buy fresh root ginger in most Oriental foodstores and keep it moist by burying it in soil in a pot or in

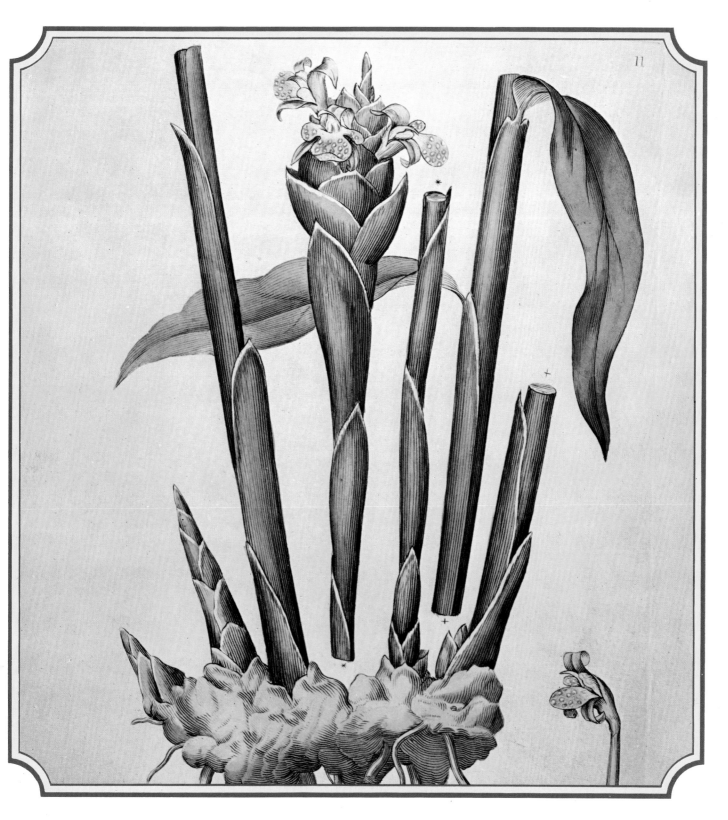

the garden.

Uses Dried root (green) ginger, which is hard and shrivelled, needs lightly crushing, or 'bruising', to extract the flavour for use in chutneys, pickles and curries. Ground ginger is the dried rhizome which is scraped, boiled and peeled. This is used in cakes, especially gingerbread, puddings, biscuits (cookies) and candy. Preserved, candied and crystallized ginger are processed from the fresh green rhizome and are eaten as sweetmeats or as a garnish for cakes and desserts. Stem ginger, preserved in a thick sugar syrup, is a popular dessert after a Chinese meal.

Ginger is the root of a perennial plant and is available ground, dried, preserved, candied, fresh and crystallized. It is used for a wide variety of purposes ranging from curries and chutneys to cakes and candy, and is popular in Oriental cooking.

AT-A-GLANCE

SPICE	PART OF PLANT	FLAVOUR
Allspice	Dried berry, whole or ground. Berries retain freshness if stored whole and crushed or pounded when needed	Fragrant, like mixture of cinnamon, cloves and nutmeg (hence name)
Aniseed	Whole dried seed	Faintly liquorice
Caraway	Whole dried seed	Slightly sharp and peppery
Cardamom	Usually bought as dried seed capsules, still containing very hard black seed. Remove seeds and crush before using	Slightly lemony and bitter-sweet
Chillis	Whole dried pod; ground, as chilli pepper or cayenne pepper. Use very sparingly. Also sold mixed with other spices as chilli seasoning—less hot	The hottest of all peppery spices. Can be very fiery indeed
Cinnamon and Cassia	Cinnamon—dried inner bark, in curled sticks, or ground. When infusing sticks in cooked dishes, remove before serving. Cassia buds, dried leaves and ground powder available	Gentle, sweet, musky flavour
Cloves	Dried unopened bud. Whole or ground. To impart flavour in savoury dish, stud cloves into an onion, then they are easy to remove	Sweet and tangy

SPICE CHART

MEAT AND FISH DISHES	VEGETARIAN	FRUIT AND DESSERTS	BAKING
Whole, in stock for poaching meat and fish, pot roasts, marinades. Ground, in beef and game casseroles	Whole, in pickles, chutneys, when cooking beetroot (beets). Crushed in sauerkraut, and cabbage dishes. Ground, with cream cheese, cream soups	Whole, in fruit pickles and stewed apples, pears, rhubarb. Ground, in mincemeat and in rose-flavoured confections	Ground, in cakes, especially fruit cakes, buns and biscuits (cookies), and in baked sponge puddings
Rich meat dishes, such as beef stews, casserole of hare or pigeon, or with sausages	Sparingly in cheese dishes, with braised red cabbage, carrots, parsnips. In salad dressings	With stewed apples, apple and other fruit pies	The seeds are used in cakes, especially coffee cake, bread, biscuits (cookies)
In Hungarian goulash, rich game, meat and offal dishes, to offset fattiness. Good with pork and goose	As a flavouring in some manufactured cheeses. Used in pickling vegetables and in vegetable soups and to garnish potato, cabbage, swede. In sauerkraut and coleslaw salad. In dumplings and cheese dips	With apple dishes of all kinds. Traditional with baked apples	Caraway cake (said to aid digestion) is traditional farm fare. Seeds used in other cakes, bread, biscuits (cookies), as ingredient or garnish. Particularly in rye bread. Eaten on bread and butter
In curry powder, and added to curries. Good with beef, pork and goose. Used to flavour pickled herrings	Used in pickling vegetables. In Indian rice dishes, with sauerkraut, in vegetable soups	With stewed fruit, in rice pudding and moulds, infused to make custards. Add lightly crushed seeds to black coffee and mulled wine and ale	Crushed seeds in Danish pastries, and in cakes and buns, especially gingerbread and coffee cakes
Whole, in classic, highly-spiced Mexican dishes, curries and some Chinese cooking. Ground, in beef casseroles, sprinkled on meat for grilling (broiling) or barbecue. With seafood such as prawn (shrimp) cocktail or grilled (broiled) lobster	Whole, in pickling spices, for onions, red cabbage. Infused in oil and vinegar for salad dressings and in barbecue sauces. Ground, as a garnish for egg and cheese dishes, especially mousses, soufflés and some cream soups. In tomato and pasta dishes		
Cinnamon sticks in pickling. Ground, sprinkled on meat for grilling (broiling) and in casseroles. Cassia leaves crumbled into curries. Whole cassia buds used in curries. Ground cassia sometimes sold as cinnamon	Cinnamon sticks in pickling. Ground, in vegetable curries and as garnish to mashed potatoes and some cream soups	Cinnamon sticks with stewed fruit such as apples, pears, rhubarb. And in mulled wine and ale. Ground, with fruit salad, bananas, peaches, and stirred into whipped cream. Sprinkled on milk puddings— rice and junket. In steamed puddings, especially Christmas pudding	Ground cinnamon in cakes, especially fruit cake, buns, biscuits (cookies). Mixed with sugar and sprinkled on hot, buttered toast or buns
Whole, used in brine to souse herrings, studded in ham and gammon. In stock, to pickle meat such as pork or beef, and in beef stew and *coq au vin*	Whole, in pickling vegetables such as onions, beetroot (beets). Infused in milk to make savoury sauces. Ground, as garnish to mashed vegetables and cream soups	Whole, in pickled and bottled fruits, with apples and pears, especially in pies and puddings. In mulled wine and ale and fruit punch. Ground, to garnish milk puddings. In mincemeat	Whole, as decoration for children's fancy confections, such as eyes on sugar mice, buttons of gingerbread men. Ground in cakes, especially fruit cakes, buns, biscuits (cookies). Often combined with ginger

SPICE	PART OF PLANT	FLAVOUR
 Coriander (dhania)	Dried seed, whole or ground. Whole seeds are more aromatic if lightly toasted before use. Are usually lightly crushed	Mild, sweet and pungent
 Cumin (jeera)	Dried seed, whole or ground. Flavour of whole seeds improved by lightly toasting	Strong and aromatic with lingering flavour
 Curry powder	A blend of ground spices, can be turmeric, coriander, ginger, cloves, cinnamon, mustard, cardamom, fenugreek, cayenne, cumin, salt and others, according to region	The taste varies from mild to hot according to proportion of different spices
 Fenugreek (methi)	Whole dried seed. The flavour is improved by lightly toasting	Slightly bitter and caramel-like
Garam masala	A spice blend (not the same as curry powder) which could contain any of the following: cumin, black pepper, cloves, cardamom and others, ground together. They are added towards the end of cooking	Blends vary but are never hot
Ginger	Fresh or dried rhizome, 'root' ginger, can be bought in pieces; ground ginger is made from the dried rhizome	Hot, rich flavour. Ground ginger less pungent than the root
Juniper	Dried berries. Lightly crush the whole berries before use	Sweet, aromatic and pine-like
Mace	Dried outer shell of nut, whole or ground	An exotic spice with strong nutmeg flavour
Mixed spice	A blend of ground spices, usually cinnamon, cloves, allspice, sometimes with ginger	Flavour depends on the proportions used of each spice
Mustard seed	Whole seeds of black or white mustard; or ground to a yellow powder	Seed has slightly sharp and hot flavour. Strength of powder depends on proportion of the different seeds

MEAT AND FISH DISHES	VEGETARIAN	FRUIT AND DESSERTS	BAKING
Crushed in casseroles, stuffings, curries. Often used in spiced sausages and in meat loaf. Ground, peppery addition to seasoned flour	Crushed seeds in thick vegetable soups such as green pea, lentil, carrot. In chutney, and Greek rice dishes and stuffings. As garnish on egg and cheese dishes. With mushrooms *à la grecque*. Infused in oil and vinegar for salad dressing	Crushed, in apple pie or pudding, fruit crumbles, with quince. Can be added to preserves such as marrow or rhubarb jam	Crushed, in apple cake, cakes, fruit breads
An ingredient of curry powder and chilli seasoning. In marinades for lamb and beef kebabs, and to spice seasoned flour	Whole, with cream cheese in dips, and with cabbage, carrots and savoury rice. Used in pickles and chutneys and sweet and sour sauce	Ground, used sparingly in fruit pies	Whole, in rye bread
Apart from curries, can be used to season flour, and lightly season meat and fish, and garnish rice dishes	Apart from curries, can be used to flavour cottage or cream cheese dips, omelettes and other egg dishes, and as a garnish to cream soups		In sweet and savoury breads and biscuits (cookies), particularly cheese straws
Whole, in stock for poaching fish. Ground, in meat casseroles, curries and sauces	Whole, in pickles and chutneys, and with boiled rice	Seeds are used to flavour imitation maple syrup. In Middle Eastern sweetmeat, *halva*	
Use in meat and fish curries, with other spices in varying proportions according to taste, or in seasoned flour in Western cooking. Also as a garnish	Use with other spices in egg or vegetable curries, in *dhal* (lentils) and in savoury rice, or as a light garnish to cheese and egg dishes (e.g. mousse) and cream soups		
Whole, in pickling. Ground, in curries and meat dishes, especially beef, and sprinkled on grilled (broiled) and baked white fish	Whole, in pickling and chutneys, and in Chinese dishes	The fresh, whole root is used to make ginger beer. Whole, in marrow and rhubarb jams, and in baked and stewed fruit, especially mixed dried fruits. Ground, with melon and to flavour steamed sponge puddings and treacle tart	Ground, in cakes. Specialities, gingerbread, ginger snaps (cookies), and brandy snaps. Usually added to fruit cakes and to spice some sweet pastries
Good with all game, poultry and pork, and in stuffings for them. In pâté, meat loaf, and all meat and fish marinades	Used in vegetable dishes, especially sauerkraut. Whole, in pickles, chutneys, infused in Béchamel sauce	A few berries infused in milk to make puddings and sauces— e.g. chocolate sauce	
Whole, in soups and casseroles, with pork, veal, sausages. Ground, in meat loaf, pâté, with minced beef	In savoury rice, egg and cheese dishes, and with root vegetables	Whole, in fruit preserves and stewed fruit. Ground, in fruit salads and sprinkled on milk puddings	Ground, in light fruit cakes, chocolate cakes, buns and biscuits (cookies)
Rubbed into pickled spiced beef, and used in rich beef and game casseroles and meat loaf	As a garnish for egg and cheese dishes and some cream soups	With stewed apples, pears and rhubarb. In steamed sponge puddings. With fresh melon	In cakes, especially fruit cakes, buns, biscuits (cookies)
Whole seed in pickling meat and fish, especially herring and mackerel, in fish dishes and sauces. In casserole of pork, veal, rabbit and in offal dishes. Mustard powder rubbed into meat and fish before grilling (broiling) or baking. Used to flavour sauce to serve with ham	Whole seed in pickling and chutneys, and in vegetable dishes such as braised celery. With cabbage, broccoli, and in coleslaw. Mustard powder in sauce to serve with cauliflower, and in cheese and egg dishes. With cream cheese in savoury dips		

SPICE	PART OF PLANT	FLAVOUR
Nutmeg	Dried kernel, whole (to be grated before use), or can be bought ground	Exotic, sweet, musky flavour
Paprika	Dried ground sweet red peppers	Mild and slightly sweet. Not at all hot
Pepper, black	Whole, dried peppercorns more pungent if freshly ground in a mill. Can be bought ready-ground	Strong, pungent, spicy
Pepper, white	Whole dried inner peppercorns best if freshly ground. Can be bought ready-ground	Milder and less 'exotic' than black pepper
Pickling spice	Can be bought ready-mixed, a selection of dried black and white whole peppercorns, chillis, mustard seed, cloves, allspice, ginger, mace, coriander	The flavour depends on the proportions of the various ingredients. Better to control it by mixing your own
Poppy seed	Whole dried seed. Lightly toast before grinding. Needs special grinder, or firm rolling with rolling pin	Scant flavour, nutty texture
Saffron	Whole dried strands, or ground (buy a reputable brand to avoid adulteration). Crush dry threads before infusing in hot liquid	Exotic golden colour, slightly sweet taste
Sesame	Whole seed, dried or toasted	Sweet, nutty flavour and crunchy texture
Tamarind	Bought as fibrous black, sticky pulp, broken seed pods. Extract sour flavour by soaking in hot water, then squeezing	Sour, acidy flavour
Turmeric (haldi)	Ground yellow rhizome, sold as powder. Is slight thickening agent	Bright yellow colour, rather bitter
Vanilla	Whole, dried pod, or pure bottled extract	Sweet, chocolate-like flavour

MEAT AND FISH DISHES	VEGETARIAN	FRUIT AND DESSERTS	BAKING
Grated into fish cakes, fish sauces, and 'white' chicken dishes. To spice pâté and meat loaf	Grated over broad (lima) beans, potatoes, cabbage, and egg and cheese dishes, cheese sauce, cream soups	Grated on to milk puddings, custard and ice cream, and in stewed fruit such as apples or pears	In fruit cakes, spiced buns and biscuits (cookies)
In Hungarian goulash (beef stew), with pork and chicken. Meat dishes with tomatoes. As a garnish to canapés. With shellfish, especially prawns (shrimp), crab, lobster	As a garnish to potatoes, cauliflower, celery. In sauce to cook potatoes or mixed vegetables. In tomato, egg or cheese dishes, and cream soups. And in Waldorf salad		Used in cheese shortbread, cheese straws and biscuits (cookies)
Whole peppercorns for pickling and in boiling meat and fish, and in marinades. Ground black pepper in all 'dark' meat dishes, some fish dishes, sauces. Crushed on steak *au poivre*	Whole peppercorns for pickling and chutneys. Ground black pepper in almost all vegetable, egg and cheese dishes, salads and salad dressings		
Whole white peppercorns in pickled meat and fish. Ground, in 'white' fish and poultry dishes where dark pepper would affect appearance	Whole white peppercorns in pickles. Ground, in cream soups, white sauces, egg and cheese dishes where paler colour is preferred		
Use to pickle beef and pork and to souse or pickle fish, and in liquor to boil fish or meat, particularly ham	Use to pickle single or mixed vegetables and in chutneys	To pickle fruit and nuts, omit hot spices such as red chillis	
Whole seed used in some curries and in savoury rice	Used whole to give nutty texture to cream cheese dips and spreads; some egg and cheese dishes. Sprinkled on carrots, potatoes, parsnips, and to garnish vegetable soups		Whole seed sprinkled on bread, buns, cakes, sweet and savoury biscuits (cookies). Crushed seed used in some baked goods
A powerful colourant. For colour alone, turmeric is cheaper. Saffron is used in rice dishes, particularly *paella*, and with fish. Is essential in *bouillabaisse*	Saffron transforms rice dishes, in both colour and flavour. Good in cheese and egg dishes and cream of vegetable soups		Ground saffron used in traditional saffron cakes and buns
Toasted, as topping to creamed fish dishes, and chicken	Gives nuttiness to cream cheese dips, and as a garnish to cream soups and some vegetables	Toasted, as topping to fruit crumble and cobbler, and on chocolate sauce to serve with ice cream	Toasted, sprinkled on bread, buns, biscuits (cookies) before baking
Authentic sour taste in meat and fish curries. Stronger than lemon or lime juice	Use in vegetable and egg curries, too		
Used in most curries and in rice-and-fish dishes such as kedgeree (but *not paella*)	Especially used in vegetable curries. Very small pinch adds colour to egg and cheese dishes. Essential in mustard pickles		Used very sparingly to colour cakes and buns. Too much will give a bitter taste
		Infuse whole dry pods in jar of sugar or in milk for sauces, puddings, ice cream, custards. More subtle than flavour of the extract	Vanilla sugar (see previous column) used in all baked goods, fillings, frostings, toppings and baked puddings, especially with chocolate

COOKING
WITH SPICES

SOUPS & STARTERS
FISH & SHELLFISH
POULTRY & GAME
MEAT & MAIN COURSES
VEGETABLES & SALADS
ETHNIC DISHES
PUDDINGS & DESSERTS
BREADS & CAKES
PRESERVES

SOUPS & STARTERS

Marinated artichoke hearts

	Metric/UK	US
Cooked or canned and drained artichoke hearts, quartered	6	6
Juice of 2 lemons		
Salt	½ tsp	½ tsp
Black peppercorns, crushed	3	3
White wine vinegar	4 Tbs	¼ cup
Olive oil	75ml/3floz	6 Tbs
Coriander seeds, crushed	2 Tbs	2 Tbs
Chopped parsley	1 Tbs	1 Tbs
Garlic clove, crushed	½	½
Onion, thinly sliced into rings	1	1

Put the artichoke hearts in a bowl and add the lemon juice, salt, peppercorns, vinegar, oil, coriander seeds, parsley and garlic. Fold together gently until the ingredients are well combined. Fold in the onion rings.

Cover and leave to marinate in a cool place for 2 hours, basting occasionally.

Transfer the artichoke hearts and onion rings to a serving dish using a slotted spoon. Sprinkle over about 4 tablespoons of the marinade and discard the remainder. Serve at room temperature or lightly chilled.

6 Servings

Potted salmon

	Metric/UK	US
Fresh salmon	½kg/1lb piece	1lb piece
Salt	1½ tsp	1½ tsp
Black pepper	1½ tsp	1½ tsp
Ground mace	½ tsp	½ tsp
Ground cloves	¼ tsp	¼ tsp
Butter	150g/5oz	10 Tbs
Black peppercorns	4	4
Bay leaves	2	2

Preheat the oven to moderate 180°C (Gas Mark 4, 350°F).

Rub the salmon with half the salt and pepper and the mace and cloves. Put the fish in a baking dish. Cut 25g/1oz (2 tablespoons) of the butter into small pieces and dot them over the fish. Sprinkle over the peppercorns and lay the bay leaves on top. Bake for 30 to 40 minutes or until the fish is cooked.

Remove the fish from the baking dish and allow to cool slightly. Strain the liquid from the dish and reserve.

Skin the fish and remove all bones. Pound the fish with a wooden spoon or using a mortar and pestle, gradually work in 50g/2oz (¼ cup) of the remaining butter and the reserved cooking liquid. Alternatively, purée the fish with the butter and liquid in a blender. Beat in the remaining salt and pepper.

Pack the fish into small pots or ramekins, leaving space at the top. Allow to cool.

Melt the remaining butter. Allow to cool slightly, then pour it over the salmon mixture in the pots. Cover with foil and chill for at least 2 hours before serving.

6 Servings

Chicken liver pâté

	Metric/UK	US
Celery stalk	1	1
Parsley sprigs	3	3
Peppercorns	8	8
Salt		
Chicken livers	½kg/1lb	1lb
Tabasco sauce	½ tsp	½ tsp
Butter or rendered chicken fat	225g/8oz	1 cup
Grated nutmeg	¼ tsp	¼ tsp
Dry mustard	2 tsp	2 tsp
Ground cloves	¼ tsp	¼ tsp
Onion, finely minced	1	1
Garlic clove, minced	1	1
Brandy or dry sherry	2 Tbs	2 Tbs
Stuffed olives, sliced	50g/2oz	¼ cup

Bring a saucepan of water to the boil and add the celery, parsley, peppercorns and salt. Simmer for 10 minutes. Add the chicken livers, cover and simmer gently for 10 minutes.

Drain the livers, then mince (grind) them, or purée in a food mill or blender. Transfer to a bowl and beat in the Tabasco, butter or chicken fat, nutmeg, mustard, cloves, onion, garlic and brandy or sherry. Add salt to taste.

Put the pâté into a serving dish and make a decorative pattern on top with the prongs of a fork. Garnish with the

Mace, the outer covering of nutmeg, is an essential ingredient in potted salmon.

olive slices. Chill for at least 6 hours before serving.

6-8 Servings

Spiced fish

	Metric/UK	US
Flour	75g/3oz	¾ cup
Salt and black pepper		
Cod fillets, skinned and cut into 5cm/2in pieces	1½kg/3lb	3lb
Oil	4 Tbs	4 Tbs
SAUCE		
Flour	1 Tbs	1 Tbs
Green chilli (chili pepper), seeded and finely chopped	1	1
Hot chilli powder	¼ tsp	¼ tsp
Ground coriander	½ tsp	½ tsp
Ground cumin	½ tsp	½ tsp
Ground cardamom	½ tsp	½ tsp
Ground ginger	½ tsp	½ tsp
Ground cloves	¼ tsp	¼ tsp
Turmeric	1 tsp	1 tsp
Garlic cloves, crushed	2	2
Salt and black pepper		
Soft brown sugar	2 Tbs	2 Tbs
White wine vinegar	450ml/15floz	2 cups
Water	450ml/15floz	2 cups
Large onions, sliced	2	2
Bay leaves	2	2
Fennel seeds	½ tsp	½ tsp
Black peppercorns	12	12

Mix the flour with salt and pepper and use to coat the fish pieces. Heat the oil in a frying pan. Add the fish pieces, in batches, and fry for 3 to 4 minutes on each side or until well browned and cooked through. Drain on paper towels and place in a deep serving dish.

Mix together the flour, chilli, spices, garlic, salt and pepper to taste and the sugar in a saucepan. Stir in 4 table-spoons of the vinegar to make a smooth paste. Gradually stir in the remaining vinegar and the water. Add the remaining sauce ingredients and bring to the boil, stirring occasionally. Cover and simmer for 30 minutes.

Strain the sauce over the fish and leave to cool. Cover and chill in the refrigerator for at least 24 hours before serving.

8 Servings

Avocados with prawns (shrimp)

	Metric/UK	US
Large avocados	2	2
Lemon juice	1 Tbs	1 Tbs
Mayonnaise	75ml/3floz	6 Tbs
Double (heavy) cream	2 Tbs	2 Tbs
Salt and black pepper		
Cayenne pepper	¼ tsp	¼ tsp
Mild curry powder	2 tsp	2 tsp
Canned pineapple rings, drained and finely chopped	2	2
Shelled prawns (shrimp)	125g/4oz	4 oz

Spiced Fish, a cold dish soused in a piquant sauce, is an appetizing first course.

85

Cut the avocados in half lengthways and remove the stones (seeds). Rub the cut surfaces with the lemon juice to prevent discolouration. Place the halves in serving dishes.

Mix together the mayonnaise, cream, salt and pepper to taste, the cayenne, curry powder and pineapple. Fold in the prawns (shrimp). Spoon the prawn (shrimp) mixture into the avocado hollows and serve.

4 Servings

Hot spiced grapefruit

	Metric/UK	US
Soft brown sugar	50g/2oz	$\frac{1}{3}$ cup
Ground allspice or mixed spice	$\frac{1}{4}$ tsp	$\frac{1}{4}$ tsp
Ground cinnamon	$\frac{3}{4}$ tsp	$\frac{3}{4}$ tsp
Butter, softened	1 Tbs	1 Tbs
Dark rum	1 Tbs	1 Tbs
Large grapefruit, halved and flesh loosened	2	2

Preheat the grill (broiler) to fairly hot.

Mix together the sugar, spices, butter and rum, and cream to a smooth paste. Divide the paste between the grapefruit halves, spreading it evenly

over the cut surfaces. Arrange the grapefruit halves in the grill (broiler) pan, cut sides up. Grill (broil) for 6 to 8 minutes or until the tops are browned and bubbling. Serve hot.

4 Servings

Baked stuffed aubergines (eggplants)

	Metric/UK	US
Medium aubergines (eggplants)	2	2
Salt		
Olive oil	6 Tbs	6 Tbs
Large onion, finely chopped	1	1
Mushrooms, sliced	$\frac{1}{2}$kg/1lb	1lb
Cooked pork, minced (ground)	175g/6oz	$\frac{3}{4}$ cup
Sour cream	6 Tbs	6 Tbs
Black pepper		
Ground allspice	$\frac{1}{2}$ tsp	$\frac{1}{2}$ tsp
Fresh breadcrumbs	25g/1oz	$\frac{1}{2}$ cup
Parmesan cheese, grated	25g/1oz	$\frac{1}{4}$ cup
Paprika	$\frac{1}{2}$ tsp	$\frac{1}{2}$ tsp
Butter, cut into small pieces	1 Tbs	1 Tbs

Cut the aubergines (eggplants) in half lengthways and sprinkle the cut sur-

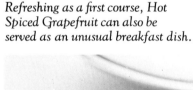

Refreshing as a first course, Hot Spiced Grapefruit can also be served as an unusual breakfast dish.

faces with salt. Set aside for 30 minutes.

Squeeze the aubergines (eggplants) to remove as much liquid as possible, then rinse and pat dry with paper towels.

Heat 4 tablespoons of the oil in a frying pan. Put in the aubergine (eggplant) halves, cut sides down, and cook for 7 to 8 minutes or until lightly browned. Turn over and cook the other sides for 8 to 10 minutes. Remove from the pan and allow to cool slightly.

Preheat the oven to fairly hot 190°C (Gas Mark 5, 375°F).

Heat the remaining oil in the pan. Add the onion and fry until softened. Add the mushrooms and fry for 2 minutes. Stir in the pork, sour cream, salt and pepper to taste and the allspice and cook for a further 3 minutes. Remove from the heat.

Scoop out the aubergine (eggplant) flesh, leaving the skins intact. Finely chop the flesh and add it to the pork mixture. Stir well, then stuff the aubergine (eggplant) skins with the pork mixture. Arrange the stuffed aubergines (eggplants) in a greased baking dish.

Mix together the breadcrumbs, cheese and paprika and sprinkle over the aubergines (eggplants). Dot the tops with the pieces of butter. Bake for 10 to 15 minutes or until the topping is golden brown. Serve hot.

4 Servings

Roquefort mousse

	Metric/UK	US
Roquefort cheese, crumbled	$\frac{1}{2}$kg/1lb	1lb
Single (light) cream	250ml/8floz	1 cup
Ground cinnamon	$\frac{1}{2}$ tsp	$\frac{1}{2}$ tsp
Double (heavy) cream, whipped until thick	350ml/12floz	1$\frac{1}{2}$ cups
Unflavoured gelatine dissolved in 4 Tbs hot water	15g/$\frac{1}{2}$oz	2 envelopes
Mustard and cress (garden cress) to garnish		

Rub the cheese through a strainer with the back of a wooden spoon into a heatproof bowl. Beat in the single (light) cream and cinnamon and place the bowl over a pan of hot water. Stir the mixture until it is smooth and creamy, then remove from the heat. Allow to cool, then chill for 1 hour.

Fold the double (heavy) cream and

gelatine into the cheese mixture. Divide between eight dishes or moulds and chill for 1 hour or until the mousse is firm.

Serve cold garnished with the cress.

8 Servings

Turkish lamb and lemon soup

	Metric/UK	US
Lean lamb, cut into cubes	$\frac{1}{2}$kg/1lb	1lb
Flour	50g/2oz	$\frac{1}{2}$ cup
Olive oil	3 Tbs	3 Tbs
Water	1$\frac{1}{4}$l/2 pints	5 cups
Onions, quartered	2	2
Carrots, quartered	2	2
Salt and black pepper		
Cayenne pepper	$\frac{1}{2}$ tsp	$\frac{1}{2}$ tsp
Egg yolks	3	3
Lemon juice	2 Tbs	2 Tbs
Butter, melted	50g/2oz	4 Tbs
Paprika	2 tsp	2 tsp
Ground cinnamon	$\frac{1}{2}$ tsp	$\frac{1}{2}$ tsp
Chopped mint	2 Tbs	2 Tbs

Coat the lamb cubes with the flour. Heat the oil in a saucepan. Add the lamb cubes and brown on all sides. Stir in the water and bring to the boil. Skim any scum from the surface, then add the onions, carrots, salt and pepper to taste and the cayenne. Cover and simmer for 1$\frac{1}{2}$ to 2 hours or until the meat is tender.

Beat the egg yolks and lemon juice together. Beat in a few spoonfuls of the hot soup, then add this egg yolk mixture to the pan. Heat very gently, stirring. Do not allow the soup to boil or it will curdle. Pour the soup into a warmed tureen.

Mix together the melted butter, paprika and cinnamon. Pour this over the soup and sprinkle with the mint. Serve hot.

6 Servings

Iced carrot and orange soup

	Metric/UK	US
Butter	25g/1oz	2 Tbs
Large onion, thinly sliced	1	1
Flour	3 Tbs	3 Tbs
Chicken stock	900ml/1$\frac{1}{2}$ pints	3$\frac{3}{4}$ cups
Orange juice	600ml/1 pint	2$\frac{1}{2}$ cups
Chopped chives	2 Tbs	2 Tbs
Salt and pepper		
Grated nutmeg	$\frac{1}{4}$ tsp	$\frac{1}{4}$ tsp
Ground allspice	$\frac{1}{4}$ tsp	$\frac{1}{4}$ tsp
Carrots, cut into 2.5cm/1in pieces	$\frac{1}{2}$kg/1lb	1lb

Melt the butter in a saucepan. Add the

onion and fry until softened. Stir in the flour and cook, stirring, for 1 minute. Gradually stir in the stock and orange juice, then add the remaining ingredients with salt and pepper to taste and stir well.

Bring to the boil, stirring. Cover and simmer for 1 hour, stirring occasionally.

Purée the soup in a blender or with a food mill or strainer. Allow to cool, then chill for at least 2 hours before serving.

6 Servings

Mulligatawny soup

	Metric/UK	US
Water	3l/5 pints	6 pints
Salt		
Chicken, cut into 6 pieces and giblets removed (excluding liver)	1 × 1½kg/3lb	1 × 3lb
Root ginger, peeled and bruised	5cm/2in piece	2in piece
Bay leaves	2	2
Creamed coconut	4cm/1½in slice	1½in slice
Butter	40g/1½oz	3 Tbs
Onions, finely chopped	2	2
Garlic cloves, crushed	2	2
Hot chilli powder	½ tsp	½ tsp
Ground coriander	1 Tbs	1 Tbs
Ground cumin	1 tsp	1 tsp
Black pepper		
Ground almonds	25g/1oz	¼ cup
Gram or chick-pea flour	1½ Tbs	1½ Tbs

Put the water, 1 teaspoon salt, the chicken pieces and giblets, ginger and bay leaves in a saucepan and bring to the boil. Cover and simmer for 45 minutes or until the chicken is cooked. Remove the chicken pieces from the pan.

Continue to simmer the stock, uncovered, until it is reduced to about 1¼l/3 pints (4 pints). Strain the stock, discarding all the giblets and flavourings. Add the coconut to the stock and mix well.

Skin the chicken pieces and remove the meat from the bones. Cut the meat into dice.

Melt the butter in the cleaned-out saucepan. Add the onions and garlic and fry until the onions are golden. Stir in the chilli powder, coriander, cumin and salt and pepper to taste and fry for 5 minutes. Add the ground almonds and flour and cook, stirring, for 1 minute. Gradually stir in the stock and coconut mixture and bring

to the boil, stirring. Add the diced chicken. Cook, stirring occasionally, for 15 minutes longer.

Serve hot.

6 servings

Pumpkin soup

	Metric/UK	US
Butter	25g/1oz	2 Tbs
Onions, chopped	2	2
Flour	2 Tbs	2 Tbs
Chicken stock	1¼l/2 pints	5 cups
Pumpkin flesh, chopped	½kg/1lb	1lb
Grated nutmeg	¼ tsp	¼ tsp
Ground cloves	1/8 tsp	1/8 tsp
Salt and black pepper		
Tomatoes, skinned, seeded and chopped	225g/8oz	8oz
Milk	300ml/10floz	1¼ cups
Sour cream (optional)	4 Tbs	4 Tbs

Melt the butter in a saucepan. Add the onions and fry until softened. Stir in the flour and cook, stirring, for 1 minute. Gradually stir in the stock and bring to the boil, stirring. Add the pumpkin, spices, salt and pepper to taste, tomatoes and milk and stir well. Cover and simmer for 30 minutes.

Purée the soup in a blender or using a food mill or strainer and return to the saucepan. Heat through gently until the soup is piping hot. Serve hot, with croûtons, or allow to cool and serve chilled, topped with a spoonful of sour cream.

4-6 Servings

Chilled fruit soup

	Metric/UK	US
Mixed fruit, peeled and chopped	1kg/2lb	2lb
Sugar	50g/2oz	¼ cup
Salt	pinch	pinch
Clove	1	1
Cinnamon stick	1 × 5cm/2in	1 × 2in
Juice and grated rind of 1 lemon		
Water	1¼l/2 pints	5 cups

Put all the ingredients in a large saucepan and bring to the boil, stirring occasionally. Cover and simmer for 10 to 15 minutes or until the fruit is tender.

Discard the cinnamon stick and clove and purée the soup in a blender or with a food mill or strainer. Chill for at least 1 hour before serving.

4 Servings

Lentil and fish chowder

	Metric/UK	US
Lentils, soaked overnight and drained	225g/8oz	1 cup
Water	900ml/ 1½ pints	3¾ cups
Salt	2 tsp	2 tsp
Lemon sole fillets	6	6
Turmeric	1 tsp	1 tsp
Butter	50g/2oz	4 Tbs
Large onions, finely chopped	2	2
Garlic clove, crushed	1	1
Ground ginger	½ tsp	½ tsp
Mild chilli powder	½ tsp	½ tsp
Ground coriander	1 tsp	1 tsp
Black pepper		
Large green pepper, pith and seeds removed and cut into rings	1	1
Celery stalks, cut into 5cm/2in pieces	2	2
Creamed coconut dissolved in 500ml/ 16floz (1 pint) water	5cm/2in slice	2in slice

Put the lentils in a saucepan with the water and 1 teaspoon salt. Bring to the boil, then cover and simmer for 40 minutes or until all the water has been absorbed. Purée the lentil mixture in a blender.

Rub the sole fillets with the turmeric and remaining salt. Melt the butter in another saucepan. Add the fillets, in batches, and fry for about 2 minutes on each side. Remove from the pan and cut the fillets into 5cm/ 2in pieces.

Add the onions, garlic and ginger to the pan and fry until the onions are softened. Stir in the chilli powder, coriander and pepper to taste and cook for a further 4 minutes. Add the green pepper and celery, then gradually stir in the coconut mixture. Add the lentil purée in spoonfuls, stirring well. Bring to the boil, then add the fish pieces. Cover and simmer for 10 to 15 minutes.

Serve hot.

6-8 Servings

Iced Fruit Soup is just the thing to serve on hot, summer days either as a starter or as a dessert.

FISH & SHELLFISH

Herrings with mustard sauce

	Metric/UK	US
Herrings, filleted and halved	8	8
Lemon juice	1 Tbs	1 Tbs
Eggs, lightly beaten	2	2
Dry mustard	2 tsp	2 tsp
Salt and black pepper		
Flour	50g/2oz	$\frac{1}{2}$ cup
Butter	75g/3oz	6 Tbs
Lemon wedges	6	6
MUSTARD SAUCE		
Butter	125g/4oz	8 Tbs
Salt	$\frac{1}{2}$ tsp	$\frac{1}{2}$ tsp
White pepper	$\frac{1}{4}$ tsp	$\frac{1}{4}$ tsp
Dry mustard	1 tsp	1 tsp

Sprinkle the herring fillets with the lemon juice and set aside.

Mix together the eggs, mustard and salt and pepper to taste. Dip the fillets in the egg mixture, then coat with the flour.

Melt the butter in a frying pan. Add the fillets and fry for 2 to 3 minutes on each side or until cooked through.

Meanwhile, melt the butter for the sauce in a saucepan. Add the salt, pepper and mustard and stir well.

Arrange the herring fillets on a warmed serving platter and pour over the mustard sauce. Garnish with the lemon wedges and serve hot.

8 Servings

Cold seafood salad

	Metric/UK	US
RICE		
Long-grain rice	350g/12oz	2 cups
Canned sweetcorn kernels, drained	300g/10oz	10oz
Cooked peas	225g/8oz	1 cup
SAUCE		
Mayonnaise	300ml/10floz	$1\frac{1}{4}$ cups
Cayenne pepper	$\frac{1}{8}$ tsp	$\frac{1}{8}$ tsp
Tomato purée (paste)	1 Tbs	1 Tbs
Hot chilli powder	$\frac{1}{4}$ tsp	$\frac{1}{4}$ tsp
Salt and white pepper		
SEAFOOD		
Cooked lobster meat, diced	$\frac{1}{2}$kg/1lb	1lb
Shelled prawns (shrimp)	225g/8oz	8oz
Cooked white crabmeat, flaked	225g/8oz	8oz
Large unshelled prawns (shrimp), to garnish	6	6

Cook the rice in boiling salted water until it is tender. Drain, if necessary, and allow to cool. Stir in the corn and peas and pile the mixture on a serving platter.

Mix the mayonnaise with the cayenne, tomato purée (paste), chilli powder and salt and pepper to taste. Chill well.

Arrange the seafood on top of the rice and pour over the sauce. Garnish with the unshelled prawns (shrimp) and serve.

6 Servings

Polynesian mullet

	Metric/UK	US
Grey mullet, filleted	1 × 2kg/4lb	1 × 4lb
Salt and black pepper		
Root ginger, peeled and finely chopped	1cm/$\frac{1}{2}$in piece	$\frac{1}{2}$in piece
Garam masala	1 tsp	1 tsp
Butter	50g/2oz	4 Tbs
Onion, finely chopped	1	1
Medium pineapple, peeled, cored and thinly sliced	1	1
Flaked almonds	50g/2oz	$\frac{1}{2}$ cup
Bananas, cut into 4 slices lengthways	4	4
Sesame seeds, blanched	50g/2oz	$\frac{1}{4}$ cup
Creamed coconut dissolved in 250ml/8floz (1 cup) water	5cm/2in slice	2in slice

Preheat the oven to moderate 180°C (Gas Mark 4, 350°F).

Rub the mullet fillets with salt and pepper, the ginger and garam masala.

Melt the butter in a frying pan. Add the onion and fry until softened. Add the fillets and fry for 5 minutes on each side. Remove from the heat.

Arrange half the pineapple slices in a greased baking dish. Place the fillets on top, skin sides down. Cover the fish with the onion, remaining pineapple, almonds, banana slices and sesame seeds. Pour over the dissolved coconut mixture.

Cover the dish and bake for 20 minutes. Uncover and bake for a further 15 minutes or until the fish is cooked through.

Serve hot.

4-6 Servings

Snapper with tomato chilli sauce

	Metric/UK	US
Flour	50g/2oz	½ cup
Salt and black pepper		
Mild chilli powder	1 tsp	1 tsp
Red snapper fillets	1kg/2lb	2lb
Olive or peanut oil	75ml/3floz	6 Tbs
Onion, finely chopped	1	1
Garlic cloves, crushed	2	2
Canned pimientos, drained and finely chopped	125g/4oz	4oz
Red chilli (chili pepper), finely chopped	1	1
Canned tomatoes	425g/14oz	14oz
Pimiento-stuffed olives, chopped	50g/2oz	⅔ cup
Ground coriander	1 tsp	1 tsp
Hard-boiled egg yolks, sieved (strained)	2	2

Preheat the oven to moderate 180°C (Gas Mark 4, 350°F).

Mix the flour with salt and pepper and the chilli powder and use to coat the fillets. Heat 4 tablespoons of the oil in a frying pan. Add the fillets, and fry until golden on both sides.

Add the remaining oil to the pan. When it is hot, add the onion, garlic, pimientos and chilli and fry until the onion is softened. Stir in the tomatoes, olives, coriander and salt and pepper to taste. Bring to the boil, then simmer for 5 minutes.

Arrange the fillets in a baking dish and pour over the tomato chilli sauce. Bake for 10 to 15 minutes or until the fish is cooked through. Sprinkle over the egg yolks and serve hot, in the dish.

4-6 Servings

Snapper with Tomato Chilli Sauce is a spicy dish from Mexico.

Shrimp baked with lettuce

	Metric/UK	US
Double (heavy) cream	250ml/8floz	1 cup
Prepared French mustard	2 tsp	2 tsp
Worcestershire sauce	1 tsp	1 tsp
Cayenne pepper	$\frac{1}{8}$ tsp	$\frac{1}{8}$ tsp
Grated nutmeg	$\frac{1}{4}$ tsp	$\frac{1}{4}$ tsp
Salt and black pepper		
Tabasco sauce	$\frac{1}{8}$ tsp	$\frac{1}{8}$ tsp
Cornflour (cornstarch) dissolved in 1 Tbs cream	1 tsp	1 tsp
Small lettuces, shredded	2	2
Shelled shrimp	225g/8oz	8oz
Tomatoes, skinned, seeded and chopped	4	4
Lemon juice	2 tsp	2 tsp
Parmesan cheese, grated	50g/2oz	$\frac{1}{2}$ cup

Preheat the oven to fairly hot 190°C (Gas Mark 5, 375°F).

Put the cream, mustard, Worcestershire sauce, cayenne, nutmeg, salt and pepper to taste, Tabasco and dissolved cornflour (cornstarch) in a saucepan and heat gently, stirring, until the mixture thickens. Remove from the heat and fold in the shredded lettuces.

Spread half the lettuce mixture on the bottom of a greased baking dish (or use four individual ovenproof dishes). Make a layer of the shrimp on top and cover with the tomatoes. Spread over the remaining lettuce mixture. Sprinkle with the lemon juice and cheese.

Bake for 35 to 40 minutes or until the top is lightly browned. Serve hot.

4 Servings

Haddock morsels

	Metric/UK	US
Flour	75g/3oz	$\frac{3}{4}$ cup
Salt	1 tsp	1 tsp
Dry mustard	$\frac{1}{2}$ tsp	$\frac{1}{2}$ tsp
Ground ginger	$\frac{1}{2}$ tsp	$\frac{1}{2}$ tsp
Egg, separated	1	1
Egg yolk	1	1
Oil	1 Tbs	1 Tbs
Milk	225ml/7floz	Scant 1 cup
Sufficient oil for deep-frying		
Smoked haddock fillets, cut into small pieces	700g/1$\frac{1}{2}$lb	1$\frac{1}{2}$lb

Sift the flour, salt, mustard and ginger into a mixing bowl. Add the egg yolks,

A subtle combination of shrimps, cream, lettuce and spices, Shrimp Baked with Lettuce is delicious either on its own or as an accompaniment to roast main courses.

1 tablespoon oil and 4 tablespoons of the milk. Beat well, gradually beating in the remaining milk to form a smooth batter. Beat the egg white until stiff and fold into the batter.

Heat the oil in a deep-frying pan (deep fat fryer) until it is 185°C/360°F, or until a small cube of stale bread dropped into the oil turns golden in 50 seconds.

Coat the haddock pieces in the batter, then fry them, a few at a time, in the hot oil until they are deep golden brown. Drain on paper towels and serve hot with a piquant sauce.

4 Servings

Salmon kedgeree

	Metric/UK	US
Canned salmon, drained and flaked	700g/1½lb	1½lb
Béchamel or white sauce	450ml/15floz	2 cups
Grated nutmeg	¾ tsp	¾ tsp
Butter	50g/2oz	4 Tbs
Small onion, finely chopped	1	1
Cooked rice	300g/10oz	4 cups
Hard-boiled eggs, finely chopped	2	2
Salt and black pepper		
Curry powder	2 tsp	2 tsp

Mix together the salmon, sauce and nutmeg in a saucepan and heat through gently, stirring occasionally.

Meanwhile, melt the butter in another pan. Add the onion and fry until softened. Stir in the rice and half the chopped eggs, then stir in the salmon mixture, salt and pepper to taste and the curry powder. When the mixture is very hot, pile it on a warmed serving platter and sprinkle over the remaining egg. Serve hot.

4 Servings

Soused mackerel

	Metric/UK	US
Dry white wine	1l/1¾ pints	4½ cups
Carrots, thinly sliced	2	2
Onions, thinly sliced	2	2
Mackerel, filleted and rolled with the skins outside	8	8
Dried marjoram	2 tsp	2 tsp
Cloves	2	2
Bay leaves	4	4
Black peppercorns	1 tsp	1 tsp
Allspice berries	1 tsp	1 tsp
Salt	1 tsp	1 tsp
Lemon, sliced	1	1

Preheat the oven to cool 150°C (Gas Mark 2, 300°F).

Put the wine, carrots and onions in a saucepan and bring to the boil. Simmer for 10 minutes.

Put the fish rolls in a baking dish. Strain over the wine and sprinkle with the marjoram, cloves, bay leaves, peppercorns, allspice berries and salt. Arrange the lemon slices around the edge of the dish.

Bake for 1½ to 2 hours or until the fish is thoroughly cooked. Allow to cool completely and serve at room temperature.

8 Servings

Carp in paprika sauce

	Metric/UK	US
Carp, cut into 6 serving pieces	1 × 1½kg/3lb	1 × 3lb
Salt		
Butter	40g/1½oz	3 Tbs
Onions, finely chopped	2	2
Green peppers, pith and seeds removed and chopped	3	3
Tomatoes, skinned and chopped	8	8
Paprika	1 Tbs	1 Tbs
Oil	3 Tbs	3 Tbs

Sprinkle the carp pieces with salt and set aside.

Preheat the oven to moderate 180°C (Gas Mark 4, 350°F).

Melt the butter in a saucepan. Add the onions and fry until softened. Stir in the green peppers, tomatoes, paprika and salt to taste and cook for 20 to 25 minutes or until the sauce is thick.

Meanwhile, heat the oil in a frying pan. Add the carp pieces and brown on all sides. Transfer the carp pieces to a baking dish and pour over the paprika sauce. Bake for 30 to 40 minutes or until the fish is cooked through. Serve hot, in the dish.

4 Servings

Paprika is the ingredient which adds pungency to this recipe for Carp in Paprika Sauce.

POULTRY & GAME

West African chicken and peanut butter stew

	Metric/UK	US
Peanut oil	2 Tbs	2 Tbs
Onion, chopped	1	1
Garlic clove, crushed	1	1
Green pepper, pith and seeds removed and chopped	1	1
Chicken, cut into serving pieces	1 × 2kg/4lb	1 × 4lb
Peanut butter	225g/8oz	1 cup
Chicken stock	600ml/1 pint	2½ cups
Salt and black pepper		
Turmeric	1 tsp	1 tsp
Ground coriander	1 Tbs	1 Tbs
Ground cumin	1 tsp	1 tsp
Hot chilli powder	½ tsp	½ tsp
Tomatoes, skinned and chopped	2	2
Chopped parsley	1 Tbs	1 Tbs

Heat the oil in a saucepan. Add the onion, garlic and green pepper and fry until the onion is softened. Add the chicken pieces and brown on all sides. Mix together the peanut butter, stock, salt and pepper to taste, the turmeric, coriander, cumin and chilli powder and add to the pan. Stir well, then stir in the tomatoes. Bring to the boil. Cover and simmer for 30 minutes.

Uncover and simmer for a further 15 minutes or until the chicken is cooked through. Serve hot, sprinkled with the parsley.

4 Servings

Venezuelan chicken

	Metric/UK	US
Chicken pieces, skinned	8	8
Butter	50g/2oz	4 Tbs
Green beans	175g/6oz	1 cup
Canned sweetcorn kernels, drained	225g/8oz	8oz
MARINADE		
Orange juice	175ml/6floz	¾ cup
Grapefruit juice	4 Tbs	¼ cup
Grated rind of 1 large orange		
Garlic cloves, crushed	2	2
Shallots, chopped	2	2
Cumin seeds, crushed	½ tsp	½ tsp
Ground allspice	¼ tsp	¼ tsp
Ground mace	¼ tsp	¼ tsp
Salt and black pepper		
Mild chilli powder	¼ tsp	¼ tsp

Put all the ingredients for the marinade in a shallow dish and mix well. Add the chicken pieces and turn over to coat. Leave to marinate for 8 hours or overnight, turning occasionally.

Preheat the oven to moderate 180°C (Gas Mark 4, 350°F).

Remove the chicken pieces from the marinade and pat them dry with paper towels. Reserve the marinade.

Melt the butter in a flameproof casserole. Add the chicken pieces and brown on all sides. Add the reserved marinade, green beans and corn and stir gently to mix. Bring to the boil.

Cover the casserole and transfer it to the oven. Bake for 1 hour or until the chicken is cooked through. Serve hot, in the casserole.

4 Servings

Greek chicken in tomato and cinnamon sauce

	Metric/UK	US
Chicken pieces, skinned	8	8
Salt and black pepper		
Butter	50g/2oz	4 Tbs
Olive oil	2 Tbs	2 Tbs
Small onion, finely chopped	1	1
Garlic clove, crushed	1	1
Prepared mustard	1 tsp	1 tsp
Tomato purée (paste)	2 Tbs	2 Tbs
Canned tomatoes, chopped	425g/14oz	14oz
Chicken stock	4 Tbs	¼ cup
Juice of ½ lemon		
Ground cinnamon	1 tsp	1 tsp
Dried marjoram	½ tsp	½ tsp

Rub the chicken pieces with salt and pepper. Melt the butter with the oil in a flameproof casserole. Add the chicken pieces and brown them on all sides. Remove them from the pot.

Add the onion and garlic to the pot and fry until golden. Stir in the mustard, tomato purée (paste), tomatoes, stock, lemon juice, cinnamon and marjoram. Bring to the boil and simmer for 10 minutes.

Return the chicken pieces to the casserole, cover and simmer for 40 minutes or until tender.

Serve hot, with boiled noodles.

4 Servings

Hawaiian chicken

	Metric/UK	US
Butter	25g/1oz	2 Tbs
Oil	1 Tbs	1 Tbs
Chicken pieces, skinned	8	8
Medium onions, sliced into rings	2	2
Flour	2 Tbs	2 Tbs
Chicken stock	450ml/15floz	2 cups
Green peppers, pith and seeds removed and chopped	2	2
Large red pepper, pith and seeds removed and chopped	1	1
Canned pineapple chunks, drained	425g/14oz	14oz
Salt and black pepper		
Caraway seeds	1 Tbs	1 Tbs
Double (heavy) cream	150ml/5floz	$\frac{2}{3}$ cup
RICE		
Long-grain rice	350g/12oz	2 cups
Butter	40g/1½oz	3 Tbs
Lean cooked ham, diced	4 slices	4 slices
Canned sweetcorn kernels, drained	425g/14oz	14oz
Cayenne pepper	$\frac{1}{4}$ tsp	$\frac{1}{4}$ tsp
Grated nutmeg	$\frac{1}{8}$ tsp	$\frac{1}{8}$ tsp

Melt the butter with the oil in a flame-proof casserole. Add the chicken pieces and brown them on all sides. Remove them from the pot. Add the onions to the pot and fry until softened. Stir in the flour and cook, stirring, for 1 minute. Gradually stir in the stock.

Return the chicken pieces to the casserole with the peppers, pineapple chunks, salt and pepper to taste and the caraway seeds. Stir well and bring to the boil. Cover and simmer for 40 minutes or until the chicken pieces are tender.

Meanwhile, prepare the rice. Cook the rice in plenty of boiling salted water until it is tender.

Melt the butter in a saucepan. Add the ham, corn, cayenne and nutmeg and cook gently for 5 minutes, stirring occasionally. Stir in the rice, mixing thoroughly, and continue to cook until the rice is hot.

Spread the rice on a warmed serving platter. Arrange the chicken pieces on top and keep hot.

Stir the cream into the cooking liquid in the casserole and heat through gently. Pour this sauce over the chicken and rice and serve hot.

4 Servings

Hawaiian Chicken is a filling main course made from a combination of pineapple, chicken, peppers and rice.

Spiced honey chicken

	Metric/UK	US
Butter	50g/2oz	4 Tbs
Clear honey	125ml/4floz	½ cup
Prepared German mustard	4 Tbs	4 Tbs
Salt	1 tsp	1 tsp
Mild curry powder	1 tsp	1 tsp
Chicken pieces, skinned	8	8

Preheat the oven to moderate 180°C (Gas Mark 4, 350°F).

Melt the butter in a saucepan. Remove from the heat and stir in the honey, mustard, salt and curry powder. Mix well.

Arrange the chicken pieces in one layer in a roasting pan and pour over the honey mixture. Turn the chicken pieces so they are coated on all sides.

Bake for 1 hour, turning the chicken pieces at least once during that time. Serve hot.

4 Servings

Danish Christmas goose

	Metric/UK	US
Goose	1 × 3½–4kg/ 8–9lb	1 × 8– 9lb
Lemon	½	½
Salt and black pepper		
Cooking apples, peeled, cored and chopped	4	4
Prunes, stoned (pitted)	350g/12oz	2 cups
Dry breadcrumbs	50g/2oz	⅔ cup
Ground cardamom	1 tsp	1 tsp
GARNISH		
Prunes, soaked for 3 hours in 300ml/10floz (1¼ cups) port	225g/8oz	1¼ cups
Sugar	125g/4oz	½ cup
Water	300ml/10floz	1¼ cups
Cooking apples, peeled, cored and halved	4	4
Cornflour (cornstarch) dissolved in 1 Tbs port	1 tsp	1 tsp
Double (heavy) cream	250ml/8floz	1 cup

Preheat the oven to very hot 230°C (Gas Mark 8, 450°F).

Rub the goose, inside and out, with the lemon, then sprinkle all over with salt and pepper. Mix together the apples, prunes, breadcrumbs and cardamom and use to stuff the goose. Secure the opening with trussing needle and string or skewers. Prick the skin of the goose all over.

Place the goose, on its breast, on a rack in a roasting pan. Roast for 15 minutes, then reduce the oven temperature to moderate 180°C (Gas Mark

A fragrant dish made with honey, German mustard and chicken pieces, Spiced Honey Chicken should be served with fresh vegetables.

4, 350°F). Continue roasting for 3 to 3¼ hours, removing the fat from the pan occasionally. After 1½ hours roasting, turn the goose onto the other side.

Just before the goose is ready, prepare the garnish. Put the prunes and port mixture into a saucepan and simmer for 15 minutes.

Meanwhile, in another saucepan dissolve the sugar in the water. Bring to the boil and boil for 3 minutes or until this syrup has thickened slightly. Add the apples to the mixture and poach gently for 10 minutes or until just tender.

Transfer the goose to a warmed serving platter. Arrange the poached apple halves around it, cut sides up, and fill the hollows with the prunes. Stir the cornflour (cornstarch) and cream into the port in which the prunes were soaked and cooked, and simmer until thick and smooth. Pour this sauce into a sauceboat and serve at once, as an accompaniment to the goose.

6-8 Servings

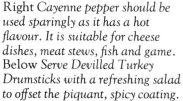

Right *Cayenne pepper should be used sparingly as it has a hot flavour. It is suitable for cheese dishes, meat stews, fish and game.* Below *Serve Devilled Turkey Drumsticks with a refreshing salad to offset the piquant, spicy coating.*

Devilled turkey drumsticks

	Metric/UK	US
French mustard	2 tsp	2 tsp
Prepared English mustard	2 tsp	2 tsp
Tomato ketchup	1 Tbs	1 Tbs
Ground ginger	¼ tsp	¼ tsp
Salt and black pepper		
Cayenne pepper	¼ tsp	¼ tsp
Turkey drumsticks, cooked	4	4
Butter, melted	25g/1oz	2 Tbs

Mix together the mustards, ketchup,

ginger, salt and pepper to taste and the cayenne. Score the drumsticks on both sides. Brush them with the melted butter, then coat with the mustard mixture. Leave for 30 minutes.

Preheat the grill (broiler) to moderate.

Place the drumsticks on the grill (broiler) rack and cook for about 10 minutes or until crisp and golden brown. Serve hot.

4 Servings

Normandy duck

	Metric/UK	US
Fresh white breadcrumbs	225g/8oz	4 cups
Strong (hard) cider	300ml/10floz	1¼ cups
Butter	50g/2oz	4 Tbs
Olive oil	2 Tbs	2 Tbs
Cooking apples, peeled, cored and sliced	1kg/2lb	2lb
Celery stalks, finely chopped	3	3
Ground cinnamon	½ tsp	½ tsp
Ground cloves	½ tsp	½ tsp
Salt and black pepper		
Duck	1 × 3kg/6lb	1 × 6lb
Calvados or applejack	75ml/3floz	⅓ cup
Double (heavy) cream	175ml/6floz	¾ cup

Preheat the oven to moderate 180°C (Gas Mark 4, 350°F).

Put the breadcrumbs in a bowl and sprinkle over 4 tablespoons of the cider. Squeeze the breadcrumbs gently so that they become completely moistened.

Melt the butter with the oil in a saucepan. When hot, add the apples and celery. Cook for about 10 minutes or until just tender. Stir in the cinnamon, cloves and salt and pepper to taste. Remove the saucepan from the heat and stir in the breadcrumb mixture.

Spoon the stuffing into the duck and secure the opening with trussing needle and string or skewers. Place the duck on a rack in a roasting pan and prick it all over. Roast for about 15 minutes.

Pour the rest of the cider over the duck and continue roasting for 1¾ hours or until the duck is tender, basting every 15 minutes with the juices in the pan.

Transfer the duck to a warmed serving platter. Remove the string or skewers, set the platter aside and keep hot.

Skim the fat from the surface of the cooking juices and place the pan over heat on top of the stove. Bring to the boil and boil until reduced to half the original quantity. Stir in the Calvados or applejack and cream and heat through gently. Pour this sauce into a sauceboat and serve at once with the duck.

4 Servings

Pigeons with chestnuts

	Metric/UK	US
Butter	25g/1oz	2 Tbs
Pigeons	4	4
Dried chestnuts, soaked overnight and cooked until almost tender	16	16
Garlic clove, crushed	1	1
Grated nutmeg	¼ tsp	¼ tsp
Ground allspice	¼ tsp	¼ tsp
Flour	1 Tbs	1 Tbs
Salt and black pepper		
Dry red wine	250ml/8floz	1 cup
Beef stock	250ml/8floz	1 cup

Preheat the oven to moderate 180°C (Gas Mark 4, 350°F).

Melt the butter in a frying pan. Add the pigeons and brown on all sides. Transfer the pigeons to a casserole. Add the chestnuts to the casserole.

Add the garlic, nutmeg and allspice to the frying pan and cook, stirring, for 2 minutes. Stir in the flour with salt and pepper to taste and cook, stirring, for a further 2 minutes. Gradually stir in the wine and stock and bring to the boil, stirring. Simmer until thickened, then pour over the pigeons in the casserole.

Cover the casserole and bake the pigeons for 1 hour or until they are cooked through. Serve hot.

4 Servings

Nutmeg is a popular spice since it can be used in many sweet and savoury dishes.

MEAT & MAIN COURSES

Spiced steak

	Metric/UK	US
Salt	1 tsp	1 tsp
Black peppercorns, crushed	4	4
Garlic clove, crushed	1	1
Turmeric	1 tsp	1 tsp
Cardamom seeds, crushed	2	2
Cayenne pepper	$\frac{1}{4}$ tsp	$\frac{1}{4}$ tsp
Ground cumin	$\frac{1}{2}$ tsp	$\frac{1}{2}$ tsp
Butter, melted	25g/1oz	2 Tbs
Soy sauce	1 Tbs	1 Tbs
Medium steaks (sirloin, porterhouse, rump, etc)	4	4

Preheat the grill (broiler) to high.

Mix together the salt, peppercorns, garlic, turmeric, cardamom, cayenne, cumin, butter and soy sauce.

Put the steaks on the rack in the grill (broiler) pan and brush with the spice mixture. Grill (broil) for 5 to 6 minutes on each side (for rare steaks), basting frequently with the spice mixture. Serve hot.

4 Servings

Empanadas

	Metric/UK	US
PASTRY		
Flour	175/6oz	1$\frac{1}{2}$ cups
Salt	$\frac{1}{4}$ tsp	$\frac{1}{4}$ tsp
Butter	140g/4$\frac{1}{2}$oz	9 Tbs
Iced water	3–4 Tbs	3–4 Tbs
FILLING		
Oil	2 Tbs	2 Tbs
Onion, finely chopped	1	1
Tomatoes, skinned, seeded and chopped	2	2
Small green pepper, pith and seeds removed and chopped	$\frac{1}{2}$	$\frac{1}{2}$
Minced (ground) beef	225g/8oz	8oz
Raisins	50g/2oz	$\frac{1}{3}$ cup
Salt and black pepper		
Hot chilli powder	$\frac{1}{2}$ tsp	$\frac{1}{2}$ tsp
Ground cumin	$\frac{1}{4}$ tsp	$\frac{1}{4}$ tsp

To make the pastry, sift the flour and salt into a mixing bowl. Add the butter and cut it into small pieces. Mix in enough water just to bind the mixture to a dough, which will be lumpy.

Turn out the dough onto a floured surface and roll it out into an oblong. Fold it in three and turn it so that the open edges face you. Roll it out again into an oblong, then fold and turn as before. Repeat this once again to make three folds and turns in all. Chill for 30 minutes.

Preheat the oven to fairly hot 190°C (Gas Mark 5, 375°F).

To make the filling, heat the oil in a frying pan. Add the onion, tomatoes and green pepper and fry until the onion is softened. Add the beef and cook until browned.

Stir in the raisins, salt and pepper to taste, the chilli powder and cumin and cook for 10 minutes. Remove from the heat and allow the mixture to cool slightly.

Roll out the dough into a large square and cut it into eight 13cm/5in circles. Divide the filling between the dough circles. Fold over the circles to enclose the filling.

Dampen the dough edges and press together to seal.

Arrange the empanadas on a greased baking sheet and bake for 35 minutes or until the pastry is golden brown. Serve hot.

4 Servings

Hungarian goulash

	Metric/UK	US
Butter	40g/1$\frac{1}{2}$oz	3 Tbs
Oil	2 Tbs	2 Tbs
Lean stewing (chuck) steak, cut into cubes	1kg/2lb	2lb
Onions, sliced	$\frac{1}{2}$kg/1lb	1lb
Garlic clove, crushed	1	1
Paprika	2 Tbs	2 Tbs
Salt and black pepper		
Water	150ml/5floz	$\frac{2}{3}$ cup
Bay leaf	1	1
Potatoes, peeled and sliced	$\frac{1}{2}$kg/1lb	1lb
Sour cream	150ml/5floz	$\frac{2}{3}$ cup

Melt the butter with the oil in a saucepan. Add the beef cubes and brown them on all sides. As the cubes brown, remove them from the pan. Add the onions to the pan and fry until golden. Stir in the garlic, paprika, salt and pepper to taste, the water and bay leaf. Return the beef cubes to the pan and

turn to coat them thoroughly with the sauce.

Bring to the boil, then cover and simmer for 1 hour.

Stir in the potatoes and continue simmering the mixture for a further 1 hour.

Remove the bay leaf and spoon the goulash into a warmed serving bowl. Spoon the sour cream on top and serve hot.

4 Servings

German beef and clove casserole

	Metric/UK	US
Lean topside (top round) beef, in one piece	1 × 1½kg/3lb	1 × 3 lb
Garlic clove, crushed	1	1
Dried marjoram	1 tsp	1 tsp
Salt and black pepper		
Salt pork	25g/1oz	1 oz
Cloves	8	8
Butter	50g/2oz	4 Tbs
Oil	4 Tbs	¼ cup
Red wine	250ml/8floz	1 cup
Beef stock	250ml/8floz	1 cup
Onion, chopped	1	1
Carrots, chopped	3	3
Celery stalk, chopped	1	1

Lay the meat on a working surface and pound it flat with a meat mallet. Mix together the garlic, marjoram and a little salt and pepper. Cut the salt pork into thin strips and coat the strips with the garlic mixture. Make incisions in the beef and insert the pork strips and cloves. Roll up the meat and tie with string.

Melt the butter with the oil in a flameproof casserole. Add the meat and brown it on all sides. Add the remaining ingredients with salt and pepper to taste and bring to the boil. Cover and simmer for 1¾ to 2 hours or until the beef is cooked through and tender.

Transfer the beef to a warmed serving platter. Skim the fat from the cooking liquid and strain some of it over the meat. If you like, the remainder may be thickened with cornflour (cornstarch) and served as a gravy with the meat. Serve hot.

6 Servings

A delicious dish of beef spiced with cloves, German Beef and Clove Casserole makes an appetizing lunch or supper.

Chilean meat and corn pie

	Metric/UK	US
Oil	3 Tbs	3 Tbs
Onions, thinly sliced	2	2
Red chilli (chili pepper), seeded and finely chopped	1	1
Garlic clove, crushed	1	1
Minced (ground) beef	350g/12oz	$\frac{3}{4}$lb
Minced (ground) pork	350g/12oz	$\frac{3}{4}$lb
Salt	1 tsp	1 tsp
Ground cumin	1 tsp	1 tsp
Hot chilli powder	$\frac{1}{2}$ tsp	$\frac{1}{2}$ tsp
Flour	1 Tbs	1 Tbs
Black olives, stoned (pitted)	50g/2oz	$\frac{1}{2}$ cup
Raisins, soaked in water for 15 minutes and drained	75g/3oz	$\frac{1}{2}$ cup
TOPPING		
Oil	2 Tbs	2 Tbs
Onion, finely chopped	1	1
Canned sweetcorn kernels, drained and puréed in a blender or food mill	350g/12oz	12oz
Salt	$\frac{1}{2}$ tsp	$\frac{1}{2}$ tsp

Preheat the oven to fairly hot 190°C (Gas Mark 5, 375°F).

Heat the oil in a frying pan. Add the onions, chilli and garlic and fry until the onions are softened. Add the beef and pork and fry until browned. Stir in the salt, cumin, chilli powder and flour, then mix in the olives and raisins. Spoon the mixture into a greased 1$\frac{1}{4}$l/2 pint (2$\frac{1}{2}$ pint) baking dish.

To make the topping, heat the oil in another frying pan. Add the onion and fry until softened. Stir in the sweetcorn purée and salt and cook, stirring, for 5 minutes.

Spoon the topping over the meat mixture in the dish. Bake for 20 to 25 minutes or until the top is golden brown. Serve hot, in the dish.

4 Servings

Chillis should always be used with great caution in cooking as they have a very hot flavour and over-zealous use can ruin carefully prepared dishes.

Marinated beef fillet (tenderloin)

	Metric/UK	US
Beef fillet (tenderloin roast)	1 × 2kg/4lb	1 × 4lb
Salt and black pepper		
Streaky bacon rashers (slices)	8	8
MARINADE		
Red wine	300ml/10floz	1$\frac{1}{4}$ cups
Tarragon vinegar	125ml/4floz	$\frac{1}{2}$ cup
Grated nutmeg	1 tsp	1 tsp
Ground cloves	1 tsp	1 tsp
Bay leaves	2	2
Onion, sliced into rings	1	1
Lemon, thinly sliced	$\frac{1}{2}$	$\frac{1}{2}$
Large carrot, thinly sliced	1	1
SAUCE		
Oil	2 Tbs	2 Tbs
Onions, finely chopped	2	2
Large carrot, finely chopped	1	1
Brandy	4 Tbs	$\frac{1}{4}$ cup
Beef stock	350ml/12floz	1$\frac{1}{2}$ cups
Bouquet garni	1	1
Black peppercorns	6	6
Butter	40g/1$\frac{1}{2}$oz	3 Tbs
Flour	2 Tbs	2 Tbs
Salt	$\frac{1}{4}$ tsp	$\frac{1}{4}$ tsp

Rub the beef with salt and pepper and place it in a shallow dish. Mix together all the marinade ingredients and pour over the meat. Turn to coat, then leave to marinate for 24 hours.

Preheat the oven to hot 220°C (Gas Mark 7, 425°F).

Remove the beef from the marinade and dry with paper towels. Put the beef in a roasting pan. Strain the marinade and reserve 125ml/4floz ($\frac{1}{2}$ cup).

Lay the rashers (slices) of bacon over the beef and roast for 1 hour for rare meat; increase the time by 30 minutes if you prefer it well done.

Meanwhile, make the sauce. Heat the oil in a saucepan. Add the onions and carrot and fry until the onions are softened. Stir in the reserved marinade and the brandy and bring to the boil. Boil until reduced to one-third. Add the stock and bouquet garni, stir well, cover and simmer for 30 minutes.

Add the peppercorns to the sauce. Mix 1 tablespoon of the butter with the flour to form a paste and add to the sauce in small pieces. Simmer, stirring, until thickened. Add the salt and remaining butter. Stir until the butter melts, then pour the sauce into a sauceboat. Keep hot.

Transfer the beef to a warmed serving platter. Remove the bacon. Carve and serve with the sauce.

8 Servings

Pakistani lamb chops

	Metric/UK	US
Juice of ½ lemon		
Salt	2 tsp	2 tsp
Cayenne pepper	1 tsp	1 tsp
Lamb chops	8	8
Butter	50g/2oz	4 Tbs
Onion, finely chopped	1	1
Garlic cloves, crushed	2	2
Root ginger, peeled and finely chopped	2.5cm/1in piece	1in piece
Ground cumin	1 tsp	1 tsp
Ground fenugreek	½ tsp	½ tsp
Ground pomegranate seed	1 Tbs	1 Tbs
Hot chilli powder	½ tsp	½ tsp
Plain yogurt	150ml/5floz	⅔ cup
Saffron threads soaked in 2 Tbs boiling water	½ tsp	½ tsp
Chopped fresh coriander leaves	1 Tbs	1 Tbs

Mix together the lemon juice, salt and cayenne and rub into the chops. Leave them for 30 minutes.

Melt the butter in a frying pan. Add the chops, in batches, and brown on both sides. Remove the chops from the pan.

Add the onion, garlic and ginger to the pan and fry until the onion is golden. Mix together the cumin, fenugreek, pomegranate seed, chilli powder, yogurt and saffron-coloured water. Add to the pan and stir well. Bring to the boil.

Return the chops to the pan and turn them over in the sauce. Cover and cook gently for 15 minutes. Uncover and continue cooking for 20 to 25 minutes or until the chops are tender and the sauce is thick. Serve hot, sprinkled with the coriander leaves.

4 Servings

Arabian stewed lamb

	Metric/UK	US
Oil	2 Tbs	2 Tbs
Boned lamb leg or shoulder, cut into large cubes	1kg/2lb	2lb
Large onion, sliced	1	1
Garlic clove, crushed	1	1
Turmeric	1 tsp	1 tsp
Cinnamon stick	1 × 5cm/2in	1 × 2in
Salt and pepper		
Flour	1 Tbs	1 Tbs
Beef stock	350ml/12floz	1½ cups
Brown sugar	1 Tbs	1 Tbs
Prunes, stoned (pitted) and soaked in water for 2 hours	16	16

Heat the oil in a large saucepan. Add the lamb cubes, in batches, and fry until evenly browned. As the cubes are browned, remove them from the pan.

Add the onion and garlic to the pan and fry until softened. Stir in the turmeric, cinnamon and salt and pepper to taste and cook, stirring, for 5 minutes. Stir in the flour, cook for 1 minute, then gradually stir in the stock. Bring to the boil, stirring.

Return the lamb cubes to the pan and simmer for 1 hour or until the meat is tender. Ten minutes before the lamb is ready, stir in the sugar and prunes. Remove the cinnamon stick and serve hot.

4 Servings

Lamb pie

	Metric/UK	US
Lemon juice	1 tsp	1 tsp
Dessert apples, peeled, cored and sliced	1kg/2lb	2lb
Best end of neck of lamb (rib chops), boned and cut into slices	1kg/2lb	2lb
Soft brown sugar	2 Tbs	2 Tbs
Prunes, stoned (pitted) and chopped	10	10
Large onions, chopped	2	2
Grated nutmeg	2 tsp	2 tsp
Ground mace	1 tsp	1 tsp
Ground cinnamon	1 tsp	1 tsp
Salt and black pepper		
Beef stock	175ml/6floz	¾ cup
PASTRY		
Flour	225g/8oz	2 cups
Salt	¼ tsp	¼ tsp
Butter, lard or vegetable fat	75g/3oz	6 Tbs
Iced water	4-6 Tbs	4-6 Tbs
Egg, lightly beaten	1	1

To make the pastry, sift the flour and salt into a bowl. Add the fat and cut into small pieces, then rub the fat into the flour until the mixture resembles breadcrumbs. Mix in enough of the water to bind the ingredients to a dough. Chill for 20 minutes.

Preheat the oven to fairly hot 190°C (Gas Mark 5, 375°F).

Meanwhile, mix the lemon juice into the apple slices. Put one-third of the meat on the bottom of a pie dish (casserole) and cover with one-third of the apples. Sprinkle over a little of the sugar and about one-third of the prunes. Top with one-third of the onions. Mix together the spices and salt and pepper to taste and sprinkle about one-third of this mixture over the onions. Continue making layers in this way until all the ingredients are used up. Pour in the stock.

*Delicious Syrian Stuffed Lamb
Breasts is an exotic main course.*

Roll out the dough and use to cover
the dish (casserole). Make a large cross
in the centre to allow steam to escape
and decorate the top with leaves made
from the dough trimmings. Brush with
the beaten egg.

Bake for 1¼ to 1½ hours or until the
pastry is golden brown. Serve hot.

4 Servings

Syrian stuffed lamb breasts

	Metric/UK	US
Large, whole breasts of lamb, boned	2	2
Salt and pepper		
Olive oil	2 Tbs	2 Tbs
Dried apricots, soaked in water overnight	275g/9oz	1½ cups
Sugar	2 Tbs	2 Tbs
STUFFING		
Oil	2 Tbs	2 Tbs
Large onion, finely chopped	1	1
Minced (ground) beef	225g/8oz	8oz
Long-grain rice	1½ Tbs	1½ Tbs
Ground cumin	1 tsp	1 tsp
Turmeric	1 tsp	1 tsp
Water	175ml/6floz	¾ cup
Chopped parsley	3 Tbs	3 Tbs
Salt and black pepper		
Almonds, chopped	50g/2oz	½ cup
Raisins	50g/2oz	⅓ cup

To make the stuffing, heat the oil in a
saucepan. Add the onion and fry until
golden. Add the beef and fry until
browned. Stir in the rice and cook for
4 minutes. Stir in the cumin, turmeric,
water, parsley, and salt and pepper to
taste and bring to the boil. Cover and
simmer for 25 minutes or until the
rice is tender and all the water has
been absorbed. Remove from the
heat and add the almonds and raisins.
Allow to cool.

Preheat the oven to moderate 180°C
(Gas Mark 4, 350°F).

Lay the lamb breasts flat on a
working surface and spread them with
the stuffing. Roll up each breast and
tie securely with string. Rub the meat
with salt and pepper and brush with
the oil.

Place the breasts in a roasting pan
and roast for 1½ hours or until the
meat is well browned and tender.

Meanwhile, put the apricots in a
saucepan with the water in which they
were soaked and the sugar. Bring to
the boil and simmer for 30 minutes
or until the apricots are pulpy.

When the lamb is cooked, pour off
the liquid from the roasting pan.
Increase the oven temperature to very
hot 230°C (Gas Mark 8, 450°F). Pour
the apricot mixture over the lamb
breasts and roast for a further 10
minutes or until glazed and golden
brown. Serve hot.

6 Servings

Leg of lamb with coriander and garlic

	Metric/UK	US
Leg of lamb	1×3kg/6lb	1×6lb
Garlic cloves	6	6
Crushed coriander seeds	1 Tbs	1 Tbs
Salt and black pepper		
Butter, cut into small pieces	25g/1oz	2 Tbs

Preheat the oven to fairly hot 190°C (Gas Mark 5, 375°F).

Make shallow incisions in the lamb and insert the garlic cloves and crushed coriander seeds. Rub the lamb with salt and pepper and place it in a roasting pan. Dot with the butter.

Roast for 20 minutes, then reduce the heat to moderate 180°C (Gas Mark 4, 350°F) and roast for a further 1½ hours, or a little longer if you do not like lamb to be pink. Serve hot.

6-8 Servings

Moussaka

	Metric/UK	US
Medium aubergines (eggplants), sliced	3	3
Salt		
Flour	50g/2oz	½ cup
Oil	175ml/6floz	¾ cup
Butter	25g/1oz	2 Tbs
Shallots, finely chopped	4	4
Lean lamb, minced (ground)	½kg/1lb	1lb
Tomatoes, skinned, seeded and chopped	2	2
Red wine	4 Tbs	¼ cup
Lemon juice	1 tsp	1 tsp
Dried sage	¼ tsp	¼ tsp
Black pepper		
Ground allspice	½ tsp	½ tsp
Fresh white breadcrumbs	50g/2oz	1 cup
SAUCE		
Mizithra or ricotta cheese	175g/6oz	6oz
Egg yolks	3	3
Single (light) cream	350ml/12floz	1½ cups
Salt		
Ground allspice	½ tsp	½ tsp
Kefalotiri or Parmesan cheese, grated	50g/2oz	½ cup

Put the aubergine (eggplant) slices in a colander and sprinkle with salt. Leave for 30 minutes, then rinse and pat dry with paper towels. Coat the aubergine (eggplant) slices with the flour.

Heat 4 tablespoons of the oil in a frying pan. Add the aubergine (eggplant) slices, in batches, and fry until they are golden brown on each side. Drain the slices on paper towels.

Preheat the oven to fairly hot 190°C (Gas Mark 5, 375°F).

Melt the butter in the cleaned-out frying pan. Add the shallots and fry until they are softened. Stir in the lamb and cook, stirring, until it is browned. Add the tomatoes, wine, lemon juice, sage, salt and pepper to taste and the allspice and mix well. Cook for 4 minutes, remove from the heat and stir in the breadcrumbs.

To make the sauce, mash the mizithra or ricotta cheese until it is smooth. Beat in the egg yolks, then gradually stir in the cream. Add salt to taste, the allspice and kefalotiri or Parmesan cheese.

Make alternate layers of aubergine (eggplant) slices and meat mixture in a baking dish. Pour over the sauce. Bake for 45 to 50 minutes or until the top is golden. Serve hot.

4-6 Servings

Hungarian veal escalopes (scallops)

	Metric/UK	US
Veal escalopes (scallops), pounded thin	4	4
Lemon juice	2 Tbs	2 Tbs
Flour	2 Tbs	2 Tbs
Salt and black pepper		
Butter	75g/3oz	6 Tbs
Onions, finely chopped	2	2
Paprika	1 Tbs	1 Tbs
Dry white wine	75ml/3floz	⅓ cup
Sour cream	125ml/4floz	½ cup

Put the escalopes (scallops) in a shallow dish and sprinkle with the lemon juice. Leave to marinate for 30 minutes, turning occasionally. Pat the veal dry with paper towels.

Mix the flour with salt and pepper and use to coat the veal. Melt 50g/2oz (¼ cup) of the butter in a frying pan. Add the escalopes (scallops), two at a time, and brown on both sides. Cook gently until the veal is cooked through. Remove from the pan and arrange on a warmed serving platter. Keep hot.

Add the remaining butter to the pan. When it has melted, add the onions and fry until they are softened. Stir in the paprika, then the wine. Bring to the boil, stirring. Simmer for 3 to 4 minutes.

Remove the pan from the heat and stir in the sour cream. Pour this sauce over the veal and serve hot.

4 Servings

Allspice veal roll

Allspice has great versatility and can be used in a number of sweet and savoury dishes.

	Metric/UK	US
Fresh white breadcrumbs	50g/2oz	1 cup
Raisins or sultanas	1 Tbs	1 Tbs
Grated rind of 1 orange		
Finely chopped parsley	1 Tbs	1 Tbs
Dried sage	¼ tsp	¼ tsp
Dried thyme	¼ tsp	¼ tsp
Finely chopped onion	1 Tbs	1 Tbs
Salt and pepper		
Boned breast of veal, trimmed of excess fat	1 × 1kg/2lb	1 × 2lb
Butter	125g/4oz	8 Tbs
Ground allspice	1 Tbs	1 Tbs
Orange juice	3 Tbs	3 Tbs

Preheat the oven to moderate 180°C (Gas Mark 4, 350°F).

Mix together the breadcrumbs, raisins or sultanas, orange rind, parsley, sage, thyme, onion and salt and pepper to taste. Lay the veal flat on a work surface, fat side down, and spread with the breadcrumb mixture. Cut 40g/1½oz (3 tablespoons) of the butter into small pieces and dot them over the stuffing. Roll up the meat tightly and tie with string at 2.5cm/1in intervals.

Cream 25g/1oz (2 tablespoons) of the remaining butter with the allspice. Grease a baking dish with the remaining butter and place the veal roll in it. Rub the veal with the allspice butter. Sprinkle over the orange juice.

Cook for 1¼ hours, basting occasionally and adding more orange juice if necessary. Remove the string and serve hot.

4 Servings

Pork chops with apricots

	Metric/UK	US
Large pork chops	6	6
Garlic cloves, crushed	2	2
Ground coriander	½ tsp	½ tsp
Ground ginger	½ tsp	½ tsp
Grated nutmeg	½ tsp	½ tsp
Salt and black pepper		
Butter	125g/4oz	8 Tbs
Onions, finely chopped	2	2
Potatoes, peeled and cut into 1cm/½in thick slices	6	6
Canned apricot halves	½ kg/1lb	1lb
Soft brown sugar	1 Tbs	1 Tbs

Preheat the oven to moderate 180°C (Gas Mark 4, 350°F).

Rub the chops with the garlic, coriander, ginger, nutmeg and salt and pepper. Melt half the butter in a frying pan. Add the onions and potatoes and fry until the onions are golden. Transfer the vegetables to a casserole.

Add the remaining butter to the pan. When it has melted, add the chops and fry until browned on both sides. Arrange the chops on top of the onions and potatoes in the casserole and cover them with the apricot halves. Pour the syrup from the can of apricots over the top and sprinkle with the sugar.

Cover and bake for 30 minutes. Uncover and bake for a further 15 minutes or until the chops are cooked through. Serve hot, in the casserole.

6 Servings

Pork with grapes

	Metric/UK	US
Seedless green grapes	1¼kg/2½lb	2½lb
Boned loin of pork, trimmed of excess fat, rolled and tied	1 × 2½kg/5lb	1 × 5lb
Salt and black pepper		
Ground coriander	1 tsp	1 tsp
Juniper berries, crushed	16	16
Garlic clove, crushed	1	1
Shallots, finely chopped	2	2
Worcestershire sauce	4 tsp	4 tsp
Butter	50g/2oz	4 Tbs
Dry white wine	150ml/5floz	⅔ cup
Cayenne pepper	⅛ tsp	⅛ tsp
Gin	4 Tbs	¼ cup
Cornflour (cornstarch) dissolved in 1 Tbs white wine	1 Tbs	1 Tbs
GARNISH		
Butter	50g/2oz	4 Tbs
Seedless green grapes	1kg/2lb	2lb

Purée the grapes in a blender or food mill and strain. Put the pork in a shallow dish and rub with salt and pepper and the coriander. Pour over the grape juice and add the juniper berries, garlic, half the shallots and 3 teaspoons of the Worcestershire sauce. Leave to marinate for 8 hours or overnight, turning occasionally.

Remove the pork from the marinade and pat dry with paper towels. Reserve the marinade.

Melt the butter in a flameproof casserole. Add the remaining shallot and fry until softened. Put the pork in the casserole and brown on all sides. Add half the reserved marinade with all the juniper berries, the wine, cayenne and remaining Worcestershire sauce. Discard the remaining marinade.

Right A dish fit to grace any dinner table, Allspice Veal Roll looks and is mouth-wateringly good.

Pork Meatballs with Spicy Sauce should be served on a bed of pasta or rice for a substantial meal.

Bring to the boil, then cover and simmer for 2½ hours or until the pork is cooked through.

Ten minutes before the pork is ready, prepare the garnish. Melt the butter in a frying pan. Add the grapes and fry until they are lightly browned all over. Remove from the heat and keep warm.

Warm the gin, pour it over the pork and set alight. When the flames die down, transfer the pork to a warmed serving platter. Arrange the grape garnish around the meat and keep the mixture hot.

Skim the fat from the surface of the cooking liquid in the casserole. Stir in the dissolved cornflour (cornstarch) and bring back to the boil. Simmer, stirring, until thickened. Strain the sauce into a sauceboat. Pour a little over the pork.

Serve hot.

8–10 Servings

Pork meatballs with spicy sauce

	Metric/UK	US
Minced (ground) pork	1kg/2lb	2lb
Large onion, finely grated	1	1
Garlic cloves, crushed	2	2
Ground almonds	50g/2oz	½ cup
Fresh breadcrumbs	50g/2oz	1 cup
Egg, lightly beaten	1	1
Chopped parsley	1 Tbs	1 Tbs
Ground cinnamon	¾ tsp	¾ tsp
Salt and black pepper		
Medium dry sherry	3 Tbs	3 Tbs
Butter	1 Tbs	1 Tbs
Olive oil	2 Tbs	2 Tbs
SAUCE		
Large onion, finely chopped	1	1
Garlic clove, crushed	1	1
Soft brown sugar	1½ tsp	1½ tsp
Tomatoes, skinned, seeded and chopped	6	6
Green pepper, pith and seeds removed and thinly sliced	1	1
Red pepper, pith and seeds removed and thinly sliced	1	1
Green chilli (chili		

pepper), finely chopped	1	1
Cayenne pepper	$\frac{1}{4}$ tsp	$\frac{1}{4}$ tsp
Paprika	1 tsp	1 tsp
Chopped parsley	1 Tbs	1 Tbs
Beef stock	150ml/5floz	$\frac{2}{3}$ cup
Cornflour (cornstarch) dissolved in 4 Tbs dry sherry	2 tsp	2 tsp

Mix together the pork, onion, garlic, almonds, breadcrumbs, egg, parsley, cinnamon, salt and pepper to taste and the sherry. Combine the ingredients thoroughly, then shape the mixture into about 36 walnut-sized balls.

Melt the butter with the oil in a frying pan. Add the meatballs, in batches, and fry until well browned. Remove the balls from the pan.

Add the onion, garlic and brown sugar for the sauce to the pan and fry until the onion is golden. Stir in the tomatoes, green and red peppers, chilli, cayenne, paprika and parsley and cook for a further 3 minutes. Add the stock and salt and pepper to taste and bring to the boil, stirring occasionally. Stir in the dissolved cornflour (cornstarch) and simmer, stirring until the sauce thickens.

Add the meatballs to the sauce and coat well. Cover and cook gently for 20 to 25 minutes or until the meatballs are cooked through. Serve hot.

4–6 Servings

Pork and beef loaf

	Metric/UK	US
Fresh breadcrumbs	75g/3oz	1$\frac{1}{2}$ cups
Milk	250ml/8floz	1 cup
Minced (ground) pork	$\frac{1}{2}$kg/1lb	1lb
Minced (ground) beef	$\frac{1}{2}$kg/1lb	1lb
Large onions, finely chopped	2	2
Canned pimientos, drained and chopped	125g/4oz	4oz
Prepared French mustard	3 Tbs	3 Tbs
Dried basil	1 tsp	1 tsp
Cayenne pepper	$\frac{1}{4}$ tsp	$\frac{1}{4}$ tsp
Paprika	1 Tbs	1 Tbs
Salt and black pepper		
Eggs, lightly beaten	2	2

Preheat the oven to moderate 180°C (Gas Mark 4, 350°F).

Soak the breadcrumbs in the milk for 15 minutes. Add the remaining ingredients, with salt and pepper to taste, to the breadcrumb mixture and knead well together with your fingers. Pack the mixture into a greased 1kg/2lb loaf pan and smooth the top.

Place the loaf pan in a roasting pan and pour enough boiling water into the roasting pan to come halfway up the loaf pan. Bake for 1$\frac{1}{2}$ hours, or until a skewer comes out clean.

Turn the meat loaf out of the pan and serve hot or cold.

4–6 Servings

Serve Pork and Beef Loaf hot surrounded by an elegant layer of creamed potatoes or cold with a mixed salad.

Loin of pork with oranges and pineapple

	Metric/UK	US
Boned loin of pork, trimmed of excess fat, rolled and tied	1 × 2kg/4lb	1 × 4lb
Oil	2 Tbs	2 Tbs
Large oranges, peeled and sliced	2	2
Small pineapple, peeled, cored and cut into chunks	1	1
MARINADE		
Root ginger, peeled and finely grated	2.5cm/1in piece	1in piece
Ground allspice	½ tsp	½ tsp
Crushed coriander seeds	1 tsp	1 tsp
Salt	1 tsp	1 tsp
Crushed black peppercorns	1 tsp	1 tsp
Prepared French mustard	1 tsp	1 tsp
Grated rind of 1 orange		
Garlic cloves, crushed	2	2
Soy sauce	5 Tbs	5 Tbs
Lemon juice	4 Tbs	¼ cup

Mix together the ingredients for the marinade in a shallow dish. Add the pork and turn to coat. Leave to marinate for about 3 hours, turning occasionally.

Preheat the oven to fairly hot 190°C (Gas Mark 5, 375°F).

Remove the pork from the marinade and pat it dry with paper towels. Reserve the marinade.

Put the oil in a roasting pan and place it in the oven. When the oil is hot, put the pork in the pan, fat side up. Roast for 1¾ hours. While the pork is roasting, put the marinade in a saucepan and bring it to the boil. Baste the pork with the hot marinade every 20 minutes during the roasting period.

Cover the pork with the orange slices and add the pineapple chunks to the pan. Continue roasting for 45 minutes, basting as before.

Carve the pork and arrange the slices on a warmed serving platter. Add the fruit. Skim any fat from the cooking liquid in the pan and pour over the pork.

Serve hot.

8 Servings

A highly seasoned dish originating from Central America, Mexican Pork and Veal Stew is delicious accompanied by crunchy, salted popcorn.

Peruvian pork stew

	Metric/UK	US
Oil	4 Tbs	4 Tbs
Pork fillet (tenderloin), cut into 5cm/2in pieces	1kg/2lb	2lb
Onions, thinly sliced	2	2
Garlic clove, crushed	1	1
Dried red chillis (chili peppers), chopped	2	2
Cumin seeds, crushed	1½ tsp	1½ tsp
Canned sweetcorn kernels, drained	425g/14oz	14oz
Canned tomatoes	425g/14oz	14oz
Orange juice	175ml/6floz	¾ cup
Grated orange rind	1 tsp	1 tsp
Salt and black pepper		
Sweet potatoes, parboiled for 15 minutes, peeled and cubed	½kg/1lb	1lb

Heat the oil in a saucepan. Add the pork cubes and brown on all sides. Remove the pork from the pan.

Add the onions, garlic, chillis and cumin to the pan and fry until the onions are softened. Stir in the sweetcorn, tomatoes, orange juice, orange rind and salt and pepper to taste. Bring to the boil.

Return the pork to the pan and stir well. Cover and simmer for 50 minutes.

Stir in the sweet potatoes and continue to cook, covered, for 20 minutes or until the pork is cooked through. Serve hot.

4 Servings

Mexican pork and veal stew

	Metric/UK	US
Butter	50g/2oz	4 Tbs
Oil	2 Tbs	2 Tbs
Boneless veal, cut into cubes	1kg/2lb	2lb
Boneless pork, cut into cubes	1kg/2lb	.2lb
Onions, finely chopped	2	2
Garlic cloves, crushed	3	3
Green tomatoes, skinned, seeded and chopped (if unavailable substitute ordinary ones)	1kg/2lb	2lb
Green peppers, pith and seeds removed and chopped	3	3
Green chillis (chili peppers), chopped	4	4
Tomato purée (paste)	2 Tbs	2 Tbs
Dried marjoram	2 tsp	2 tsp
Chopped chives	1 Tbs	1 Tbs
Dried basil	2 tsp	2 tsp
Grated nutmeg	2 tsp	2 tsp
Salt and black pepper		
Sugar	1 tsp	1 tsp
Chicken stock	250ml/8floz	1 cup
Dry sherry	250ml/8floz	1 cup
Double (heavy) cream	6 Tbs	6 Tbs

Melt the butter with the oil in a saucepan. Add the veal and pork, in batches, and brown on all sides. Remove the meat from the pan.

Add the onions and garlic to the pan and fry until softened. Stir in the tomatoes, green peppers, chillis, tomato purée (paste), herbs, nutmeg, salt and pepper to taste and the sugar. Cook, stirring, for 5 minutes. Stir in the stock and sherry.

Return the meat to the pan and bring to the boil. Cover and simmer for 1½ hours or until the meat is tender.

Remove from the heat and stir in the cream. Serve hot.

8 Servings

Left To bring out the flavour of cumin, heat gently without fat and then use accordingly.

Pork and ham balls

	Metric/UK	US
Fresh breadcrumbs soaked in 2 Tbs milk	25g/1oz	½ cup
Lean pork, minced (ground)	350g/12oz	12oz
Uncooked ham, minced (ground)	300g/10oz	10oz
Hard-boiled eggs, finely chopped	2	2
Chopped parsley	1½ Tbs	1½ Tbs
Dry mustard mixed with 2 tsp milk	1 tsp	1 tsp
Salt and black pepper		
Ground cinnamon	¼ tsp	¼ tsp
Egg, lightly beaten	1	1
Flour	25g/1oz	¼ cup
Butter	25g/1oz	2 Tbs
Oil	2 Tbs	2 Tbs
Red wine	125ml/4floz	½ cup
Chicken stock	125ml/4floz	½ cup

Mix together the breadcrumbs, pork, ham, eggs, parsley, mustard, salt and pepper to taste and the cinnamon. Add the beaten egg and combine thoroughly. Form the mixture into 24 balls and coat them with all but 2 teaspoons of the flour.

Melt all but 1 teaspoon of the butter with the oil in a frying pan. Add the balls, in batches, and fry for 8 minutes or until they are brown on all sides. Drain the balls on paper towels and transfer them to a baking dish.

Preheat the oven to moderate 180°C (Gas Mark 4, 350°F).

Put the wine and stock in a saucepan and bring to the boil. Mix together the remaining flour and butter to make a paste and add to the liquid in small pieces, stirring constantly. Simmer until thickened.

Pour the wine mixture over the ham balls and bake for 15 minutes or until the ham balls are thoroughly cooked. Serve hot.

4–6 Servings

Tunisian scrambled eggs and sausages

	Metric/UK	US
Olive oil	2 Tbs	2 Tbs
Spicy sausage, such as Spanish chorizo, cut into 2.5cm/1in thick slices	½ kg/1lb	1lb
Garlic clove, finely chopped	1	1
Cayenne pepper	½ tsp	½ tsp
Ground cumin	¼ tsp	¼ tsp
Salt and pepper		
Canned tomatoes	425g/14oz	14oz
Cold water	4 Tbs	¼ cup
Green peppers, pith and seeds removed and cut into strips	4	4
Eggs, lightly beaten	6	6

Heat the oil in a frying pan. Add the sausage slices and fry until they are evenly browned. Stir in the garlic, cayenne, cumin, salt and pepper to taste, tomatoes and water and bring to the boil. Simmer until the mixture is thick, stirring occasionally.

Stir in the pepper strips, cover and cook gently for a further 5 minutes.

Pour over the beaten eggs and cook gently, stirring lightly, until the eggs are just set and scrambled. Serve hot.

4 Servings

Ox tongue with hot raisin sauce

	Metric/UK	US
Butter	50g/2oz	4 Tbs
Flour	25g/1oz	¼ cup
Beef stock	125ml/4floz	½ cup
Water	425ml/14floz	1¾ cups
Raisins	125g/4oz	⅔ cup
Salt and black pepper		
Juice of ½ lemon		
Soft brown sugar	1 tsp	1 tsp
Hot chilli powder	¼ tsp	¼ tsp
Ground cinnamon	¼ tsp	¼ tsp
Ground ginger	¼ tsp	¼ tsp
Ground cloves	⅛ tsp	⅛ tsp
Salted ox tongue, soaked for 36 hours, cooked, skinned and kept warm	1 × 2–2½kg/ 4–5lb	1 × 4– 5lb
Single (light) cream	2 Tbs	2 Tbs

Melt the butter in a saucepan. Add the flour and cook, stirring, for 1 minute. Gradually stir in the stock and water and bring to the boil, stirring. Simmer until smooth and thickened.

Stir in the raisins, salt and pepper to taste, the lemon juice, sugar, chilli powder, cinnamon, ginger and cloves. Continue to cook gently for 10 minutes.

Slice the tongue into 6mm/¼in thick slices, discarding the bones and gristle. Arrange the slices on a warmed serving platter. Stir the cream into the sauce and pour a little over the tongue.

Put the rest into a sauceboat and then serve hot.

8–10 Servings

VEGETABLES & SALADS

Algerian carrots

	Metric/UK	US
Carrots, cut into 1cm/½in slices	1kg/2lb	2lb
Olive oil	5 Tbs	5 Tbs
Salt and pepper		
Ground cinnamon	½ tsp	½ tsp
Cumin seeds	½ tsp	½ tsp
Garlic cloves, finely chopped	2	2
Dried thyme	½ tsp	½ tsp
Bay leaf	1	1
Lemon juice	1 tsp	1 tsp

Put the carrot slices into a saucepan and just cover with water. Bring to the boil and simmer until the carrots are just tender but still firm. Drain the carrots, reserving 150ml/5floz (⅔ cup) of the cooking liquid. Keep the carrots warm.

Put the oil, salt and pepper to taste, cinnamon, cumin, garlic and thyme in the saucepan and cook gently for 10 minutes. Stir in the reserved cooking liquid and the bay leaf and simmer the mixture for a further 15 minutes or until it has thickened slightly.

Add the carrots to the pan and fold them into the sauce. Reheat for 2 to 3 minutes. Remove the bay leaf from the pan and turn the carrots into a warmed serving dish.

Sprinkle over the lemon juice and serve hot.

4 Servings

Israeli pumpkin

	Metric/UK	US
Sweet potatoes, peeled	½kg/1lb	1lb
Pumpkin, sliced, peeled and seeded	½kg/1lb	1lb
Salt and black pepper		
Grated nutmeg	½ tsp	½ tsp
Ground cloves	¼ tsp	¼ tsp
Orange marmalade	6 Tbs	6 Tbs
Large cooking apples, peeled, cored and sliced	3	3
Lemon juice	2 Tbs	2 Tbs
Water	125ml/4floz	½ cup
White wine	125ml/4floz	½ cup
Grated lemon rind	2 Tbs	2 Tbs
Brown sugar	1 Tbs	1 Tbs
Butter, cut into small pieces	1 Tbs	1 Tbs

Put the sweet potatoes in a saucepan, cover with water and bring to the boil. Cook for 30 minutes or until tender but not too soft.

Meanwhile, put the pumpkin slices in another saucepan, cover with water and bring to the boil. Cook for 10 minutes.

Preheat the oven to warm 170°C (Gas Mark 3, 325°F).

Drain the sweet potatoes and pumpkin and allow to cool, then cut into thin slices. Mix together salt and pepper to taste, the nutmeg and cloves.

Arrange half the sweet potato slices in a greased baking dish. Cover with about 1 tablespoon of the marmalade

A spiced vegetable dish, Algerian Carrots are delicious with roasted or boiled meat dishes.

and sprinkle with a little of the spice mixture. Top with half the apples, then a little more marmalade and spice mixture. Add a layer of half the pumpkin, then marmalade and spices. Repeat each layer once more.

Mix together the lemon juice, water and wine and pour into the baking dish. Sprinkle the lemon rind and sugar on top and dot with the pieces of butter. Bake for 1 hour and serve hot, in the dish.

6-8 Servings

Braised red cabbage with apples

	Metric/UK	US
Small red cabbage, cored and shredded	1	1
Grated nutmeg	$\frac{1}{4}$ tsp	$\frac{1}{4}$ tsp
Ground cinnamon	$\frac{1}{4}$ tsp	$\frac{1}{4}$ tsp
Salt and black pepper		
Vinegar	3 Tbs	3 Tbs
Butter	25g/1oz	2 Tbs
Cooking apples, peeled, cored and quartered	4	4
Brown sugar	1 Tbs	1 Tbs

Mix together the cabbage, nutmeg, cinnamon, salt and pepper to taste and vinegar. Melt the butter in a saucepan

and add the cabbage mixture. Cover and cook gently for 1½ hours, stirring occasionally.

Stir in the apples and brown sugar and continue cooking for 30 minutes. Serve hot.

4 Servings

Jugged celery

	Metric/UK	US
Lean bacon rashers (slices)	8	8
Large cooking apples, halved	10	10
Water	450ml/15floz	2 cups
Sugar	2 Tbs	2 Tbs
Ground cloves	$\frac{1}{8}$ tsp	$\frac{1}{8}$ tsp
Grated nutmeg	$\frac{1}{2}$ tsp	$\frac{1}{2}$ tsp
Salt and black pepper		
Large head of celery, cut into 15cm/6in pieces	1	1
Chopped walnuts	50g/2oz	$\frac{1}{2}$ cup

Preheat the oven to moderate 180°C (Gas Mark 4, 350°F).

Lay half the bacon rashers (slices) on the bottom of a greased casserole.

Put the apple halves in a large saucepan with the water and cook until the apples are soft. Strain the apples into a mixing bowl, pressing down on the

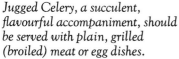
Jugged Celery, a succulent, flavourful accompaniment, should be served with plain, grilled (broiled) meat or egg dishes.

peel and core to push the pulp through to make a purée. Discard the peel and core. Stir the sugar, cloves, nutmeg and salt and pepper to taste into the apple purée. Spoon the purée over the bacon slices in the casserole.

Arrange the celery pieces in the purée so they stand upright. Sprinkle over the chopped walnuts and lay the remaining bacon slices on top. Cover and bake for 1½ to 2 hours or until the celery is cooked. Serve hot, in the casserole.

4-6 Servings

Creole potatoes

	Metric/UK	US
Sufficient oil for deep-frying		
Small new potatoes, parboiled and drained	1kg/2lb	2lb
Prepared French or German mustard	2 tsp	2 tsp
Butter, melted	40g/1½oz	3 Tbs
Cayenne pepper	¼ tsp	¼ tsp
Hot chilli powder	¼ tsp	¼ tsp
Salt and black pepper		
Chilli vinegar	2 tsp	2 tsp

Heat the oil in a deep-frying pan (deep fat fryer) until it is 185°C/360°F, or until a small cube of stale bread dropped into the oil turns golden in 50 seconds.

Deep-fry the potatoes, in batches, for 4 minutes or until golden. Drain on paper towels and keep hot.

Mix together the remaining ingredients, with salt and pepper to taste, in a saucepan. Cook, stirring, for 2 minutes. Add the fried potatoes and turn well to coat with the sauce. Continue cooking for 5 minutes, stirring frequently.

Serve hot.

4 Servings

Nut and fruit pilaff

	Metric/UK	US
Butter	75g/3oz	6 Tbs
Onion, chopped	1	1
Green pepper, pith and seeds removed and chopped	1	1
Turmeric	½ tsp	½ tsp
Grated nutmeg	¼ tsp	¼ tsp
Salt	1 tsp	1 tsp
Dried apricots, soaked for 30 minutes, drained and chopped	175g/6oz	1 cup
Raisins	75g/3oz	½ cup
Long-grain rice	350g/12oz	2 cups
Chicken stock, boiling	900ml/1½ pints	3¾ cups
Flaked almonds, toasted	125g/4oz	1 cup

Melt the butter in a saucepan. Add the onion and green pepper and fry until the onion is softened. Stir in the turmeric, nutmeg and salt, then add the apricots and raisins. Cook, stirring, for 2 minutes.

Add the rice and cook, stirring, for 5 minutes. Stir in the stock and bring to the boil. Cover and simmer for 20 to 25 minutes or until the rice is tender and has absorbed all the stock. Add a little oil to the simmering stock if the rice seems in danger of sticking to the bottom of the pan. Stir in the almonds.

Serve hot.

6-8 Servings

Jamaican beans

	Metric/UK	US
Dried white haricot (navy) beans, soaked overnight and drained	350g/12oz	2 cups
Salt pork, diced	50g/2oz	2oz
Oil	2 Tbs	2 Tbs
Onions, thinly sliced	2	2
Green pepper, pith and seeds removed and chopped	1	1
Celery stalk, thinly sliced	1	1
Canned tomatoes, drained and chopped	425g/14oz	14oz
Dark rum	6 Tbs	6 Tbs
Black treacle or molasses	3 Tbs	3 Tbs
Dry mustard	1 tsp	1 tsp
Dried thyme	½ tsp	½ tsp
Hot chilli powder	¼ tsp	¼ tsp
Salt and black pepper		

Put the beans in a saucepan and cover with plenty of water. Bring to the boil, cover and simmer for 45 to 50 minutes or until just tender.

Drain the beans well and place them in a casserole.

Preheat the oven to moderate 180°C (Gas Mark 4, 350°F).

Blanch the salt pork dice for 5 minutes, then drain well. Heat the oil in a frying pan. Add the salt pork dice, onions and green pepper and fry until the onions are softened. Stir in the celery and tomatoes, then stir this vegetable mixture into the beans in the casserole. Add the rum, treacle or molasses, mustard, thyme, chilli powder and salt and pepper to taste and mix well.

Bake for 30 to 40 minutes or until the beans are very tender. Serve hot.

4 Servings

Korean vegetable salad

	Metric/UK	US
Small turnip, peeled and cut into strips	1	1
Salt		
Oil	4 Tbs	4 Tbs
Small onion, finely chopped	1	1
Mushrooms, sliced	125g/4oz	1 cup
Celery stalks, thinly sliced	2	2
Spring onions (scallions), chopped	3	3
Carrot, cut into strips	1	1
Finely chopped pine nuts	1 Tbs	1 Tbs
DRESSING		
Soy sauce	3 Tbs	3 Tbs
Brown sugar	1 Tbs	1 Tbs
Vinegar	1 Tbs	1 Tbs
Black pepper	$\frac{1}{4}$ tsp	$\frac{1}{4}$ tsp
Ground ginger	$\frac{1}{4}$ tsp	$\frac{1}{4}$ tsp

Sprinkle the turnip strips with salt and leave for 15 minutes.

Heat half the oil in a frying pan. Add the turnip strips and fry until crisp. Drain on paper towels and leave to cool.

Add the onion to the pan and fry until golden brown. Drain on paper towels and leave to cool.

Add the mushrooms to the pan and fry until tender, adding the remaining oil if necessary. Drain on paper towels and leave to cool.

Fry the celery until golden, then drain on kitchen paper towels and leave to cool.

Mix all the fried vegetables together with the spring onions (scallions) and carrot. Combine the ingredients for the dressing and add to the vegetables. Toss well, then spoon into a serving dish. Sprinkle with the finely chopped pine nuts and serve.

4 Servings

Coleslaw with caraway

	Metric/UK	US
Large white cabbage, cored and shredded	1	1
Onion, finely chopped	1	1
Green pepper, pith and seeds removed and finely chopped	$\frac{1}{2}$	$\frac{1}{2}$
Lemon juice	$\frac{1}{2}$ tsp	$\frac{1}{2}$ tsp
Caraway seeds	1 Tbs	1 Tbs
DRESSING		
Double (heavy) cream	175ml/6floz	$\frac{3}{4}$ cup
Sour cream	75ml/3floz	$\frac{1}{3}$ cup
Prepared French mustard	1 Tbs	1 Tbs
Lemon juice	3 Tbs	3 Tbs
Sugar	1 Tbs	1 Tbs
Salt and white pepper		

Put the cabbage, onion, green pepper and lemon juice in a mixing bowl. In another bowl, mix together the dressing ingredients with salt and pepper to taste. Add the dressing to the cabbage mixture and toss well until all

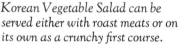

Korean Vegetable Salad can be served either with roast meats or on its own as a crunchy first course.

the vegetables are well coated. Fold in the caraway seeds until well mixed into the salad.

Chill for at least 1 hour before serving.

8 Servings

Tunisian aubergines (eggplants)

	Metric/UK	US
Aubergines (eggplants), cut into cubes	4	4
Salt		
Olive oil	4 Tbs	$\frac{1}{4}$ cup
Onions, sliced	2	2
Garlic clove, chopped	1	1
Cayenne pepper	$\frac{1}{4}$ tsp	$\frac{1}{4}$ tsp
Ground cloves	$\frac{1}{4}$ tsp	$\frac{1}{4}$ tsp
Ground cumin	$\frac{1}{2}$ tsp	$\frac{1}{2}$ tsp
Tomatoes, skinned and chopped	$\frac{1}{2}$kg/1lb	1lb
Ground coriander	1 tsp	1 tsp
Chopped fresh mint	1 Tbs	1 Tbs
Raisins	2 Tbs	2 Tbs
Black pepper		
Chopped parsley	2 Tbs	2 Tbs

Put the aubergine (eggplant) cubes into a colander and sprinkle with salt. Leave for 20 minutes, then drain, rinse and pat dry with kitchen paper towels.

Heat the oil in a frying pan. Add the onions and garlic and fry until softened. Stir in the cayenne, cloves and cumin and cook for 2 minutes. Add the aubergine (eggplant) cubes and brown carefully on all sides, stirring well.

Stir in the tomatoes, coriander, mint, raisins, and salt and pepper to taste. Cook gently until almost all the liquid has evaporated and the aubergines (eggplants) are tender. Stir in the parsley. Serve hot or cold.

4 Servings

Tunisian Aubergines (Eggplants), accompanying an eastern dish such as lamb kebabs, creates a meal with a foreign flavour.

117

ETHNIC DISHES

Seekh kabab

	Metric/UK	US
Minced (ground) meat	700g/1½lb	1½lb
Fresh white breadcrumbs	50g/2oz	1 cup
Root ginger, peeled and grated	2.5cm/1in piece	1in piece
Green chilli (chili pepper), finely chopped	1	1
Garlic cloves, crushed	2	2
Ground cumin	1 tsp	1 tsp
Hot chilli powder	½ tsp	½ tsp
Salt	½ tsp	½ tsp
Finely grated lemon rind	1 tsp	1 tsp
Lemon juice	1 tsp	1 tsp

Mix together all the ingredients, using your fingers to combine them thoroughly. Divide the mixture into 16 portions. With dampened hands, mould each portion into a sausage shape. Thread the sausages onto greased skewers (two or three to a skewer), pressing them on well.

Preheat the grill (broiler) to high.

Grill (broil) the kebabs for 6 minutes or until they are cooked through and browned on all sides.

Serve hot.

4 Servings

Tandoori chicken

	Metric/UK	US
Chicken, skinned	1 × 1½kg/3lb	1 × 3lb
Hot chilli powder	1 tsp	1 tsp
Salt and black pepper		
Lemon juice	2 Tbs	2 Tbs
Butter, melted	50g/2oz	4 Tbs
MARINADE		
Plain yogurt	3 Tbs	3 Tbs
Garlic cloves	4	4
Raisins	1 Tbs	1 Tbs
Root ginger, peeled and chopped	5cm /2in piece	2in piece
Cumin seeds	1 tsp	1 tsp
Coriander seeds	1 Tbs	1 Tbs
Dried red chillis (chili peppers)	2	2
Red food colouring	½ tsp	½ tsp

Make gashes all over the chicken. Mix together the chilli powder, salt and pepper to taste and the lemon juice and rub all over the chicken. Leave for 20 minutes.

Meanwhile, put all the marinade ingredients, except the food colouring, into a blender and blend to a smooth purée. Mix in the red food colouring.

Place the chicken in a large bowl and spread it with the yogurt marinade. Cover and leave in the refrigerator for 24 hours.

Preheat the oven to fairly hot 200°C (Gas Mark 6, 400°F).

Put the chicken, on its back, on a rack in a roasting pan. Put enough water in the tin just to cover the bottom. Spoon all the marinade from the bowl over the chicken, then 1 tablespoon of the melted butter. Roast for 1 hour, basting frequently with the remaining melted butter and the drippings in the pan.

Carve the chicken and serve hot.

3 Servings

Marinated lamb kebabs

	Metric/UK	US
Root ginger, peeled and finely chopped	10cm/ 4in piece	4in piece
Onions, chopped	3	3
Small bunch fresh coriander leaves	1	1
Coriander seeds	1 Tbs	1 Tbs
Juice of 1 lemon		
Green chillis (chili peppers)	2	2
Black peppercorns	½ tsp	½ tsp
Boned leg of lamb, cut into 2.5cm/1in cubes	1kg/2lb	2lb
Salt	1 tsp	1 tsp
Butter, melted	25g/1oz	2 Tbs

Put the ginger, onions, coriander leaves and seeds, lemon juice, chillis and peppercorns in a blender and blend to a purée. Add a little more lemon juice, if necessary. Put the spice mixture in a shallow dish and add the lamb cubes. Turn to coat well. Leave to marinate for 4 hours, turning occasionally.

Preheat the grill (broiler) to high.

Thread the lamb cubes onto skewers and sprinkle with the salt and melted butter. Grill (broil) for 8 to 10 minutes, turning occasionally.

Serve hot.

4 Servings

Marinated Lamb Kebabs is a subtly flavoured meat dish from India.

Samosas, savoury meat-filled parcels, are ideal either as a pre-dinner snack with drinks or as a piquant side dish to a main course.

Samosas

	Metric/UK	US
PASTRY		
Flour	225g/8oz	2 cups
Salt	½ tsp	½ tsp
Butter	25g/1oz	2 Tbs
Water	4-6 Tbs	4-6 Tbs
FILLING		
Butter	25g/1oz	2 Tbs
Onion, finely chopped	1	1
Garlic cloves, crushed	2	2
Green chillis (chili peppers), chopped	2	2
Root ginger, peeled and finely chopped	2.5cm/1in piece	1in piece
Turmeric	½ tsp	½ tsp
Hot chilli powder	½ tsp	½ tsp
Lean minced (ground) meat	350g/12oz	12oz
Salt	1 tsp	1 tsp
Garam masala	2 tsp	2 tsp
Juice of ½ lemon		
Sufficient oil for deep-frying		

To make the pastry, sift the flour and salt into a bowl. Rub in the butter until the mixture resembles breadcrumbs. Mix in enough of the water to bind the ingredients to a dough. Knead well for about 10 minutes, then set aside.

To make the filling, melt the butter in a frying pan. Add the onion, garlic, chillis and ginger and fry until the onion is golden. Stir in the turmeric and chilli powder, then add the meat and salt. Fry until the meat is well cooked and all the moisture has evaporated. Stir in the garam masala and lemon juice and cook for a further 5 minutes. Remove from the heat and allow to cool.

Divide the dough into 15 portions and roll each into a ball. Flatten the balls and roll out each into a circle about 10cm/4in in diameter. Cut each circle in half. Dampen the edges of each circle with water and shape them into cones. Fill the cones with the filling, then pinch them together to seal.

Heat oil in a deep-frying pan (deep-fat fryer) until it is 185°C/360°F or until a cube of stale bread dropped into the hot oil turns golden brown in 50 seconds.

Deep-fry the samosas in batches for 2 to 3 minutes or until they are golden brown. Drain on paper towels and serve hot.

30 Samosas

Vegetable kitcheri

	Metric/UK	US
Long-grain rice	225g/8oz	1⅓ cups
Moong dhal (yellow lentils)	75g/3oz	⅓ cup
Tur dhal (orange lentils)	50g/2oz	¼ cup
Masoor dhal (salmon-pink lentils)	75g/3oz	⅓ cup
Butter	50g/2oz	4 Tbs
Onions, sliced	2	2
Green chillis (chili peppers), finely chopped	2	2
Root ginger, peeled and chopped	2.5cm/1in piece	1in piece
Garlic cloves, crushed	2	2
Ground coriander	1 Tbs	1 Tbs
Turmeric	½ tsp	½ tsp
Potatoes, peeled and cubed	125g/4oz	1 cup
Carrots, cubed	125g/4oz	1 cup
Aubergine (eggplant), cubed	1	1
Green peas	125g/4oz	½ cup
Small cauliflower, broken into flowerets	½	½
Large tomatoes, skinned and chopped	2	2
Salt	1 tsp	1 tsp
Chicken stock or water, boiling	500ml/16floz	2 cups
Butter, melted	25g/1oz	2 Tbs

Cook the rice in boiling salted water for 3 minutes, then drain. Cook the dhals (lentils) in boiling salted water for 5 minutes, then remove from the heat and drain.

Melt the butter in a frying pan. Add the onions and fry until golden. Stir in the chillis, ginger and garlic and fry for 2 minutes. Add the spices and fry, stirring, for 1 minute. Add the vegetables and salt and mix thoroughly. Cover and cook the mixture gently for 20 minutes.

Preheat the oven to very cool 140°C (Gas Mark 1, 275°F).

Make layers of the vegetable mixture, rice and dhals in a greased baking dish beginning with vegetables and ending with a layer of dhal. Pour in the boiling chicken stock or water, cover and bake for 45 minutes to 1 hour or until the rice and dhals are cooked and tender and all the liquid has been absorbed.

Serve hot, straight from the dish, liberally sprinkled with the melted butter.

4-6 Servings

Vegetable Kitcheri uses three types of lentils (dhal).

Dry beef curry

	Metric/UK	US
Oil	4 Tbs	4 Tbs
Green chillis (chili peppers), finely chopped	2	2
Onions, finely chopped	2	2
Stewing (chuck) steak, cut into small cubes	1kg/2lb	2lb
Salt	½ tsp	½ tsp
Tomatoes, skinned and chopped	2	2
Turmeric	1 tsp	1 tsp
Ground cumin	1 tsp	1 tsp
Ground coriander	2 tsp	2 tsp
Garam masala	1½ tsp	1½ tsp
Plain yogurt	300ml/10floz	1¼ cups

Heat the oil in a saucepan. Add the chillis and fry for 1 minute. Add the onions and fry until softened. Add the beef cubes and salt and fry until the beef cubes are evenly browned. Stir in the tomatoes and continue cooking gently for 10 minutes.

Mix together the turmeric, cumin, coriander, 1 teaspoon of the garam masala and the yogurt. Add to the meat mixture and stir well. Half cover the pan and simmer for 1½ hours.

Remove the lid and continue cooking for 30 minutes or until the meat is covered with a thick gravy. If the curry becomes too dry, cover the pan.

Spoon the curry into a warmed serving dish and sprinkle over the remaining garam masala.

Serve hot.

4-6 Servings

Aviyal (Vegetable curry)

	Metric/UK	US
Oil	4 Tbs	4 Tbs
Mustard seeds	1 tsp	1 tsp
Root ginger, peeled and minced	5cm/2in piece	2in piece
Garlic cloves, quartered	2	2
Onion, minced	1	1
Green chilli (chili pepper), minced	1	1
Turmeric	1½ tsp	1½ tsp
Ground coriander	1 Tbs	1 Tbs
Mixed vegetables (carrots, beans, aubergines (eggplants), turnips, cauliflower, green peppers, potatoes, okra, etc.), sliced	700g/1½lb	1½lb
Salt	1 tsp	1 tsp
Fresh coconut, puréed in a blender with 175ml/6floz (¾ cup) water, or 2.5/1in slice creamed coconut	225g/8oz	8oz
Chopped coriander leaves	2 Tbs	2 Tbs

Heat the oil in a saucepan. Add the mustard seeds, ginger and garlic and fry for 30 seconds. Add the onion and chilli and fry until the onion is golden. Stir in the turmeric and coriander and fry for 1 minute.

Add the vegetables and stir well to mix with the spices. Stir in the salt and coconut purée or creamed coconut. If the mixture is too dry, add a little water. Cover and simmer for 30 minutes or until the vegetables are cooked and tender.

Serve hot, sprinkled with the coriander.

4 Servings

Pork korma

	Metric/UK	US
Butter	50g/2oz	4 Tbs
Root ginger, peeled and finely chopped	4cm/1½in piece	1½in piece
Garlic cloves, crushed	3	3
Onions, finely chopped	2	2
Hot chilli powder	½ tsp	½ tsp
Ground coriander	2 Tbs	2 Tbs
Pork fillet (tenderloin), cut into 4cm/1½in cubes	1kg/2lb	2lb
Salt	1 tsp	1 tsp
Plain yogurt	300ml/10floz	1¼ cups
Ground almonds	125g/4oz	1 cup
Double (heavy) cream	300ml/10floz	1¼ cups
Ground cinnamon	½ tsp	½ tsp
Ground mace	¼ tsp	¼ tsp
Ground cardamom	½ tsp	½ tsp
Saffron threads soaked in 2 Tbs boiling water	¼ tsp	¼ tsp
GARNISH		
Onions, thinly sliced into rings and fried until golden brown	2	2

Melt the butter in a saucepan. Add the ginger, garlic and onions and fry until the onions are golden. Stir in the chilli powder and coriander and fry for 1 minute. Add the pork cubes and brown on all sides. Continue cooking briskly until all the moisture in the pan evaporates.

Reduce the heat to moderate and add the salt and 4 tablespoons of the yogurt. Cook, stirring, until the yogurt evaporates. Add 4 more tablespoons and cook until it evaporates. Continue in this way until all the yogurt has been added and there is no liquid in the pan.

Mix together the almonds and cream and stir into the pork mixture. Add the spices and bring to the boil, stirring. Cover the pan and simmer for about 25 minutes, stirring occasionally

to prevent sticking.

Preheat the oven to moderate 180°C (Gas Mark 4, 350°F).

Transfer the pork mixture to a casserole and stir in the saffron-coloured water. Transfer to the oven and bake for 15 minutes. Serve hot, straight from the casserole, generously garnished with the onions.

4 Servings

Fruit curry

	Metric/UK	US
Apricots, peeled, stoned (pitted) and chopped	4	4
Pears, peeled, cored and chopped	4	4
Bananas, sliced	3	3
Small honeydew melon, peeled, seeded and chopped	½	½
Canned mangoes, drained and chopped	125g/4oz	½ cup
Canned pineapple chunks, drained	50g/2oz	⅓ cup
Clear honey mixed		
with 300ml/10floz (1¼ cups) boiling water	4 Tbs	¼ cup
Ground cumin	½ tsp	½ tsp
Ground coriander	½ tsp	½ tsp
Turmeric	½ tsp	½ tsp
Ground cloves	½ tsp	½ tsp
Ground fenugreek	½ tsp	½ tsp
Hot chilli powder	pinch	pinch
Lemon juice	1 tsp	1 tsp
Plain yogurt	150ml/5floz	⅔ cup
Creamed coconut	2.5cm/1in slice	1in slice

Put the fruit in a saucepan with the honey mixture. Cover and poach gently for 15 minutes. Mix together the spices, lemon juice and yogurt and stir into the fruit mixture. Continue cooking gently for 25 minutes.

Add the creamed coconut and stir until it dissolves and the liquid thickens. Simmer for a further 3 minutes.

Remove from the heat and allow to cool, then chill for at least 3 hours before serving.

Serve cold.

4 Servings

Yogurt, pork, cream and spices are the basic ingredients in Pork Korma.

Lamb and cashew nut curry

	Metric/UK	US
Root ginger, peeled and chopped	4cm/1½in piece	1½in piece
Garlic cloves	3	3
Green chillis (chili peppers)	2	2
Unsalted cashew nuts	50g/2oz	½ cup
Water	4-6 Tbs	4-6 Tbs
Cloves	4	4
Cardamom seeds	¼ tsp	¼ tsp
Coriander seeds	1 Tbs	1 Tbs
White poppy seeds	1 Tbs	1 Tbs
Butter	50g/2oz	4 Tbs
Onions, finely chopped	2	2
Boned leg or shoulder of lamb, cut into cubes	1kg/2lb	2lb
Plain yogurt	300ml/10floz	1¼ cups
Saffron threads soaked in 2 Tbs boiling water	¼ tsp	¼ tsp
Salt	1 tsp	1 tsp
Juice of ¼ lemon		
Chopped coriander leaves	1 Tbs	1 Tbs
Lemon, sliced	1	1

Put the ginger, garlic, chillis, nuts and half the water in a blender and blend to a purée. Add the cloves, cardamom seeds, coriander seeds and poppy seeds and blend again until smooth, adding just enough of the remaining water to prevent blender from sticking.

Melt the butter in a saucepan. Add the onions and fry until golden. Stir in the spice purée and fry, stirring, for 3 minutes. Add the lamb cubes and fry for 5 minutes, turning to coat them with the spice mixture.

Mix together the yogurt, saffron-coloured water and salt. Add this to the pan and stir well. When the mixture begins to bubble, reduce the heat and cook gently for 1 hour, stirring occasionally.

Stir in the lemon juice and sprinkle over the coriander leaves. Cover and continue cooking for 20 minutes. Serve hot, garnished with the lemon slices.

4 Servings

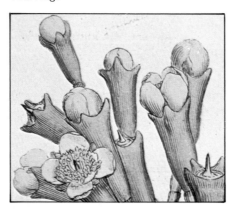

Cloves have a strong flavour and should be used with restraint.

Chicken with almonds and raisins

	Metric/UK	US
Chicken, skinned	1 × 2kg/4lb	1 × 4lb
Juice of ½ lemon		
Coriander seeds	1 Tbs	1 Tbs
Black peppercorns	1 tsp	1 tsp
Cardamom seeds	1 tsp	1 tsp
Cloves	6	6
Root ginger, peeled and very finely chopped	4cm/1½in piece	1½in piece
Salt	1 tsp	1 tsp
Hot chilli powder	½ tsp	½ tsp
Butter	75g/3oz	6 Tbs
Onions, very finely chopped	2	2
Double (heavy) cream	300ml/10floz	1¼ cups
Saffron threads soaked in 2 Tbs boiling water	¼ tsp	¼ tsp
Slivered almonds	50g/2oz	½ cup
Raisins	50g/2oz	⅓ cup

Preheat the oven to fairly hot 200°C (Gas Mark 6, 400°F).

A luxurious dish seasoned with saffron, Chicken with Almonds and Raisins is a splendid party dish.

Prick the chicken all over with a fork, then rub it all over with the lemon juice.

Crush or grind the coriander seeds, peppercorns, cardamom seeds and cloves. Sift the crushed spices, then stir in the ginger, salt and chilli powder. Cream in half the butter to make a smooth paste. Rub this spice paste over the chicken. Put the chicken in a casserole and bake for 15 minutes.

Meanwhile, melt the remaining butter in a saucepan. Add the onions and fry until golden. Stir in the cream, saffron-coloured water, almonds and raisins and remove from the heat.

Reduce the oven temperature to moderate 180°C (Gas Mark 4, 350°F). Continue roasting the chicken for 1 hour, basting every 10 minutes with the cream mixture.

Remove the chicken from the casserole and carve it. Arrange the pieces on a warmed serving platter. Keep hot.

Skim any fat from the surface of the cooking liquid in the casserole. Pour the cooking liquid into a saucepan and stir in any remaining cream mixture. Cook the sauce on top of the stove for 2 to 3 minutes or until it is very hot. Pour the sauce over the chicken and serve.

4 Servings

The pungency of chillis can be lessened by removing the small white seeds found inside the peppers.

125

Cantonese roast pork

	Metric/UK	US
Pork fillet (tenderloin), cut into strips 15cm/ 6in long and 4cm/1½in thick	1½kg/3lb	3lb
Oil	2 Tbs	2 Tbs
MARINADE		
Onion, very finely chopped	1	1
Soy sauce	5 Tbs	5 Tbs
Sugar	1 Tbs	1 Tbs
Dry sherry	1 Tbs	1 Tbs
Ground ginger	1½ tsp	1½ tsp
Hoisin sauce (optional)	1 Tbs	1 Tbs

Mix together the ingredients for the marinade in a shallow dish. Add the pork strips and leave to marinate for 2 hours, turning occasionally.

Preheat the oven to moderate 180°C (Gas Mark 4, 350°F).

Remove the pork from the marinade, reserving the marinade, and arrange the strips in a roasting pan in one layer. Baste with half the marinade and 1 tablespoon of the oil. Roast for 15 minutes.

Turn the pork strips over and baste with the remaining marinade and oil. Roast for a further 15 minutes. Cut the pork strips into 6mm/¼in thick slices and serve hot.

6-8 Servings

Beef in Chinese sauce

	Metric/UK	US
Walnut-size tamarind, soaked in 125ml/4floz (½ cup) water for 30 minutes, or 1 Tbs vinegar	1	1
Groundnut oil	4 Tbs	4 Tbs
Onions, sliced	2	2
Garlic cloves, crushed	3	3
Root ginger, peeled and finely chopped	4cm/1½in piece	1½in piece
Cloves	3	3
Grated nutmeg	¼ tsp	¼ tsp
Black pepper	¼ tsp	¼ tsp
Chuck steak, cut into 4cm/1½in cubes	1kg/2lb	2lb
Salt	1 tsp	1 tsp
Brown sugar	2 tsp	2 tsp
Black treacle or molasses	1 Tbs	1 Tbs
Dark soy sauce	2 Tbs	2 Tbs
Water	150ml/5floz	⅔ cup

Squeeze the tamarind in the water, then strain the liquid, pressing down on the pulp to extract all the liquid.

Heat the oil in a saucepan. Add the onions and fry until softened. Add the garlic, ginger, cloves, nutmeg and pepper and cook, stirring, for 3 minutes. Add the beef and fry until browned on all sides.

Stir in the salt, sugar, treacle or molasses, soy sauce, tamarind water or vinegar, and the water. Bring to the boil, then cover and simmer for 2 to 2½ hours or until the beef is cooked through and tender. Serve hot.

4 Servings

Gingered beef

	Metric/UK	US
Ground ginger	2 tsp	2 tsp
Soy sauce	5 Tbs	5 Tbs
Cornflour (cornstarch)	2 tsp	2 tsp
Sugar	½ tsp	½ tsp
Rump (sirloin) steak, thinly sliced across the grain	700g/1½lb	1½lb
Oil	4 Tbs	¼ cup
Root ginger, peeled and finely chopped	5cm/2in piece	2in piece
Canned bamboo shoots, drained and diced	125g/4oz	4oz
Large dried Chinese mushrooms, soaked for 30 minutes, drained and sliced	4	4

Mix together the ginger, soy sauce, cornflour (cornstarch) and sugar. Use to coat the steak slices and leave to marinate for 1 hour.

Remove the meat from the marinade and pat dry with paper towels. Heat the oil in a frying pan. Add the root ginger and fry for 3 minutes. Add the meat, bamboo shoots and mushrooms and cook for 6 to 8 minutes or until the meat is cooked through. Serve hot.

4 Servings

Honeyed ham with bean sprouts

	Metric/UK	US
Ham, soaked overnight (if necessary) and drained	1 × 1kg/2lb	1 × 2lb
Carrot, sliced	1	1
Onion, sliced	1	1
Star anise	1	1
Peppercorns, coarsely crushed	6	6
Unsalted peanuts	50g/2oz	⅓ cup
Clear honey	4 Tbs	¼ cup
Chicken stock	125ml/4floz	½ cup
Oil	3 Tbs	3 Tbs
Sesame seeds (optional)	1 tsp	1 tsp
Beansprouts	½kg/1lb	1lb
Cornflour (cornstarch) dissolved in 3 Tbs water	2 tsp	2 tsp

Put the ham, carrot, onion, anise and peppercorns in a saucepan and cover with water. Bring to the boil, then cover and simmer for 50 minutes. Remove the ham from the pan and allow to cool. Reserve the cooking liquid.

Preheat the oven to moderate 180°C (Gas Mark 4, 350°F).

Cut the ham into 2.5cm/1in cubes. Skim any fat from the surface of the cooking liquid, then strain it and reserve 125ml/4floz (½ cup).

Put the ham cubes, peanuts, honey and chicken stock in a casserole and stir well. Cover and bake for 30 minutes.

Five minutes before the ham is ready, heat the oil in a frying pan. Add the sesame seeds, if using, and fry for 1 minute. Add the bean sprouts and fry, stirring, for 2 minutes. Stir in the reserved ham cooking liquid and cook for a further 2 minutes. Transfer the beansprouts to a warmed serving dish, using a slotted spoon. Keep hot. Reserve the cooking liquid in the frying pan.

Remove the ham cubes from the casserole using a slotted spoon and pile them on top of the beansprouts. Keep hot.

Pour the mixture from the casserole into the frying pan. Bring to the boil, stirring well. Stir in the dissolved cornflour (cornstarch) and simmer, stirring, until thickened. Pour this sauce over the ham and beansprouts and serve hot.

4 Servings

Chinese red-cooked chicken

	Metric/UK	US
Spring onions (scallions), cut into 5cm/2in pieces	2	2
Root ginger, peeled and sliced	4cm/1½in piece	1½in piece
Chicken	1 × 1½kg/3lb	1 × 3lb
Oil	6 Tbs	6 Tbs
Soy sauce	6 Tbs	6 Tbs
Water	300ml/10floz	1¼ cups
Chicken stock cube, crumbled	½	½
Sugar	2 tsp	2 tsp
Sherry	3 Tbs	3 Tbs

Gingered Beef, made with Chinese mushrooms, beansprouts, spices and steak, is a delicious mixture of textures and flavour.

Right Curry powder is a commercial amalgamation of spices. You can, however, make your own following an appropriate recipe.

Stuff the spring onions (scallions) and ginger slices into the cavity in the chicken and secure the opening with trussing needle and string or skewers.

Heat the oil in a saucepan. Add the chicken and brown lightly on all sides. Pour off the excess oil from the pan and add the soy sauce, water, stock cube, sugar and sherry. Bring to the boil, then cover and simmer for 30 minutes. Turn the chicken over and continue to cook, covered, for a further 45 minutes.

Carve the chicken and serve with the cooking liquid as a sauce.

4 Servings

Dindings duck

	Metric/UK	US
Ground coriander	1 Tbs	1 Tbs
Ground fenugreek	2 tsp	2 tsp
Ground cumin	2 tsp	2 tsp
Turmeric	1 tsp	1 tsp
Ground cinnamon	1 tsp	1 tsp
Ground cardamom	$\frac{1}{2}$ tsp	$\frac{1}{2}$ tsp
Ground cloves	$\frac{1}{4}$ tsp	$\frac{1}{4}$ tsp
Grated nutmeg	$\frac{1}{4}$ tsp	$\frac{1}{4}$ tsp
Mild chilli powder	1 tsp	1 tsp
Salt	$\frac{1}{2}$ tsp	$\frac{1}{2}$ tsp
Black pepper	1 tsp	1 tsp
Root ginger, peeled and finely chopped	1cm/$\frac{1}{2}$in piece	$\frac{1}{2}$in piece
Juice of 1 lemon		
Small onions, minced	2	2
Garlic cloves, crushed	2	2
Desiccated (shredded) coconut, soaked in 175ml/6floz ($\frac{3}{4}$ cup) boiling water	125g/4oz	$\frac{1}{2}$ cup
Duck, split open through the breastbone	1 × 2$\frac{1}{2}$kg/5lb	1 × 5lb

Preheat the oven to fairly hot 190°C (Gas Mark 5, 375°F), or prepare the barbecue fire.

Mix together the spices, salt and pepper, ginger, lemon juice, onions garlic and coconut mixture to form a thick paste.

Tie the duck wings and legs to-

Below Barbecued Dindings Duck.

128

gether and open the duck so that it will lie flat. Place it on a rack in a roasting pan, or on the barbecue grid, skin side down. Spread with some of the spice paste. Roast for 45 minutes, basting with the spice paste every 15 minutes, then turn the duck over and continue roasting and basting for a further 45 minutes.

If you are using a barbecue, the total cooking time will be about half that for roasting, depending on how hot the fire is and how near you place the grid. The duck will need to be turned and basted more frequently.

Serve hot.

4 Servings

Malaysian fish

	Metric/UK	US
Fish fillets	700g/1½lb	1½lb
Turmeric	2 tsp	2 tsp
Salt	1½ tsp	1½ tsp
Oil	3 Tbs	3 Tbs
Onions, finely chopped	2	2
Root ginger, peeled and grated	2.5cm/1in piece	1in piece
Green or red chillis (chili peppers), finely chopped	2	2
Blachan or anchovy paste	1 tsp	1 tsp
Sereh powder or finely grated lemon rind	1 tsp	1 tsp
Sugar	1 tsp	1 tsp
Tomatoes, skinned and chopped	4	4
Small pineapple, peeled, cored and cut into chunks	1	1

Cut the fillets into finger-size pieces and rub them with 1 teaspoon each of the turmeric and salt. Heat the oil in a frying pan. Add the fish pieces and fry for 1 to 2 minutes on each side or until beginning to brown. Remove the fish pieces from the pan.

If necessary, add more oil to the pan so that the bottom is just covered. Heat the oil, then add the onions and fry until golden. Stir in the ginger, chillis, blachan or anchovy paste, sereh or lemon rind and the remaining turmeric. Fry gently for 5 minutes, stirring. Add the sugar, tomatoes and remaining salt.

Return the fish pieces to the pan with the pineapple chunks. Stir well, then cover and cook for 20 to 25 minutes or until the fish is cooked through. Serve hot.

4 Servings

Bali tamarind fish

	Metric/UK	US
Tamarind soaked in 125ml/4floz (½ cup) hot water for 20 minutes	2 Tbs	2 Tbs
Red mullet, cleaned	4	4
Peanut oil	4 Tbs	¼ cup
Red chillis (chili peppers), seeded	4	4
Onion, quartered	1	1
Garlic cloves	2	2
Root ginger, peeled	1cm/½in piece	½in piece
Water	175ml/6floz	¾ cup
Soy sauce	1 tsp	1 tsp
Salt	½ tsp	½ tsp

Strain the tamarind, pushing through as much pulp as possible. Discard all the seeds remaining in the strainer. Rub the fish all over with the tamarind pulp. Heat the oil in a frying pan. Add the fish and cook for 7 minutes on each side.

Meanwhile, put the chillis, onion, garlic, ginger and 4 tablespoons of the water in a blender and blend to a purée.

Remove the fish from the pan and set aside. Add the chilli mixture to the pan and cook, stirring, for 2 minutes. Stir in the soy sauce, salt and remaining water and bring to the boil.

Return the fish to the pan and continue cooking for 10 minutes or until cooked through. Serve hot.

4 Servings

Indonesian mackerel

	Metric/UK	US
Fresh lime juice	300ml/10floz	1¼ cups
White wine vinegar	4 Tbs	¼ cup
Salt	1 tsp	1 tsp
Black peppercorns	6	6
Mackerel, filleted	2 × 1kg/2lb	2 × 2lb
Turmeric	1 tsp	1 tsp
Peanut oil	4 Tbs	4 Tbs

Mix together the lime juice, vinegar, half the salt and the peppercorns in a shallow dish. Add the mackerel fillets and turn to coat well. Leave to marinate for 1 hour, turning occasionally.

Remove the fish from the marinade and pat dry with paper towels. Strain the marinade and reserve 4 tablespoons (¼ cup). Rub the fish all over with the remaining salt and the turmeric.

Heat the oil in a frying pan. Add the fish fillets and fry for 4 to 5 minutes on each side or until cooked through. Arrange on a warmed serving platter and sprinkle over the reserved marinade. Serve hot.

4 Servings

PUDDINGS & DESSERTS

Pineapple soufflé

	Metric/UK	US
Butter	50g/2oz	4 Tbs
Flour	50g/2oz	½ cup
Ground allspice	1 tsp	1 tsp
Single (light) cream	250ml/8floz	1 cup
Kirsch	4 Tbs	¼ cup
Sugar	50g/2oz	¼ cup
Egg yolks	4	4
Small pineapple, peeled, cored and finely chopped	1	1
Egg whites	5	5

Preheat the oven to fairly hot 190°C (Gas Mark 5, 375°F).

Melt the butter in a saucepan. Add the flour and allspice and cook, stirring, for 1 minute. Gradually stir in the cream and kirsch and bring to the boil, stirring. Simmer, stirring, until very thick and smooth. Remove from the heat and allow to cool.

Beat the sugar and egg yolks into the cooled sauce, then fold in the pineapple. Beat the egg whites until stiff and fold gently but thoroughly into the pineapple mixture. Spoon into a greased 1.8l/3 pint (2 quart) soufflé dish fitted with a paper collar. Bake for 35 to 40 minutes or until the soufflé has risen and is golden on top.

Remove the paper collar and serve immediately.

4 Servings

Apple noodle pudding

	Metric/UK	US
Eggs, lightly beaten	2	2
Milk	2 Tbs	2 Tbs
Sugar	2 Tbs	2 Tbs
Salt	¼ tsp	¼ tsp
Ground cinnamon	¼ tsp	¼ tsp
Ground allspice	¼ tsp	¼ tsp
Large cooking apples, peeled, cored and grated	2	2
Raisins	50g/2oz	⅓ cup
Fine noodles, cooked and drained	350g/12oz	12oz
Butter, melted	25g/1oz	2 Tbs

Preheat the oven to moderate 180°C (Gas Mark 4, 350°F).

Mix together the eggs, milk, sugar, salt, cinnamon and allspice. Add the apples, raisins and noodles and fold together thoroughly. Turn into a deep baking dish and pour the melted

butter on top.

Bake for 45 minutes or until the pudding is firm to the touch and lightly browned on top. Serve hot.

4-6 Servings

Armenian dried fruit dessert

	Metric/UK	US
Dried apricots, soaked overnight	225g/8oz	1⅓ cups
Prunes, stoned (pitted) and soaked overnight	225g/8oz	1⅓ cups
Sultanas or raisins, soaked overnight	125g/4oz	⅔ cup
Large cooking apples, peeled, cored and sliced	2	2
Clear honey	6 Tbs	6 Tbs
Pared rind of 1 lemon		
Grated nutmeg	½ tsp	½ tsp
Ground cinnamon	½ tsp	½ tsp
Ground ginger	½ tsp	½ tsp
Brandy	2 Tbs	2 Tbs

Drain the dried fruit, reserving 125ml/4floz (½ cup) of the soaking liquid. Put the fruit and reserved liquid in a saucepan and add the apples, honey, lemon rind, nutmeg, cinnamon and ginger. Stir well and bring to the boil. Simmer for 25 minutes or until the mixture is pulpy.

Discard the lemon rind and allow the fruit to cool, then beat the fruit with a wooden spoon to form a purée. Stir in the brandy. Chill for at least 30 minutes before serving.

6 Servings

Ginger cream-filled horns

	Metric/UK	US
Butter, melted	75g/3oz	6 Tbs
Sugar	50g/2oz	¼ cup
Flour, sifted	50g/2oz	½ cup
Ground ginger	1 tsp	1 tsp
Large egg whites	4	4
Double (heavy) cream, whipped	250ml/8floz	1 cup
Madeira	1 Tbs	1 Tbs
Chopped preserved ginger	2 Tbs	2 Tbs

Preheat the oven to fairly hot 200°C (Gas Mark 6, 400°F).

Mix together the melted butter,

sugar, flour and ginger to make a smooth batter. Beat the egg whites until stiff and fold into the batter. Drop teaspoonfuls of the batter onto a greased baking sheet, leaving space around each. Gently flatten the batter mounds. Put the baking sheet into the oven and bake gently for 3 to 5 minutes or until golden.

Shape each biscuit (cookie) into a horn with your fingers before baking the next batch. When all the horns have been baked and shaped, allow them to cool.

Whip the cream and fold in the Madeira and preserved ginger. Fill the horns with the cream mixture and serve.

38 Horns

Pears baked with cardamom

	Metric/UK	US
Large pears, peeled, cored and sliced	3	3
Soft brown sugar	2 Tbs	2 Tbs
Orange-flavoured liqueur	125ml/4floz	½ cup
Ground cardamom	2 tsp	2 tsp

Preheat the oven to moderate 180°C (Gas Mark 4, 350°F).

Arrange the pear slices in a baking dish and sprinkle with the sugar, liqueur and cardamom. Bake for 35 to 40 minutes or until cooked and very tender.

Allow the pears to cool and serve at room temperature with whipped cream.

4-6 Servings

Pears baked with Cardamom is a refreshing dessert to serve after a filling main course.

An elegant recipe to round off
a dinner party, Cinnamon
Flavoured Layer Cake is light pastry
filled with almond cream and
topped by a chocolate-covered layer
garnished with slivered almonds.

Danish cinnamon layer cake

	Metric/UK	US
PASTRY		
Butter	225g/8oz	1 cup
Sugar	125g/4oz	½ cup
Flour	225g/8oz	2 cups
Ground cinnamon	2 tsp	2 tsp
FILLING		
Dark (semi-sweet) cooking chocolate, broken into small pieces	50g/2oz	2 squares
Rum	1 Tbs	1 Tbs
Double (heavy) cream	300ml/10floz	1¼ cups
Ground almonds	75g/3oz	¾ cup
Slivered almonds	1 Tbs	1 Tbs

Preheat the oven to fairly hot 200°C
(Gas Mark 6, 400°F).

To make the pastry, cream the
butter and sugar together until the
mixture is pale and fluffy. Sift in the
flour and cinnamon and knead in
thoroughly. Divide the dough into six
portions and roll out each between
two sheets of greaseproof or wax paper
into a 20cm/8in circle. Remove the
top sheet of paper, but leave each
circle on the bottom sheet. Place two
circles on a baking sheet and bake for
6 to 8 minutes or until the pastry is
pale golden brown. Allow to cool on

the paper. Bake the remaining circles
in the same way. When the pastry
circles are completely cold, carefully
peel off the paper.

Melt the chocolate with the rum.
Spread the chocolate over one of the
pastry circles. Leave to set.

Whip the cream until it begins to
thicken. Gradually beat in the ground
almonds until the cream is stiff. Sand-
wich together the remaining five pastry
circles with the almond cream. Place
the chocolate-covered circle on top
and garnish decoratively with the
slivered almonds. Serve immediately.

6 Servings

Flummery

	Metric/UK	US
Round-grain rice	125g/4oz	⅔ cup
Milk	300ml/10floz	1¼ cups
Double (heavy) cream	300ml/10floz	1¼ cups
Sugar	50g/2oz	¼ cup
Grated lemon rind	1 Tbs	1 Tbs
Ground cinnamon	1 tsp	1 tsp

Put all the ingredients in the top of a
double saucepan (boiler) and place

over the heat. Cover and cook gently for 50 to 55 minutes, or until the rice is soft and has absorbed all the liquid. Stir occasionally during cooking and add more milk if necessary.

Pour the flummery into a serving bowl, or individual dishes, and allow to cool. Chill until set and serve cold.

4 Servings

Rhubarb and ginger compote

	Metric/UK	US
Sugar	225g/8oz	1 cup
Water	125ml/4floz	½ cup
Rhubarb, cut into 5cm/2in pieces	1kg/2lb	2lb
Gin	250ml/8floz	1 cup
Grated orange rind	1 Tbs	1 Tbs
Grated nutmeg	¼ tsp	¼ tsp
Ground ginger	½ tsp	½ tsp
Preserved ginger, finely chopped	1 Tbs	1 Tbs

Dissolve the sugar in the water in a saucepan, then bring to the boil. Add the rhubarb, gin, orange rind and spices and simmer for 20 to 30 minutes or until the rhubarb is tender, stirring occasionally. Transfer the rhubarb to a serving dish using a slotted spoon.

Return the cooking liquid to the boil and boil until reduced to about one-third. Pour the liquid over the rhubarb and stir gently. Sprinkle the preserved ginger over the top and allow to cool. Chill for at least 30 minutes before serving.

4 Servings

Oranges with cinnamon

	Metric/UK	US
Large oranges, peeled, white pith removed and thinly sliced	4	4
Sugar	2 tsp	2 tsp
Ground cinnamon	1 tsp	1 tsp
Orange-flavoured liqueur	2 Tbs	2 Tbs

Arrange the orange slices in a serving dish. Sprinkle with the sugar, cinnamon and liqueur. Chill for at least 30 minutes before serving.

4 Servings

Rhubarb and Ginger Compote is a delectable blend of gin and rhubarb.

Coriander fruit crumble

	Metric/UK	US
Cooking apples, peeled, cored and thinly sliced	700g/1½lb	1½lb
Blackberries	225g/8oz	8oz
Brown sugar	2 Tbs	2 Tbs
Ground cinnamon	1 tsp	1 tsp
TOPPING		
Flour	125g/4oz	1 cup
Sugar	125g/4oz	½ cup
Butter	125g/4oz	8 Tbs
Ground coriander	2 tsp	2 tsp

Preheat the oven to moderate 180°C (Gas Mark 4, 350°F).

Put the apples and blackberries in a greased baking dish and fold in the sugar and cinnamon.

Sift the flour into a mixing bowl and stir in the sugar. Add the butter and rub it into the flour until the mixture resembles breadcrumbs. Stir in the coriander.

Sprinkle the topping on the fruit. Bake for 45 minutes, or until the topping is golden. Serve hot.

4-6 Servings

Grumble pie

	Metric/UK	US
PASTRY		
Flour	175g/6oz	1½ cups
Sugar	1 tsp	1 tsp
Salt	pinch	pinch
Butter	50g/2oz	4 Tbs
Vegetable fat or lard	50g/2oz	¼ cup
Iced water	1-2 Tbs	1-2 Tbs
FILLING		
Raisins	75g/3oz	½ cup
Brown sugar	175g/6oz	1 cup
Water	125ml/4floz	½ cup
Eggs, lightly beaten	3	3
TOPPING		
Stale cake crumbs	50g/2oz	1 cup
Flour	50g/2oz	½ cup
Ground cinnamon	½ tsp	½ tsp
Ground ginger	¼ tsp	¼ tsp
Butter, cut into small pieces	50g/2oz	4 Tbs

First make the pastry. Sift the flour, sugar and salt into a mixing bowl. Add the butter and vegetable fat or lard and cut into small pieces, then rub the fat into the flour until the mixture resembles breadcrumbs. Mix in enough water to bind the mixture to a dough. Chill for 20 minutes.

Preheat the oven to fairly hot 200°C (Gas Mark 6, 400°F).

Roll out the dough and use to line a 23cm/9in pie dish (pan). Line the dough with foil and weigh down with dried beans. Bake for 10 minutes, then remove the foil and beans and bake for a further 5 minutes. Remove from the oven and set aside. Reduce the oven temperature to moderate 180°C (Gas Mark 4, 350°F).

Sprinkle the raisins over the bottom of the pastry shell. Dissolve the brown sugar in the water over gentle heat. Beat in the eggs and cook very gently, stirring, until the mixture thickens. Remove from the heat and cool.

To make the topping, mix together the cake crumbs, flour, cinnamon and ginger. Rub in the butter until the mixture resembles fine breadcrumbs.

Pour the cooled filling into the pastry shell and sprinkle over the topping. Bake for 30 minutes or until the topping is golden. Serve warm.

6 Servings

Green grape and apple pie

	Metric/UK	US
PASTRY		
Flour	300g/10oz	2½ cups
Salt	¼ tsp	¼ tsp
Vegetable fat or lard	125g/4oz	½ cup
Butter	50g/2oz	4 Tbs
Iced water	6 Tbs	6 Tbs
Egg, lightly beaten	1	1
FILLING		
Sugar	125g/4oz	½ cup
Salt	¼ tsp	¼ tsp
Ground cinnamon	½ tsp	½ tsp
Grated nutmeg	¼ tsp	¼ tsp
Large cooking apples, peeled, cored and thinly sliced	2	2
Seedless green grapes	350g/12oz	12oz
Cornflour (cornstarch) dissolved in 2 Tbs water	1 Tbs	1 Tbs
Butter, cut into small pieces	25g/1oz	2 Tbs

To make the pastry, sift the flour and salt into a mixing bowl. Add the vegetable fat or lard and butter and cut into small pieces, then rub the fat into the flour until the mixture resembles crumbs. Mix in enough water to bind to a dough. Chill.

Roll out about two-thirds of the dough to line a deep pie dish (pan).

Preheat the oven to hot 220°C (Gas Mark 7, 425°F).

To make the filling, mix together the sugar, salt, cinnamon and nutmeg. Add the apples, grapes and dissolved cornflour (cornstarch) and fold together thoroughly. Spoon into the pie dish (pan) and dot with the butter.

Roll out the remaining dough and use to cover the pie. Press the edges together to seal and cut two slits in the centre to allow the steam to escape. Brush with the beaten egg.

Bake for 10 minutes, then reduce the oven temperature to moderate

180°C (Gas Mark 4, 350°F). Continue baking for 45 minutes or until the crust is golden brown. Serve warm.

6-8 Servings

Italian cherries

	Metric/UK	US
Canned Morello (Bing) cherries, drained and stoned (pitted)	1kg/2lb	2lb
Marsala	150ml/5floz	⅔ cup
Grated nutmeg	½ tsp	½ tsp
Sugar	1 Tbs	1 Tbs
Double (heavy) cream, whipped	150ml/5floz	⅔ cup

Put the cherries, Marsala, nutmeg and sugar in a saucepan and bring to the boil, stirring thoroughly to dissolve the sugar. Simmer gently for 10 minutes.

Transfer the cherries to a serving bowl using a slotted spoon. Continue simmering the cooking syrup for 3 to 4 minutes or until it is thick and syrupy. Pour the syrup over the cherries.

Allow to cool, then chill for at least 1 hour. Serve at once topped with the whipped cream in individual glass dessert bowls.

4 Servings

BREADS & CAKES

Lardy cake

	Metric/UK	US
Fresh (compressed) yeast	15g/½oz	½ cake
Sugar	50g/2oz	¼ cup
Lukewarm water	300ml/10floz	1¼ cups
Flour	½kg/1lb	4 cups
Salt	1 tsp	1 tsp
Oil	1 tsp	1 tsp
Lard, cut into small pieces	125g/4oz	½ cup
Grated nutmeg	½ tsp	½ tsp
Ground cinnamon	½ tsp	½ tsp
Ground ginger	½ tsp	½ tsp
Currants	350g/12oz	2 cups
GLAZE		
Sugar	3 Tbs	3 Tbs
Water	3 Tbs	3 Tbs

Crumble the yeast into a bowl and mash in ½ teaspoon of the sugar and 1 tablespoon of the water. Leave in a warm place for 15 to 20 minutes or until puffed up and frothy.

Sift the flour and salt into another bowl. Make a well in the centre and pour in the yeast mixture, oil and remaining water. Gradually draw the flour into the liquids and mix to a dough. Turn the dough out onto a floured surface and knead until it is smooth and elastic—about 10 minutes.

Return the dough to the bowl, cover and leave to rise in a warm place for 1 to 1½ hours or until doubled in bulk.

Knead the dough lightly, then roll it out into an oblong about 6mm/¼in thick that is three times as long as it is wide. Sprinkle the upper two-thirds of the oblong with half the lard, remaining sugar, spices and currants. Fold the bottom, uncovered, third up and the top third down. Turn the dough so the open ends face you. Lightly press the open ends with the rolling pin to seal them, then roll out again into an oblong. Repeat the process with the remaining lard, sugar, spices and currants and fold and turn as before. Roll out the dough to fit a 20cm/8in round loose-bottomed cake tin (springform pan). Put the dough in the tin (pan), cover and leave to rise in a warm place for 40 to 45 minutes or until almost doubled in bulk.

Preheat the oven to fairly hot 200°C (Gas Mark 6, 400°F).

Bake for 35 minutes. Mix together the sugar and water for the glaze and brush over the cake. Continue baking for 10 minutes or until well risen and golden brown. Allow to cool on a wire rack before serving.

20cm/8in Cake

Spice and nut cake

	Metric/UK	US
Butter	75g/3oz	6 Tbs
Black treacle or molasses	3 Tbs	3 Tbs
Sugar	75g/3oz	6 Tbs
Egg	1	1
Egg white	1	1
Flour	175g/6oz	1½ cups
Baking powder	2 tsp	2 tsp
Ground allspice	¼ tsp	¼ tsp
Ground cinnamon	¼ tsp	¼ tsp
Ground ginger	¼ tsp	¼ tsp
Ground cloves	⅛ tsp	⅛ tsp
Juice of ½ lemon		
Milk	1 Tbs	1 Tbs
Walnuts, chopped	175g/6oz	1½ cups
Grated lemon rind	2 tsp	2 tsp
TOPPING		
Flour	2 Tbs	2 Tbs
Soft brown sugar	2 Tbs	2 Tbs
Grated lemon rind	1 tsp	1 tsp
Grated nutmeg	½ tsp	½ tsp
Butter	25g/1oz	2 Tbs
Walnuts, chopped	50g/2oz	½ cup

Preheat the oven to moderate 180°C (Gas Mark 4, 350°F).

First make the topping. Mix together the flour, sugar, lemon rind and nutmeg. Add the butter and rub into the flour mixture until the mixture resembles breadcrumbs. Stir in the walnuts.

Cream the butter until it is pale and fluffy. Beat in the treacle or molasses and sugar, then beat in the egg and egg white. Sift together the flour, baking powder and spices and fold into the creamed mixture. Stir in the lemon juice, milk, walnuts and lemon rind. Pour the batter into a greased and lined 18cm/7in loose-bottomed cake tin (springform pan). Sprinkle over the topping.

Bake for 1 hour or until a skewer inserted into the centre of the cake comes out clean. Cool in the tin for 5 minutes, then turn out onto a wire rack to cool completely.

18cm/7in Cake

A traditional British bread, Lardy Cake makes an excellent accompaniment to morning coffee.

Parkin

	Metric/UK	US
Flour	½kg/1lb	4 cups
Bicarbonate of soda (baking soda)	1 tsp	1 tsp
Salt	1 tsp	1 tsp
Ground ginger	2 tsp	2 tsp
Rolled oats	½ kg/1lb	4 cups
Butter	225g/8oz	1 cup
Black treacle or molasses	250ml/8floz	1 cup
Golden (light corn) syrup	250ml/8floz	1 cup
Clear honey	4 Tbs	¼ cup
Soft brown sugar	2 Tbs	2 Tbs
Milk	350ml/12floz	1½ cups

Preheat the oven to moderate 180°C (Gas Mark 4, 350°F).

Sift the flour, soda, salt and ginger into a bowl. Stir in the oats.

Melt the butter in a saucepan. Add the treacle or molasses, syrup, honey and sugar and stir well. Cook, stirring, for 1 minute. Add to the flour mixture with the milk and mix together thoroughly. Pour the batter into two greased and lined 25cm/10in square cake tins (pans).

Bake for 45 to 50 minutes or until the parkins feel firm when pressed with a fingertip. Allow to cool in the tins (pans) for 15 minutes, then cool completely on a wire rack. Store the parkins in airtight tins for at least a week before eating.

2 × 25cm/10in Square cakes

German spice cake

	Metric/UK	US
Eggs	3	3
Sugar	175g/6oz	¾ cup
Clear honey	300ml/10floz	1¼ cups
Almonds, finely chopped	125g/4oz	1 cup
Grated rind of ½ lemon		
Grated rind of ½ orange		
Chopped mixed candied peel	50g/2oz	⅓ cup
Flour	300g/10oz	2½ cups
Baking powder	1 tsp	1 tsp
Ground cloves	¼ tsp	¼ tsp
Ground cinnamon	½ tsp	½ tsp
Grated nutmeg	¼ tsp	¼ tsp

Preheat the oven to fairly hot 190°C (Gas Mark 5, 375°F).

Beat the eggs and sugar together until the mixture is pale and fluffy. Stir in the honey, almonds, grated lemon and orange rind and candied peel. Sift in the flour, baking powder and spices and mix well. Pour the batter into a greased 20cm/8in square baking tin (cake pan). Bake for 40 to 45 minutes or until a skewer inserted into the centre of the cake comes out

clean. Allow the cake to cool in the tin (pan) for 15 minutes before turning it out onto a cake rack to cool completely.

20cm/8in Square cake

Hermits

	Metric/UK	US
Butter	225g/8oz	1 cup
Soft brown sugar	175g/6oz	1 cup
Eggs	2	2
Strong black coffee	125ml/4floz	½ cup
Flour	225g/8oz	2 cups
Ground cinnamon	1 tsp	1 tsp
Grated nutmeg	½ tsp	½ tsp
Baking powder	½ tsp	½ tsp
Raisins	75g/3oz	½ cup
Walnuts, chopped	50g/2oz	½ cup

Preheat the oven to fairly hot 190°C (Gas Mark 5, 375°F).

Cream the butter and sugar together until the mixture is fluffy. Beat in the eggs, then beat in the coffee. Sift in the flour, spices and baking powder and fold in thoroughly. Stir in the raisins and walnuts.

Drop heaped teaspoonfuls of the mixture onto a greased baking sheet, leaving space around each. Bake for 10 to 15 minutes or until the biscuits (cookies) are golden brown. Cool on a wire rack.

50 Biscuits(Cookies)

Genoese sweet bread

	Metric/UK	US
Fresh (compressed) yeast	25g/1oz	1 cake
Sugar	175g/6oz plus ½ tsp	¾ cup plus ½ tsp
Lukewarm milk	425ml/14floz	1¾ cups
Flour	1kg/2lb	8 cups
Salt	1 tsp	1 tsp
Orange-flower water	3 Tbs	3 Tbs
Butter, melted	75g/3oz	6 Tbs
Pine nuts	50g/2oz	⅓ cup
Pistachio nuts	50g/2oz	⅓ cup
Raisins, soaked in 3 Tbs Marsala for 30 minutes and drained	175g/6oz	1 cup
Fennel seeds, crushed	2 tsp	2 tsp
Aniseed, crushed	½ tsp	½ tsp
Candied citron, chopped	50g/2oz	⅓ cup
Candied lemon peel, chopped	50g/2oz	⅓ cup
Grated rind of 1 orange		

Crumble the yeast into a bowl and mash in the ½ teaspoon sugar and 4 tablespoons of the milk. Leave in a warm place for 15 to 20 minutes or

until puffed up and frothy.

Sift the flour, salt and remaining sugar into another bowl. Make a well in the centre and pour in the yeast mixture, remaining milk, orange-flower water and butter. Gradually draw the flour mixture into the liquids and mix to a dough. Turn the dough onto a floured board and knead until it is elastic and smooth—about 10 minutes.

Return the dough to the bowl, cover and leave to rise in a warm place for 1 to 1½ hours or until doubled in bulk.

Knead the dough lightly, then shape it into a square about 1cm/½in thick on a floured surface. Mix together the remaining ingredients and sprinkle them evenly over the dough square. Roll it up like a Swiss (jelly) roll, then shape it into a round. Place it on a baking sheet, cover and leave to rise in a warm place for 1 hour or until almost doubled in bulk.

Preheat the oven to fairly hot 190°C (Gas Mark 5, 375°F).

Make three cuts in the top of the dough round in the shape of a triangle.

Bake for 20 minutes, then reduce the oven temperature to warm 170°C (Gas Mark 3, 325°F). Continue baking for 1 hour.

Cool the bread on a wire rack before serving.

1¼kg/2½lb Bread

An unusual bread from Northern Italy, Genoese Sweet Bread is delicately flavoured with pine nuts, fennel seeds and orange-flower water.

Treacle or molasses loaf

	Metric/UK	US
Butter, melted	125g/4oz	8 Tbs
Black treacle or molasses	125ml/4floz	½ cup
Large eggs	2	2
Flour	225g/8oz	2 cups
Baking powder	1½ tsp	1½ tsp
Ground ginger	1½ tsp	1½ tsp
Ground allspice	½ tsp	½ tsp
Ground cinnamon	¼ tsp	¼ tsp
Salt	¼ tsp	¼ tsp
Rolled oats	125g/4oz	1 cup
Sour cream	150ml/5floz	⅔ cup
Sultanas or raisins	4 Tbs	4 Tbs
Chopped walnuts	2 Tbs	2 Tbs

Preheat the oven to moderate 180°C (Gas Mark 4, 350°F).

Mix together the butter, treacle or

Black Bun is a rich pastry case filled with a choice selection of fruit and assorted spices.

molasses and eggs. Sift the flour, baking powder, spices and salt into another bowl. Stir in the oats. Gradually mix in the treacle or molasses mixture and sour cream, then fold in the sultanas or raisins and walnuts.

Spoon the batter into a greased 1kg/2lb loaf pan. Bake for 1 hour or until a skewer inserted into the centre of the loaf comes out clean. Cool in the pan for 10 minutes and then turn out on to a wire rack to cool completely.

700g/1½lb Loaf

Cumin and raspberry buns

	Metric/UK	US
Butter	175g/6oz	¾ cup
Sugar	225g/8oz plus 2 Tbs	1 cup plus 2 Tbs
Eggs	2	2
Ground cumin	1 tsp	1 tsp
Self-raising flour	350g/12oz	3 cups
Salt	pinch	pinch
Raspberry jam	125g/4oz	½ cup

Preheat the oven to fairly hot 190°C (Gas Mark 5, 375°F).

Cream the butter and all but 2 tablespoons of the sugar together until the mixture is pale and fluffy. Beat in the eggs and cumin. Sift in the flour and salt and fold into the butter mixture thoroughly. Chill for 30 minutes.

Roll the dough into walnut-sized balls. Make an indentation in each with your thumb, fill with a little jam, and seal up the dough to enclose the jam completely. Roll the balls in the remaining sugar to coat on all sides.

Place the balls in greased patty or cup cake pans and bake for 20 minutes or until risen and golden. Allow to cool before serving.

24 Buns

Black bun

	Metric/UK	US
PASTRY		
Flour	**350g/12oz**	**3 cups**
Salt	**¼ tsp**	**¼ tsp**
Butter	**75g/3oz**	**6 Tbs**
Sugar	**2 Tbs**	**2 Tbs**
Small eggs, lightly beaten	**3**	**3**
Iced water	**4-6 Tbs**	**4-6 Tbs**
FILLING		
Flour	**225g/8oz**	**2 cups**
Bicarbonate of soda (baking soda)	**1 tsp**	**1 tsp**
Baking powder	**1½ tsp**	**1½ tsp**
Soft brown sugar	**125g/4oz**	**⅔ cup**
Ground allspice	**1 tsp**	**1 tsp**
Ground cinnamon	**½ tsp**	**½ tsp**
Ground ginger	**½ tsp**	**½ tsp**
Ground mace	**¼ tsp**	**¼ tsp**
Sultanas or raisins	**350g/12oz**	**2 cups**
Currants	**350g/12oz**	**2 cups**
Almonds, chopped	**125g/4oz**	**1 cup**
Walnuts, chopped	**125g/4oz**	**1 cup**
Chopped mixed candied peel	**125g/4oz**	**⅔ cup**
Grated rind and juice of 1 lemon		
Milk	**175ml/6floz**	**¾ cup**
Brandy	**1 Tbs**	**1 Tbs**

To make the pastry, sift the flour and salt into a bowl. Add the butter and cut it into small pieces, then rub the butter into the flour until the mixture resembles breadcrumbs. Stir in the sugar. Mix in the beaten eggs with enough of the water to bind the ingredients to a dough. Chill for 20 minutes.

Roll out two-thirds of the dough and use to line a deep 18cm/7in cake pan.

Preheat the oven to fairly hot 200°C (Gas Mark 6, 400°F).

To make the filling, sift the flour, soda, baking powder, sugar and spices into a bowl. Stir in the sultanas or raisins, currants, almonds, walnuts, candied peel and lemon rind and juice. When the ingredients are thoroughly combined, moisten with the milk and brandy. Spoon the filling into the pastry case and smooth the top.

Roll out the remaining dough and use to cover the top of the cake. Cut a large cross in the centre. Brush the dough with the remaining beaten egg.

Bake for 15 minutes, then cover with foil and reduce the oven temperature to warm 170°C (Gas Mark 3, 325°F). Continue baking for 3½ hours or until a skewer inserted into the centre of the cake comes out clean.

Carefully turn the cake out onto a wire rack and leave to cool. Wrap in foil and keep for at least 1 week before eating.

18cm/7in Cake

German dried fruit bread

	Metric/UK	US
Fresh (compressed) yeast	**25g/1oz**	**1 cake**
Sugar	**125g/4oz plus ½ tsp**	**½ cup plus ½ tsp**
Lukewarm water	**750ml/1 pint 8floz**	**3½ cups**
Flour	**1½kg/3lb**	**12 cups**
Ground coriander	**½ tsp**	**½ tsp**
Ground fennel seeds	**¼ tsp**	**¼ tsp**
Ground cloves	**¼ tsp**	**¼ tsp**
Salt	**1 tsp**	**1 tsp**
Butter, melted	**125g/4oz**	**8 Tbs**
Dried apricots, chopped	**50g/2oz**	**⅓ cup**
Dried pears, chopped	**50g/2oz**	**⅓ cup**
Dried apples, chopped	**50g/2oz**	**⅓ cup**
Whole hazelnuts	**300g/10oz**	**2 cups**
Raisins	**175g/6oz**	**1 cup**
Chopped mixed candied peel	**125g/4oz**	**⅔ cup**

Crumble the yeast into a bowl and mash in the ½ teaspoon sugar and 125ml/4floz (½ cup) of the water. Leave in a warm place for 15 to 20 minutes or until puffed up and frothy.

Sift half the flour into a mixing bowl with the spices and salt. Make a well in the centre and pour in the yeast mixture, the butter and the remaining water. Gradually draw the flour mixture into the liquids and mix to a dough.

In another bowl, mix together the remaining flour with the dried fruits, nuts, raisins and candied peel. Add to the dough and knead together thoroughly to distribute the fruits and nuts evenly. Continue kneading until the dough is smooth and elastic. Cover and leave to rise in a warm place for 1½ hours or until doubled in bulk.

Knead the dough lightly and cut it into three pieces. Shape each piece into a ball. Place the balls on greased baking sheets, cover and leave to rise in a warm place for 30 to 40 minutes or until almost doubled in bulk.

Preheat the oven to hot 220°C (Gas Mark 7, 425°F).

Bake the breads for 15 minutes, then reduce the oven temperature to fairly hot 190°C (Gas Mark 5, 375°F). Continue baking for 30 minutes or until crusty and golden brown. Cool on a wire rack.

3 × 1kg/2lb Loaves

Chocolate cinnamon biscuits (cookies)

	Metric/UK	US
Butter	**225g/8oz**	**1 cup**
Sugar	**125g/4oz**	**½ cup**
Self-raising flour	**225g/8oz**	**2 cups**
Cocoa powder	**50g/2oz**	**½ cup**
Ground cinnamon	**¾ tsp**	**¾ tsp**
Vanilla essence (extract)	**1 tsp**	**1 tsp**

Preheat the oven to moderate 180°C (Gas Mark 4, 350°F).

Cream the butter until it is pale and fluffy. Beat in the sugar gradually, then sift in the flour, cocoa powder and cinnamon. Fold into the butter until the mixture is smooth. Stir in the vanilla.

Roll small spoonfuls of the dough into balls and place them on a greased baking sheet, about 5cm/2in apart. Flatten the balls using the prongs of a fork.

Bake for 12 minutes. Allow to cool slightly before removing from the baking sheet.

25 Biscuits (Cookies)

Spice doughnuts

	Metric/UK	US
Fresh (compressed) yeast	**15g/½oz**	**½ cake**
Brown sugar	**50g/2oz plus ½ tsp**	**⅓ cup plus ½ tsp**
Lukewarm milk	**150ml/5floz plus 2 Tbs**	**⅔ cup plus 2 Tbs**
Flour	**½kg/1lb**	**4 cups**
Ground allspice	**1 tsp**	**1 tsp**
Ground cinnamon	**½ tsp**	**½ tsp**
Ground cloves	**½ tsp**	**½ tsp**
Ground mace	**½ tsp**	**½ tsp**
Butter, melted	**25g/1oz**	**2 Tbs**
Currants	**50g/2oz**	**⅓ cup**
Sufficient oil for deep-frying		

Crumble the yeast into a bowl and mash in the ½ teaspoon sugar and 2 tablespoons milk. Leave in a warm place for 20 minutes or until frothy.

Sift the flour and spices into another bowl. Make a well in the centre and pour in the yeast mixture, remaining milk and butter. Gradually draw the flour mixture into the liquids and mix to a dough. Cover and leave to rise in a warm place for 1 to 1½ hours or until doubled in bulk.

Knead the dough lightly, then work in the currants until they are distributed evenly. Shape the dough into about 30 balls. Cover and leave to rise in a warm place for 30 minutes.

Heat oil in a deep-frying pan (deep fat fryer) until it is 180°C/350°F, or until a small cube of stale bread dropped into the oil turns golden in 55 seconds. Deep-fry the doughnuts, a few at a time, for 5 to 6 minutes or until golden brown. Drain on paper towels and serve hot.

30 Doughnuts

Hot cross buns

	Metric/UK	US
Fresh (compressed) yeast	**15g/½oz**	**½ cake**
Sugar	**50g/2oz plus ¼ tsp**	**¼ cup plus ¼ tsp**
Lukewarm milk	**250ml/8floz plus 2 Tbs**	**1 cup plus 2 Tbs**
Flour	**½kg/1lb**	**4 cups**
Salt	**½ tsp**	**½ tsp**
Ground mixed spice or allspice	**1 tsp**	**1 tsp**
Ground cinnamon	**1 tsp**	**1 tsp**
Eggs	**2**	**2**
Unsalted butter, melted	**50g/2oz**	**4 Tbs**
Raisins	**50g/2oz**	**⅓ cup**
Chopped mixed candied peel	**50g/2oz**	**⅓ cup**
CROSSES		
Butter	**1 Tbs**	**1 Tbs**
Flour	**25g/1oz**	**¼ cup**
Cold water	**1 tsp**	**1 tsp**
GLAZE		
Milk	**2 Tbs**	**2 Tbs**
Sugar	**1 tsp**	**1 tsp**

Crumble the yeast into a bowl and mash in the ¼ teaspoon sugar and 2 tablespoons milk. Leave in a warm place for 15 to 20 minutes or until puffed up and frothy.

Sift the flour, remaining sugar, salt and spices into another bowl. Make a well in the centre and pour in the yeast mixture, remaining milk, the eggs and butter. Gradually draw the flour mixture into the liquids and mix

to a dough. Turn the dough out onto a floured board and knead until it is smooth and elastic—about 10 minutes.

Return the dough to the bowl, cover and leave to rise in a warm place for 1 hour or until doubled in bulk.

Knead the dough lightly and work in the raisins and candied peel. Divide the dough into 16 portions and shape each into a bun. Arrange the buns, about 5cm/2in apart, on greased baking sheets. Cover and leave to rise in a warm place for 15 to 20 minutes or until almost doubled in bulk.

Preheat the oven to very hot 230°C (Gas Mark 8, 450°F).

Make the dough for the crosses by rubbing the butter into the flour until the mixture resembles breadcrumbs. Add the water and mix to a firm dough. Roll out the dough thinly and cut it into thin strips 5cm/2in long. Press the dough strips into the tops of the buns in the shape of a cross.

Mix together the milk and sugar for the glaze and brush over the buns. Bake for 15 minutes or until golden brown. Cool on a wire rack.

16 Buns

Apple muffins

	Metric/UK	US
Flour	225g/8oz	2 cups
Salt	½ tsp	½ tsp
Baking powder	2 tsp	2 tsp
Sugar	50g/2oz	¼ cup
Ground cinnamon	½ tsp	½ tsp
Grated nutmeg	¼ tsp	¼ tsp
Ground allspice	¼ tsp	¼ tsp
Eggs, lightly beaten	2	2
Butter, melted	50g/2oz	4 Tbs
Buttermilk	150ml/5floz	⅔ cup
Lemon juice	1 Tbs	1 Tbs
Medium dessert apples, peeled, cored and grated	2	2

Preheat the oven to very hot 230°C (Gas Mark 8, 450°F).

Sift the flour, salt, baking powder, sugar and spices into a mixing bowl. Beat together the eggs, butter, buttermilk and lemon juice and add to the flour mixture. Stir but do not overmix. Fold in the apples.

Spoon the batter into greased muffin tins and bake for 15 to 20 minutes or until cooked through.

Allow to cool in the tins for 5 minutes, then serve warm, or cool completely on a wire rack.

12 Muffins

Traditionally eaten at Easter, Hot Cross Buns are delicious toasted and served with butter and jam.

143

PRESERVES

Pickled cucumbers

	Metric/UK	US
Small pickling cucumbers	1kg/2lb	2lb
Fresh dill sprigs	4	4
White wine vinegar	600ml/1 pint	2½ cups
Dill seed	1 tsp	1 tsp
Allspice berries, bruised	½ tsp	½ tsp
Mace blade	1	1
Mustard seeds, bruised	1 tsp	1 tsp
Mixed black and white peppercorns, bruised	1 tsp	1 tsp
Celery seed	½ tsp	½ tsp
Garlic cloves	2	2
Dried red chillis (chili peppers)	4	4
Bay leaf, crumbled	1	1
Rock salt	2 Tbs	2 Tbs

Prick the cucumbers all over with a fork. Pack them tightly into four preserving (canning) jars. Put a dill sprig in each jar.

Put the vinegar, dill seed, allspice berries, mace blade, mustard seeds, peppercorns, celery seed, garlic, chillis, bay leaf and salt in a saucepan and bring to the boil. Boil for 5 minutes. Remove from the heat and allow to cool, then remove the garlic cloves.

Half fill each preserving (canning) jar with water, then top up with the spiced vinegar. The liquid should cover the cucumbers completely. Leave the jars, covered but not sealed, in a warm place for 4 days, then seal and label. Store in a cool dark place for at least 3 or 4 weeks before serving.

About 2kg/4lb

Mushroom ketchup

	Metric/UK	US
Button mushrooms, chopped	1½kg/3lb	3lb
Salt	125g/4oz	½ cup
Small onion, finely chopped	1	1
Pickling spices	2 tsp	2 tsp
Black peppercorns, crushed	6	6
Ground mace	1 tsp	1 tsp
Ground allspice	¼ tsp	¼ tsp
Juice of 2 lemons		
Brandy	6 Tbs	6 Tbs

Make layers of mushrooms and salt in a casserole. Cover and leave for 24 hours, stirring occasionally.

Preheat the oven to cool 150°C (Gas Mark 2, 300°F).

Stir the onion into the mushrooms. Re-cover the casserole and bake for 30 minutes.

Purée the mushrooms and onion in a blender or with a food mill. Pour the purée into a saucepan and add the pickling spices, peppercorns, mace, allspice and lemon juice. Bring to the boil, stirring, and simmer for 3 to 5 minutes or until the purée is thick.

Allow the ketchup to cool completely, then stir in the brandy. Use immediately, or store in tightly sealed bottles.

About 900ml/1½ pints (2 pints)

Orange pickle

	Metric/UK	US
Oranges	6	6
Salt	1 tsp	1 tsp
Sugar	½kg/1lb	2 cups
Golden (light corn) syrup	2 Tbs	2 Tbs
Malt vinegar	175ml/6floz	¾ cup
Water	500ml/16floz	2 cups
Seeds of 6 cardamoms		
Black peppercorns, crushed	6	6
Ground cinnamon	½ tsp	½ tsp
Ground allspice	¼ tsp	¼ tsp
Cloves	12	12

Put the oranges and salt into a saucepan and cover with hot water. Bring to the boil and simmer for 50 minutes or until the oranges are tender. Drain the oranges and allow to cool.

Put the remaining ingredients in the cleaned-out saucepan and bring to the boil, stirring occasionally. Simmer for 10 minutes, then remove from the heat and leave to cool for 20 minutes.

Thinly slice the oranges.

Strain the cooled spice mixture into another saucepan. Add the orange slices and bring to the boil. Simmer for 20 minutes. Remove from the heat and allow to cool for 5 minutes before ladling into warm jars.

Seal and label and store in a cool, dry place.

About 2kg/4lb

It is always useful to have a variety of sauces to hand such as those illustrated here: Mushroom Ketchup, Mustard, Tomato, Horseradish, Mint, and Worcestershire sauces.

Piccalilli

	Metric/UK	US
Medium cauliflower, broken into flowerets	1	1
Cucumber, cut into 1cm/½in pieces	1	1
Pickling (pearl) onions	225g/8oz	8oz
Large Spanish (Bermuda) onion, chopped	1	1
Green tomatoes, skinned and chopped	4	4
Coarse salt	175g/6oz	1½ cups
Malt vinegar	600ml/1 pint	2½ cups
SAUCE		
Malt vinegar	600ml/1 pint	2½ cups
Mustard seed, bruised	3 Tbs	3 Tbs
Root ginger, peeled and chopped	5cm/2in piece	2in piece
Garlic cloves, halved	4	4
Black peppercorns, bruised	1 Tbs	1 Tbs
Turmeric	1 Tbs	1 Tbs
Dry mustard	1 Tbs	1 Tbs
Sugar	125g/4oz	½ cup
Flour dissolved in 4 Tbs water	3 Tbs	3 Tbs

Put the vegetables in a bowl. Sprinkle them with the salt and leave for 4 hours. Drain the vegetables well and pat dry with paper towels.

Bring the vinegar to the boil in a saucepan. Add the vegetables, cover and simmer for 15 minutes or until almost tender. Remove from the heat and drain the vegetables. Put them in a bowl.

To make the sauce, put the vinegar, mustard seed, ginger, garlic, peppercorns, turmeric, mustard and sugar in the cleaned-out saucepan and bring to the boil, stirring to dissolve the sugar and spices. Simmer for 15 minutes.

Strain the sauce and return it to the saucepan. Bring back to the boil and stir in the dissolved flour. Simmer, stirring, until smooth and thickened.

Pour the sauce over the vegetables and turn and toss gently so they become well coated. Spoon the piccalilli into warm jars. Allow to cool completely before sealing and labelling. Store in a cool, dry place.

About 1½kg/3lb

Fruit chutney

	Metric/UK	US
Apricots, stoned (pitted) and chopped	1kg/2lb	2lb
Cooking apples, peeled, cored and chopped	1kg/2lb	2lb
Peaches, peeled, stoned (pitted) and chopped	4	4
Onions, finely chopped	2	2
Raisins	225g/8oz	1⅓ cups
Root ginger, peeled and diced	5cm/2in piece	2in piece
Grated nutmeg	¾ tsp	¾ tsp
Ground allspice	¾ tsp	¾ tsp
Dry mustard	¾ tsp	¾ tsp
Finely grated rind of 1 large lemon		
Finely grated rind and juice of 2 oranges		
White wine vinegar	750ml/1¼ pints	1½ pints
Sugar	½kg/1lb	2 cups
Soft brown sugar	½kg/1lb	2⅔ cups

Put the apricots, apples, peaches, onions, raisins, ginger, nutmeg, allspice, mustard, lemon rind, orange rind and juice and 600ml/1 pint (2½ cups) of the vinegar in a saucepan. Stir well and bring to the boil. Simmer, stirring occasionally, for 1 to 1½ hours

Far Left Piccalilli *is a delicious, pungent pickle usually served with cold meats. It owes its bright colouring to turmeric and mustard, two of its ingredients.*

Near Top Left and Bottom Right Black and white mustard are the two basic varieties, the seeds either being ground to provide the ready-made mustard or used bruised in Indian cooking and pickles. Whole seeds are more aromatic than the ready-made variety.

or until the mixture is very soft and pulpy.

Stir in the sugars and the remaining vinegar and continue simmering, stirring occasionally, for 40 to 50 minutes or until the chutney is very thick.

Ladle the chutney into jars, cover and seal. Label and store in a cool dry place for 6 weeks before serving.

About 4kg/8lb

Nectarine chutney

	Metric/UK	US
Large nectarines, peeled, stoned (pitted) and quartered	10	10
Large dessert apples, peeled, cored and chopped	2	2
Grated rind and juice of 3 lemons		
Soft brown sugar	175g/6oz	1 cup
Walnuts, chopped	175g/6oz	1½ cups
Sultanas or raisins	275g/9oz	1½ cups
Root ginger, bruised	5cm/2in piece	2in piece
Garlic cloves, crushed	2	2
Black peppercorns	6	6
Cayenne pepper	¼ tsp	¼ tsp
Ground cinnamon	1 tsp	1 tsp
White wine vinegar	175ml/6floz	¾ cup

Put the nectarines, apples, lemon rind and juice, sugar, walnuts, sultanas or raisins, ginger, garlic, peppercorns, cayenne, cinnamon and half the vinegar in a saucepan. Stir well and bring to the boil. Simmer for 30 minutes, stirring occasionally.

Stir in the remaining vinegar and continue simmering, stirring occasionally, for 1½ hours or until the chutney is thick.

Ladle the chutney into jars, cover and seal. Label and store in a cool dry place.

About 2kg/4lb

Coconut chutney

	Metric/UK	US
Desiccated (shredded) coconut, soaked in 150ml/5floz (⅔ cup) plain yogurt for 1 hour	50g/2oz	½ cup
Juice and grated rind of 1 lemon		
Root ginger, peeled and sliced	2.5cm/1in piece	1in piece
Green chilli (chili pepper), chopped	1	1
Garlic clove, sliced	1	1
Onion, chopped	1	1

Put the coconut mixture and lemon juice in a blender and blend to a smooth purée. Add the lemon rind, ginger, chilli, garlic and onion and blend until smooth again.

If you do not have a blender, very finely chop or mince (grind) all the ingredients.

Serve immediately, or keep, covered, in the refrigerator. This chutney will keep for 2 to 3 days.

About 125g/4oz (1 cup)

Apple chutney

	Metric/UK	US
Cooking apples, peeled and cored	2kg/4lb	4lb
Sultanas or raisins	½kg/1lb	2⅔ cups
Onions	4	4
Chilli (chili pepper), chopped	1	1
Mustard seeds	1 Tbs	1 Tbs
Lemon juice	3 Tbs	3 Tbs
Chopped lemon rind	3 Tbs	3 Tbs
Ground ginger	2 tsp	2 tsp
Vinegar	900ml/1½ pints	3¾ cups
Brown sugar	1kg/2lb	5⅓ cups

Mince (grind) the apples, sultanas or raisins, onions and chilli into a preserving pan. Add the mustard seeds, lemon juice and rind, ginger and 600ml/1pint (2½ cups) of the vinegar. Stir well and bring to the boil. Simmer for 1 to 1½ hours, stirring occasionally, or until very soft and pulpy.

Dissolve the sugar in the remaining vinegar in another saucepan, then add to the apple mixture. Continue to simmer, stirring occasionally, until the chutney is thick.

Ladle the chutney into jars, cover and seal. Label and store in a cool dry place.

About 2kg/4lb

Peach jam

	Metric/UK	US
Medium cooking apple, chopped	1	1
Thinly pared rind of 2 lemons		
Cloves	2	2
Peaches, stoned (pitted) and sliced	1½kg/3lb	3lb
Water	300ml/10floz	1¼ cups
Ground allspice	1 tsp	1 tsp
Sugar	1½kg/3lb	3lb (6 cups)

Tie the apple, lemon rind and cloves in a double piece of muslin or cheese-

cloth. Skin the peaches and put the peaches, water and flavourings bag in a preserving pan and bring to the boil, stirring.

Simmer until the peaches are just soft but be careful not to overcook.

Remove the flavourings bag and press it against the side of the pan to extract all the liquid. Add the allspice and sugar and stir continuously until the sugar has dissolved. Return to the boil and boil rapidly for 15 to 20 minutes or until setting point (jell point) is reached.

To test for setting, put a spoonful of the jam on a saucer. Allow it to cool, then push it with your finger. If the jam is ready, it will crinkle and the surface should feel set. If it is still runny, continue boiling and testing as described.

Leave the jam off the heat for 10 minutes, then ladle it into jars, cover, seal and label. Store in a cool, dry place.

About 2½kg/5lb

Quince jelly

	Metric/UK	US
Ripe quinces, sliced	2kg/4lb	4lb
Water	600ml/1 pint	2½ cups
Allspice berries, bruised	6	6
Lemon juice		
Sugar		

Put the quinces, water and allspice berries in a preserving pan and bring to the boil. Simmer for 50 minutes or until tender. Pour into a jelly bag and drain overnight. Discard the pulp.

Measure juice and return to the pan. Add 1 tablespoon of lemon juice and 425g/14oz (1¾ cups) of sugar to every 600ml/1 pint (2½ cups) of liquid. Place over low heat and stir until the sugar has dissolved. Bring to the boil and boil for 10 minutes or until setting (jell) point is reached.

Skim surface of jelly with a metal spoon. Ladle into hot pots, cover, label and store in a dark, cool place.

About 1.2kg/2½lb

Peach jam is delicious either on hot toast at breakfast or thickly spread on pieces of bread.

INDEX